PERSONAS MEXICANAS

Chicano High Schoolers in a Changing Los Angeles

James Diego Vigil, Ph.D.

Department of Anthropology
UCLA

CASE STUDIES IN CULTURAL ANTHROPOLOGY

HARCOURT BRACE COLLEGE PUBLISHERS

Fort Worth   Philadelphia   San Diego   New York   Orlando   Austin   San Antonio
Toronto   Montreal   London   Sydney   Tokyo

Publisher	Christopher P. Klein
Senior Acquisitions Editor	Stephen T. Jordan
Developmental Editor	Rick Carruth
Project Editors	Pam Hatley/Tamara Neff Vardy
Senior Production Manager	Kathleen Ferguson
Art Director	Bill Brammer
Electronic Publishing Supervisor	Paul Zinn
Electronic Publishing Coordinator	Kathi Embry

Address editorial correspondence to:
Harcourt Brace College Publishers
301 Commerce Street, Suite 3700
Fort Worth, TX 76102

Address orders to:
Harcourt Brace & Company
Permissions Department
6277 Sea Harbor Drive
Orlando, FL 32887-6777
1-800-782-4479 or 1-800-433-0001 (in Florida)

Harcourt Brace may provide complimentary instructional aids and supplements or supplement packages to those adopters qualified under our adoption policy. Please contact your sales representative for more information. If as an adopter or potential user you receive supplements you do not need, please return them to your sales representative or send them to:

Attn: Returns Department
Troy Warehouse
465 South Lincoln Drive
Troy, MO 63379

Printed in the United States of America

ISBN: 0-15-503838-9

Library of Congress Catalog Card Number: 96-077233

6 7 8 9 0 1 2 3 4 5 090 9 8 7 6 5 4 3 2 1

To my wife Polly, with appreciation and affection.

Foreward

ABOUT THE SERIES

These case studies in cultural anthropology are designed for students in beginning and intermediate courses in the social sciences, to bring them insights into the richness and complexity of human life as it is lived in different ways, in different places. The authors are men and women who have lived in the societies they write about and who are professionally trained as observers and interpreters of human behavior. Also, the authors are teachers; in their writing, the needs of the student reader remain foremost. It is our belief that when an understanding of ways of life very different from one's own is gained, abstractions and generalizations about the human condition become meaningful.

The scope and character of the series have changed constantly since we published the first case studies in 1960, in keeping with our intention to represent anthropology as it is. We are concerned with the ways in which human groups and communities are coping with the massive changes wrought in their physical and sociopolitical environments in recent decades. We are also concerned with the ways in which established cultures have solved life's problems. Also, we want to include representation of the various modes of communication and emphasis that are being formed and reformed as anthropology itself changes.

We think of this series as an instructional series, intended for use in the classroom. We, the editors, have always used case studies in our teaching, whether for beginning students or advanced graduate students. We start with case studies, whether from our own series or from elsewhere, and weave our way into theory, and then turn again to cases. For us, they are the grounding of our discipline.

ABOUT THE AUTHOR

James Diego Vigil is a native of Los Angeles with long-standing family roots in the American Southwest. His paternal grandfather was born in 1842 to a teamster's family that plied the trail from Santa Fe, New Mexico to Chihuahua just before the Mexican American War. As a "zero" generation Chicano, Vigil speaks Spanish primarily because he recaptured its usage in his earlier research in Southern Mexico (self-taught archaeology) and Guatemala (peasant studies). He was reared to be moderately "assimilated."

Beginning as a public school teacher in the early 1960s, he has taught at all levels, including elementary, junior high, and senior high school. He soon became active in the Chicano Movement, a period which marked a major turning point in his life. The experience and ferment of the Civil Rights Era stimulated his interest and motivation to know more about his people—his own family and friends as well as the students and local youth with whom he was working. Thus, he returned to graduate school to pursue advanced study. Because of the support of many fine people, faculty and peers alike, and affirmative action opportunities, he was able to complete his studies at UCLA in anthropology in 1976.

From that point on, he continued investigations focused on ethnohistory, education, and urban youth, especially street gangs and family life. More recently, he has directed his attention to comparative issues affecting urban youth in various ethnic communities such as Black, Vietnamese, Salvadorean, and Mexican nationals. With this urban youth focus, he has regularly integrated applied strategies into his research agenda to help shape public policy on the many problems of the inner city. After many years at the University of Southern California, he is now in anthropology at the University of California at Los Angeles and is Director of the Center for the Study of Urban Poverty.

ABOUT THE CASE STUDY

Personas Mexicanas serves a high purpose—to bring the reader a better understanding of Mexican-American high school students and their struggles with ethnicity, Americanization, prejudice, schools, and life's purposes. In most Anglo minds, these students are characterized by exceptionally high dropout rates and poor school performance in general, without any explanation for this performance other than the fact that they are Mexican. In *Personas Mexicanas,* Diego Vigil explores the real-life situations in a sample of young people of Mexican descent in both a suburban and an urban high school during two time periods separated by fourteen years (1974 and 1988).

In this study, Vigil provides some surprises for the reader. For example, there is much more diversity among the Mexican-American population than ordinarily thought. His sample of "thumbnail" sketches (short-term autobiographies) shows this clearly, as he divides his selected students for each period into culturally Mexican-oriented, Intermediate, and Anglo-oriented. It is fascinating to see how personal adaptation varies not only with each category, but also *within* each category. This is especially true in the Intermediate category. No one, after reading this case study, will thoughtlessly make generalizations about students of Mexican descent.

Vigil's methodology is impressive. Its strength lies in his strong comparative procedure. Not only are different schools compared (urban/suburban), but there also is a comparison of the same high schools in 1974 and in 1988. These comparisons lead to sound interpretations that avoid premature statements about Chicano adaptations to life in the United States, particularly in that part of the greater Los Angeles area.

His methodology is also impressive because it combines quantitative and qualitative approaches. Ethnography and statistics are often thought of as strange bedfellows. In fact, some analysts regard them as hopelessly antithetical. In actuality, the two approaches supplement each other, as Diego Vigil clearly demonstrates. The short autobiographic sketches provide an opportunity to meet the young people directly and the quantitative aspect of the study provides essential background.

The last twenty years of demographics and political change in this country are reflected in the situation of these school populations. For these young people, being

Mexican is losing its stigma. Ethnicization, in the form of Mexicanization, is in. However, the number of families and children living under poverty levels has increased, and the rising middle class—which has become more suburban and Anglicized—moves further away from the inner city poor and the larger mass of working class. These trends mirror the movement in the mainstream of the larger society and among all ethnic minorities in the United States.

There are many other dimensions of this rich study of the adaptations that Chicano high school students are making that could be mentioned. We leave the reader to find them in what should be an interesting trip.

George and Louise Spindler
Series Editors
P.O. Box 38
Calistoga, California 94515

PREFACE AND ACKNOWLEDGEMENTS

Personas Mexicanas primarily addresses one of the many educational issues that urgently need attention and scrutiny. The focus of this work is on acculturation and educational performance, but I have long been aware that teacher training, curriculum, counseling, teaching methods, community involvement, and institutional change are also in need of examination and reconsideration. In addition to my personal experiences and insights that have guided my investigation on culture and academics, I have also been strongly influenced by the training I received and the thinkers and writers to whom I was exposed and from whom I have learned.

Before outlining the events and people which have influenced my approach to this work, let me first acknowledge the school district officials and school administrators and teachers most responsible for making this investigation a success. They, of course, are not accountable for the findings and interpretations of the book, but their easy and ready advice and counsel certainly helped me to rethink and reformulate certain points throughout. Among those school personnel who assisted me and offered feedback are: Alex Avilez, Lee Eastwood, Maria Tostado, Bob Tafoya, Gil Campos, Jose Ramos, Domingo Rodriquez, and Dick Torres, among many others. Students at USC also helped at different stages of the process and added important insights to what characterizes adolescent dynamics.

At Sacramento State, Clark Taylor and Sue Ellen Jacobs were instructors in the Experienced Teachers Fellowship Program that addressed the educational issues and problems of the Mexican American child. The courses they developed gave me a solid grounding in educational theory on culture, culture change, and academic achievement. Particularly influential during my fellowship at Sacramento were the collegial relations and interactions that allowed for debate and dissent on any number of educational problems affecting ethnic minority children.

Steve Arvizu figures prominently in this circle, since he first introduced me to bilingual education and the practical importance of allowing immigrant and non-English speaking children to learn in their own language while they gradually but forthrightly mastered English. Through the decades his support and counsel have been invaluable. The Cross Cultural Resource Center (CCRC), which Steve founded at Sacramento State in the 1970s, was also a touchstone for me, as it was for other budding scholars at the time. My experience in the CCRC put me in contact with many other writers in the field of culture and education, such as Robert Alvarez, Juan Garcia, Margaret Gibson, Henry Trueba, John Ogbu, and many other public school teachers and community practitioners at the local and statewide level. The CCRC workshops I and others conducted throughout the state and the feedback I received from participants was invaluable in deepening my appreciation of how place and time affected cultural orientation and schooling patterns.

The support I received from the National Institute of Mental Health which funded my graduate studies at UCLA in anthropology was also instrumental during this time. The dissertation that resulted from this effort was guided by my faculty advisors, among them, Pete Snyder and Tom Weisner.

By the early 1980s, I had turned my attention to the issue of cultural marginality, an offshoot from the earlier work on education, and wrote extensively on cholos and street gangs. In 1985, a group of scholars at the Tomas Rivera Center in Clare-mont, California, asked me to participate in a conference on Hispanic females and educational achievement. Adelaida del Castillo and Teresa McKenna, along with the Center's director Arturo Madrid, deserve my special thanks for this invitation, for it reminded me of my unfinished work on acculturation and school performance. With the aid of a Ford Postdoctoral Fellowship for Minority Scholars in 1987–1988, I completed the longitudinal research on which this book is based. The stay and guidance I received at the University of California at Santa Barbara under Henry Trueba in the School of Education, with George and Louise Spindler in residence teaching their seminar as part of a yearly nomadic cycle, sharpened my theoretical formulation in the exchanges we had together.

As with all long journeys, when the traveler begins to wear down, the help re-ceived at the end seems to loom larger and, of course, is most warmly appreciated. Steve C. Yun, the research associate I stole from the University of Wisconsin, Madison, was especially helpful in putting the manuscript together, offering words and advice at all steps of the process. To him I am forever grateful, even though he decided to become a medical doctor first before striving for the Ph.D. in one of those rare efforts to become a "Double Doctor." Robert Alvarez read an early and rough draft of the manuscript and provided keen, analytical feedback to point me in the right direction. His support and friendship over the years has lifted my sagging spirits many times. Joan and Burt Moore provided sound advice for changes to im-prove the book, and as my friends and associates I am indebted to them. David Vic-torin's editorial work on the first chapters was also appreciated. My daughter, Joan E. Vigil-Rakhshani added some fine tuning to the case histories and my son, Nick Vigil provided advice on graphics.

Thanks also to the University of Southern California for the sabbatical in 1993 and to my secretary there, Mae Horie, who unflinchingly typed and retyped ad nau-sem to produce this final product. It was at USC that most of the thinking and work on this project was formulated and conducted.

Through all these years my wife, Polly, has been by my side helping craft the questionnaires and do the fieldwork and whatever else was necessary to pull this work off. She has been associated with all my investigations and her ideas and in-sights have made the major difference in most of my research. John M. Long is my long-time colleague and friend who has also been involved in most of the investiga-tions, and we have coauthored several articles together on this subject. Finally, I wish to extend my deepest appreciation and thanks to the "Spins", George and Louise Spindler, who motivated and shepherded me in this project in its early stages. Their initial work on culture change, culture and education, and what it is now known as educational anthropology is the basis for my thinking and analytical frameworks. To them and the editorial staff at Harcourt Brace, I owe my gratitude.

OVERVIEW

I am honored to provide the overview to *Personas Mexicanas* because I know it represents a unique labor of scholarship and analysis by a respected colleague. Diego Vigil is a dedicated and gifted practitioner and a critical scholar with special insights into cultural identity and cultural change among Chicano urban youth. He is an experienced and talented anthropologist who has lived many of the experiences described. In addition, Dr. Vigil has worked as an educator with Chicanos in Los Angeles at the high school, community college, and university levels, and he has been involved in many innovative programs and projects. He combines insider and outsider educational analyses of Chicano high schoolers as well as of the educators who try to serve them. This volume represents three decades of study and practice.

I have known the author, 'El Doctor' Vigil, for the past thirty years as we have been colleagues, fellow activists, and applied scholars in the nexus between anthropology and education. I met James Diego Vigil in the 1960s as a fellow student of anthropology when we participated together in a community-oriented project for experienced teachers interested in changing schools. Diego Vigil, even then, was a street-wise, innovative teacher with great courage and a keen, critical perspective on historical events, self-concept, pride, and survival strategies among Chicanos and on leaders of social movements.

As a part of a group of fellows in the Mexican American Education Project, we studied Mexican history and culture and the lessons of applied anthropology for the education of the Mexican American/Chicano community. Diego constantly related his historical expertise and teaching experience to understanding the cultural, social, and political behavior of Chicano youth in the Chicano Movement and to critical systemic analysis of schools and educators. I remember his early writings and lectures on Pachucos, social banditry, and guerrilla fighters as they provided alternative historical analyses of Pachuco behavior and cultural heroes such as Tiburcio Vasquez, Joaquin Murrieta, and Emiliano Zapata. He was very persistent in studying assimilation, cultural revitalization, and role models among various segments of the Latino school-age population. He took the time to complete his doctoral studies in anthropology at UCLA. Diego Vigil has throughout time, been genuinely interested in studying the process of identity formation and cultural shift among school-age youth, even while he was living the experience as an activist-educator at each level of the educational pipeline. He began his studies of assimilation by returning to his own schools and communities and conducting fieldwork among those in school and those on the streets. This particular work has the benefit of several decades of longitudinal analysis and understanding of the interrelated responsibilities of educators in the K-12 and college sectors.

Personas Mexicanas provides a comparative perspective when studying within groups which is valuable in understanding group patterns and individual variation. This volume is very timely in its topic as we understand demographic realities of the projected growth and concomitant social and educational issues related to what is becoming the largest minority group in the United States, and, in fact, the majority group in a large number of California schools. It is enriched by Diego Vigil's understanding of socio-cultural history and contexts for group identity reflected in his earlier works, *From Indian to Chicanos: The Dynamics of Mexican American Culture* and *Barrio Gangs,* and subsequent studies of alienated youth. Diego Vigil is a risk taker as a teacher and as a conscientious scholar and fieldworker. His teaching is energetic and actively engaged with substantive controversial issues. His studies on gangs and urban problems represent dangerous, yet essential, fieldwork necessary for collecting quality insider data on the non-school, community-based influences of Chicano and Asian gang cultural behavior. He literally puts his career and life at risk for his belief and commitment to bringing an understanding of complex problems involving people.

By returning to the study of schools and assimilation of *Personas Mexicanas,* our colleague provides a thoughtful analysis of identity, assimilation, and community dynamics across borders, decades, and neighborhoods. He uses ethnographic methodology and an anthropological approach to study and explain the educational and cultural experiences of an important spectrum of the Chicano population in Los Angeles. As Dr. Vigil steps back from being a teacher to become a studier and analyst, we get access to the rich text and qualitative voices of *Personas Mexicanas.*

Diego Vigil's work on education and culture is meaningful due to the critical importance of education in solving problems and opening opportunities and because of his insider understanding of teaching-learning as both a classroom teacher and a researcher.

If we are to liberate individuals or groups from severe conditions and non-responsive structures, we must understand underlying cultural processes and the role of identity in the contexts of survival and creativity. *Personas Mexicanas* insightfully and provocatively explains what is happening to students as they change as well as in positing their survival strategies of using multiple identities to maneuver through schools and urban communities.

As implied by this book, we need creative and courageous teachers who understand our diverse student populations. We need role models who can facilitate constructive marginality and wholeness of identity among future generations of students facing assimilation pressures in their lives.

STEVEN F. ARVIZU, PH. D.

BACKGROUND TO THIS STUDY

Nothing has overwhelmed me as much as an experience I had when I first taught high school in the mid-1960s at Excelsior High School. In the first week of the fall semester, two former teachers of mine who were now counselors brought me into the counseling office to discuss the plight of the Mexican-American students in the high school. They proceeded to show me the grade list printouts of all the Mexican students. Most of the students' records were D's and F's, graced with a few C's here and there. I was to be their role model as the first Chicano teacher at the school.

Neither of these counselors had an inkling of how this experience affected me. As the first and only Chicano teacher at the school, I felt somehow responsible for the pages and pages of names and poor grades. How was I going to make a difference? Where was I to begin? The first order of business, I thought, was to listen to the students and to interact with them not only in the school setting, but also in their community and homes, in order to determine whether there were differences among them that explained the school records.

The first thing I discovered was that most of these students came from one nearby barrio (Varrio Norwalk), but this did not mean they were cut out of the same cultural mold. Some of them were first-generation Mexicans who had come to the United States for a better life and the opportunity to improve themselves, but could not afford to live anywhere but the low-rent areas within the barrio. A small handful were the children of store owners and blue-collar tradesmen who had become the local "bourgeoisie." Others were longtime residents who had fashioned a street, *cholo* (marginal to both Anglo-American and Mexican cultures, a type of syncretic, hybrid subculture) style; many of these youths identified with the local gang and all its affairs. There was even a sizable group of youngsters who identified as "Chic-Anglo" (Anglicized, mostly English speaking) and dressed and talked in the "surfer" style of the time.

Cultural variation within one neighborhood was the rule, not the exception; this was reflected in the even more heterogenous surrounding city of Norwalk. In fact, there was a remarkable lack of concern about ethnic identity and hardly any consciously driven thinking about cultural orientation or style. It was as if a whole generation was moving culturally, adjusting to the pressures and requirements of life, without knowing precisely where they were going (understandable) or where they had come from (unforgivable).

Paralleling this cultural mixture, was a wide variation in the school performance of these students; perhaps, in part, a reflection of the confusion in cultural moorings or shaky socioeconomic status. Because of good behavior and attentiveness, some of them (especially the girls) were gaining satisfactory grades of C or better, which in their communities constituted being "brains." The "stigma" of success was for some reason more acceptable to their peers and the remainder of the group. Others received good grades for some subjects, such as physical education and shop classes, but fared miserably in the formal academic areas. A few frequently slipped back and forth between good and bad grades depending on personal and family stresses of the moment. Overall, however, their classroom achievement was dismal despite the "innate ability"—whatever that is and however it is measured or gauged (Valencia and Aburto 1991)—of many of the students who appeared bright enough to do well but did not.

Lack of effort, limited resources, outside interferences such as work, peer pressure, and traditional gender inequalities, among other reasons, explain this failure. However, the most important part of the equation were the schools and teachers that also strongly affected students' attitudes toward school and learning capacities. The overwhelming majority of these students lacked, in their lives and the life paths of their families, examples of education making a difference—demonstrations that good jobs and income were linearly related to school achievement. This left the students without immediate models of achieved educational success or social and economic mobility. Even the females who did well accepted the fact that their education ended with high school.

These impressions have led me through a long history of wrestling with the question: What is the status of minority student school achievement, especially in the Mexican-American case? It also demonstrates what the Spindlers refer to as the contrast and strain between one's *enduring self* (the past and continuity of experiences), the *situated self* (coping with situations in the present), and *endangered self* (when the situational and present seriously threatens and undermines one's enduring self) (Spindler and Spindler 1990, 1993: 36–37). This struggle is readily apparent in the lives of the students in this book as we scan their range of acculturation styles, noting the generational strain of moving from the Mexican to the Anglo end of the American cultural spectrum. Such difficulties, of course, are in addition to the normal adjustments associated with the passage of childhood to adulthood—the teen years (Schlegel and Barry 1991).

In a way, my life (and enduring self) has been directed toward addressing this question. Growing up in the inner city of Los Angeles during the 1940s and 1950s placed me in a special setting: a multiethnic community. My particular neighborhood, Twenty-third and Maple Avenue, included primarily Mexicans and Mexican Americans, but also many Asian Americans, African Americans, and working-class Whites. Back then, it seemed that the Chinese and Japanese students did well in school. The children of Mexican immigrants from fairly well-off backgrounds did well also. They gained inspiration from something positive (even if imagined), such as wealth and status. The Chicanos and African Americans seemed divided, one-third doing well and the rest doing average to marginal work. The latter were joined by some Japanese and Filipino students who identified with either Chicanos or Blacks. The White students were mostly of lower-income background, post-Depression transplants who did poorly in school; in some ways, they were more destitute than the other students.

I gained further personal insight into the relationship between culture and education when my parents, with my older brother's G.I. home loan, moved to a suburban, mostly White neighborhood. This further sparked my efforts to assimilate, or further acculturate, given the fact that my family is "zero generation" and were natives to the Southwest before the Anglo-American takeover. Nonetheless, in this new suburban setting, my situated self definitely interrupted the smooth flow of my enduring self. The experience downplayed my multiethnic upbringing, causing a mental distancing to speed the more normal spatial and time changes underway.

These early life impressions were deepened and elaborated upon after I became a public school teacher: three years in elementary (sixth grade, fourth grade, and fifth and sixth grades combined), one year in intermediate (seventh grade physical education and eighth grade literature and social studies), and two years in high school (ninth, tenth, and eleventh grade social studies).

Such a personal and professional life path has enabled me to read the cultural orientation and habits of students, particularly after interactions with their families in PTA, parent-teacher conferences, visits to homes, and other community and school activities. Throughout this period of teaching, I was immersed in the school environment, not only in mainstream activities such as coaching track and football, but also in more "ethnically cultural" areas such as advising the Mexican-American Club and involving myself in the Association of Mexican-American Educators (AMAE). The AMAE emphasized Mexican-American community activism and called for a change toward more culturally sensitive curriculum, counseling, and teachers. Most importantly, it created an awareness of and pride in Mexican Americans' cultural heritage in all its variations and permutations.

In 1968, I joined an Experienced Teachers Fellowship Program at Sacramento State University, which for a year intensively examined the cultural and educational issues in the Mexican-American community. This fellowship involved visiting schools throughout California, the United States, and Mexico. The nineteen other fellows were all school teachers. We spent the year in serious study, reflection, and debate on the issue of educational performance of minority children, especially Mexican Americans. This is when I began to understand my own personal experiences and that of other Mexican Americans in the context of "endangered self." This experience, which brought my teaching and community background into a research focus, was the beginning of my efforts to appraise and understand the dynamics between Mexican-American culture and education in a formal way. It led to the exploration and examination of the many cultural influences and antecedents of the Mexican people.

As a public school teacher turned graduate student, I began to investigate the educational paths of high school students in various settings. Early papers (Vigil 1971, 1972, 1973) established the preliminary groundwork to pursue an in-depth study for my dissertation in anthropology. Much of the anthropological debate of that time seemed to emphasize acculturation processes as a starting point in which to gauge and measure one's adaptation and adjustment to Anglo-American culture and society. Acculturation is a broad process which accompanies what happens when two cultures are in contact and change takes place in one or both cultures (Spindler 1984; Redfield, Linton, and Herskovits 1936; Siegel et al. 1953). It was pretty clear then, that what passed for acculturation was actually unidirectional acculturation (Teske and Nelson 1974). Thus, the dominant Anglo majority effectively forced minority populations, in different ways and with different results, to assimilate and change to the dominant culture. With this background, I embarked on a quest to explore the level and rate of acculturation and its effects on schooling among Mexican Americans.

Contents

Chapter 1   1
Introduction

Chapter 2   17
Where Goes Minority Student Achievement: Culture or Class?

Chapter 3   23
"Coming to America is the Best Thing That Has Happened to Me":
   The Urban 1974 Informants

Chapter 4   41
The 1.5 Generation, "Those Who Came as Children":
   The 1988 Urban Informants

Chapter 5   69
"We Knew We Were Mexican, but We Were Told to Say We Were White":
   The 1974 Suburban Informants

Chapter 6   87
"I Can't Speak Spanish, but I'm Mexican and Proud of It":
   The 1988 Suburban Informants

Chapter 7   113
"Snapshot" and "Cinematic" Views of the Issue

Chapter 8   123
Personas Mexicanas: Multiple and Shifting Identities

Appendix   141

References   147

Index   157

1 / Introduction

A study of Chicano* high school youths covering twenty years has revealed that the conditions for and the processes of acculturation have changed significantly. The way we examine this aspect of school achievement and success has also undergone some advances (De Vos 1982; Olmedo and Padilla 1978). It is argued that Mexican-American Anglicization is no longer a prerequisite for success in America; Mexicans can now integrate themselves structurally and culturally into the United States in ways that are different from the ways available to them in previous decades. Immigrants, for example, can learn how to act appropriately in Anglo-American settings and to communicate in English while also retaining Spanish language and Mexican cultural habits. School performance is still used as a gauge for cultural adaptation and integration, but the high school students of Mexican background in this study are also redefining themselves by taking a bilingual-bicultural approach to learning and success (Delgado-Gaitan 1991a; Garcia 1991). Even Mexican-American students in suburban areas (where pressure to assimilate was once much stronger) have incorporated a much more open, integrative ethnic persona in their identity makeup.

It is not just the radical demographic shift that is remaking the human and physical landscape of the Los Angeles area that commands our attention (Hayes-Bautista and Rodriguez 1994). As the population of the region becomes a "majority of minorities," mostly Mexican and Latino, along with other ethnic groups, new ways of behaving and succeeding are also being introduced (Trueba 1988, 1993b). Important social and cultural reworkings are under way, and this study captures a piece of this transformation. Acculturation, in its strictest sense, is what happens with contact between cultures under dominant-subordinate and native-immigrant situations and conditions (Buenker and Lorman 1992; Patthey-Chavez 1993). Historically, for Mexicans as well as other ethnic groups in the United States, this has meant to become Anglicized in order to adjust, mainstream, and be successful (Pozzeta 1991). In short, acculturation became synonymous with assimilation.

As a result, in part, of recent cultural changes in Southern California, a "Mexicanization" process has imbued the Mexican-American population with a sense of pride and dignity in things ethnic or Mexican (McLaughlin 1994). Reflecting the

---

*Chicano is used interchangeably with Mexican American and Mexican at times to refer in general to the ethnic roots of the population regardless of birthplace. When specific ethnic identity issues and patterns are discussed, more precision in ethnic labeling will be used.

cumulative and additive historical experiences of the Mexican people, Mexicanization adds to the *personas mexicanas* heritage that Jose Vasconcelos suggests with his much broader *"la raza cósmica"* notion (Vasconcelos and Gamio 1926); his idea embraced the whole of Latin America in its rich and varied regional, racial, and cultural mosaic. With influences and antecedents from multiple heritages—Indian, Spanish, Mexican, Anglo (Vigil 1984)—it is now historically opportune to recognize and think positively of *personas mexicanas,* the variety of imprints that makes for a people. Pigeonholing oneself with just one ethnic identity may have been appropriate during earlier phases of our American and international history, but our current period of introspection is drawing us together into a "global village" (Sassen 1991). It is incumbent on all of us to think multiculturally and transnationally, to become "border crossers" (Phelan, Davidson, and Cao Yu 1993), and to blur the national lines within our minds, understanding that geopolitical boundaries are on the surface and easier to maintain than psychic ones.

Thus, *personas mexicanas* is one people's way to chart a new path into a different, challenging era, helping to make America an integral part of the new world culture that is emerging from the transnational economic and commercial ties already in place and expanding (Elsass 1992). This notion is reminiscent of the "American cultural dialogue" advanced by the Spindlers: "The dialogue is a process, not a fixed entity; there is continuity and there is change" (Spindler and Spindler 1990, 167).

Because this investigation explores the relationship between school achievement and cultural style and identity, it is important to note that other factors and forces must also be accounted for (Spindler and Spindler 1993). For example, contemporary research is supporting the claim that students who are bilingual and bicultural can also be good students. Although the heretofore conventional wisdom stated that acculturating to the Anglo mold was the (only) way to succeed in American society, this is no longer true, and may never have been true (Fishman 1986). Schooling and academic achievement are being appreciated as much more complicated phenomena, particularly in light of the complex histories that ethnic minorities, such as Mexicans, have experienced in the United States (Ernst, Statzner, and Trueba 1994).

Early acculturation studies purporting to demonstrate the maladaptive effect of bilingualism in schools often ignored important factors, such as separate or segregated schools, bias in testing, labeling, and "tracking" (Donato, Menchaca, and Valencia 1991; Valencia and Aburto 1991). Acculturation investigations and analyses must have been affected by these interferences and oversights. Birthplace, number of family generations in the United States, language, ethnic and cultural practices, continuing "binational" (Chavez 1992) migratory and mobility shifts on both sides of the border, and many other culturally based factors were also often disregarded in early studies. Yet all of these phenomena, as well as socioeconomic and demographic criteria, environment, gender, and personal idiosyncrasies, must be addressed in assaying the influences of acculturation.

Many other investigators have looked into the relationship between levels of acculturation and school performance, but few have conducted such an investigation in the largest, most highly diverse city where large numbers of Mexicans and Latinos are found: Los Angeles. It is in this cultural cauldron, as in other "world cities," that the most significant, wide-ranging changes are underway.

Two locales in this area were sampled and studied. The urban environ is a coterie of *barrios,* or neighborhoods, in East Los Angeles with homes and infrastructure dating from as early as the first decades of this century (Diaz 1993). Most residents and business owners are conventional, law-abiding members of the working class, many of them immigrants. But also present in this largely Mexican-American community are gangs, crime, and other ills often associated with a low-income area. The second location, a southeastern suburban neighborhood approximately fourteen miles from East Los Angeles, contrasts sharply with the first location. It is a mix of working- and middle-class Anglos and Mexican Americans. The school and rows of tract-home developments are part of the suburban explosion that characterized greater Los Angeles in the 1950s. Problems associated with crime and gangs are minimal in comparison to the urban setting, but have been increasing of late.

Another distinguishing feature of this study is its sampling of a variety of acculturation levels from recent immigrants to members of families that have resided in the United States for several generations. The subjects of this study evince a spread of varied cultural styles. An even wider spectrum of acculturation and ethnic identity was sought by looking at urban and suburban school environments. Issues of gender (which surfaced on its own), family, and socioeconomics also figure prominently in the analysis. An additional strength of this study, however, lies in its long-term look at two high schools and the changing nature of their students and the communities that surround them. This social historical assessment helps us better understand subtle nuances of the relationships among cultural change, acculturation, ethnic identity, and schooling.

HISTORY OF CHICANO STUDENTS IN AMERICAN EDUCATION

For a good part of the late nineteenth century and through the 1930s, the dominant theory among Anglo-American educators was that immigrants should be integrated through an "Americanization" process. Educators argued that minority students needed to learn English and assimilate into American society as rapidly as possible. This policy was carried out to such extremes, however, that the native culture of minority students was often demeaned by teachers. Mexican students were often punished for speaking Spanish in school, having, for example, their mouths "washed out with soap" (U.S. Commission on Civil Rights 1972, 13). This Americanization era dominated the schooling experiences of whole cohorts of immigrant groups, especially "white ethnics," and, of course, Mexicans were centrally targeted in this ethnic cleansing effort.

For some proponents of this learning approach, racism was clearly a major factor (Menchaca and Valencia 1990; Donato, Menchaca, and Valencia 1991). However, most of the advocates of the Americanization process were motivated by a spirit of inclusiveness, although this sometimes smacked of benign racism: "These people just need the right culture to be more acceptable." Specific examples of this Americanization program for Mexican Americans in the barrios are abundant (Menchaca 1989; Gonzalez 1990; Hill 1928).

A paternalistic approach was often the only alternative to the more egregious practices of outright segregation, such as separate, inferior, or even nonexistent school facilities for minorities (Valencia 1991b). In 1930, for example, a San Diego community school board attempted to set up a "Mexican" school (see Alvarez 1987, 1988, on which the film *Lemon Grove Incident* by Paul Espinoza is based). The policies of Americanization and segregation combined to ensure problems in school for Mexican-American students—damned completely by segregation and daunted by a learning program based on a premise of "cultural deficiency" (Carter and Segura 1978).

Mexican people in the United States resisted blatant forms of racism and discrimination from the onset and regularly struggled for equality on numerous fronts. An early critic who challenged the cultural deficiency premise embedded in the Americanization perspective was George I. Sanchez, a scholar from New Mexico (Sanchez 1966; Buriel 1984). Sanchez's main contribution was in pushing scholars to reexamine the cultural and racial biases inherent in the IQ tests and other measurements then in vogue (Sanchez 1932). Mexican Americans consistently scored poorly on these tests, and their results were used to rationalize their placement in remedial classes. White ethnics in an earlier era had similarly scored poorly on such tests, because the Binet IQ test was created in part to differentiate these populations from Anglos (Kamin 1974; Blum 1978).

Sanchez argued that cultural and linguistic differences accounted for the IQ scores, and not cultural deficiency. In other words, these tests often provided a veneer of respectability for racist practices, however commendable the motivations of some Americanization advocates might have been. Sanchez's scholarship ultimately became an example for subsequent generations of Mexican Americans taking their places alongside African Americans in the civil rights struggles that focused on education.

Unfortunately, the cultural deficiency perspective outlasted more blatant forms of segregation. In the aftermath of World War II, the *Mendez v. Westminster* case in 1947 struck down separate and unequal schools in California (McWilliams 1968; Donato, Menchaca, and Valencia 1991). However, as recently as 1968, Mexican-American children (and blacks) who tested low in the San Diego School District were labeled educable mentally retarded (EMR) and placed in special classes. Many of these students spoke little English or were out of touch with the dominant Anglo culture on which the test was based (Valencia and Aburto 1991). Thus, the cultural deficit philosophy still existed, but under a different guise. Only after this practice was challenged by a coalition of leaders from the NAACP and the Mexican American Political Association (MAPA) was the EMR policy changed.

It is worth noting that most of the Mexican and working-class white students whom I taught in high school also took "R" classes with me (for example, Remedial World History). Even though "R" formally meant remedial, those with high "natural intelligence" would jokingly refer to their "retarded" courses, as if they knew they shouldn't be taking "R" classes. Other students, who perhaps were not as bright, would keep their heads down and remain quiet in their embarrassment.

Even with the great advancements that have been achieved since the 1960s, some often prejudiced practices, in the guises of testing and tracking, still hold over from earlier eras that stigmatize the mixing of Mexican and Anglo cultural forms, thereby hindering the academic growth of today's Chicano students (Valencia and Aburto 1991). The Americanization premise (and an assumption commonly held among early anthropologists and the public in general) specifies that successful school performance, and life achievements for that matter, come with acculturating to Anglo-American ways. My research on this issue, like earlier research by other scholars (Spindler and Spindler 1961; McFee 1968; Eaton 1952), confirms that bilingual-bicultural individuals do well in school and society as they move between their two worlds (Vigil and Long 1981; Vigil 1992a). Moreover, more recent research supports the appraisal that bicultural students merge both worlds into their unique repertoire of cultural ways to think and act resiliently in all types of social and emotional settings (Ramirez and Castaneda 1974; Ramirez 1985; Vigil 1991; Valencia 1991; Trueba et al. 1993; Spindler and Spindler 1990; Gibson and Ogbu 1991).

My research has also ascertained that preacculturation backgrounds affect the tone and direction of acculturation and adaptation patterns of immigrants in America. Furthermore, confounding facts and dynamics based on gender (Vigil 1987) and cultural styles (Vigil 1979) have also been illuminated in my studies. In short, what began as a rather simple, straightforward exercise of explaining Mexican high school children's achievement has now reached a much greater complexity.

This study began in 1974 as a qualitative and quantitative comparison of acculturation and school success among Mexican-American students at two high schools. In the years that followed, I returned frequently to the two schools, and especially to the areas in which they are located, either on business (for example, in interviews for my studies of area gangs, or as a guest lecturer for local institutions), or simply to catch up with old acquaintances. In 1988, I conducted a second formal comparison of students at the two locations, partially replicating the earlier investigation.

HISTORICAL BACKGROUND

The 1974 investigation, or "snapshot," took place in the aftermath of the civil rights movement, when many of the movement's reforms were in place and operating. An example is the bilingual education curriculum. Because of the groundswell of activism and pressure from the Chicano movement—including the "Blowouts" of 1968 in which more than seven thousand students in three Eastside Los Angeles high schools left their campuses to stage public protests—bilingual education and other educational reforms were enacted. Despite the fact that such programs were quickly conceived and hastily organized, improvements began to appear. By 1974, they were beginning to function fairly well, if only by beginning to break down the monolithic cultural barriers that impeded sensitivity to Mexican student needs.

Still much at issue, however, were broadly accepted formulas for ethnic self-identification among Mexican Americans. Scholars and community members spent large amounts of time and energy debating this issue. When class status was injected into the discussion, both the class advocates and the "cultural nationalist" adherents waxed rhetorical. Those emphasizing that Mexican Americans were

Chicano student activists at Belvedere Park in the early 1970s.

members of the poor and working class and a part of the larger class segment of American society suggested a broader identity that included many ethnic groups. The adherents of the cultural nationalist perspective, however, strongly promoted an identity that underscored the unique culture and history of Mexicans within the United States, particularly in connection with the continuous regeneration of Mexican culture and the Spanish language created by the flow of Mexican immigrants and proximity to Mexico.

Moreover, this period in the 1970s, marked by flux and change, signaled the first significant transition away from the Anglo promotion of Americanization or Anglo-conformity models, to advocating ethnic pluralism (Gordon 1964) or cultural democracy (Ramirez and Castaneda 1974).

In contrast, the Reagan years of the 1980s were noted for change of a different sort. A conservative backlash swept through federal government eliminating some of the last vestiges of the Great Society. The Reagan administration oversaw the phasing out of Comprehensive Employment and Training Act (CETA) programs and the reapplication of laissez-faire economics in a policy that emphasized entrepreneurship and individualism reminiscent of the nineteenth century. Paradoxically, as cultural diversity and assertiveness became the rule among Latino opinion makers and fashionable in academia (fueled by immigration but also by a political agenda), government leaders at all levels regressed and reacted by reintroducing Americanization policies. For example, the "English Only" language movement led by outraged "native" Americans became popular during this time.

Meanwhile, the educational bureaucracies, so slow to change either forward or backward, had institutionalized some of the reforms introduced in the 1960s, and now found it difficult to change or remove them. This was especially the case with certain language and curriculum programs that had made significant inroads in improving the educational experiences of many Mexican pupils. Consequently, significant tension began to develop among educators who disagreed about which direction future educational policy should go (Valencia 1991a; see Colvin 1996 for the challenge to bilingual education in California, for example).

CULTURE CHANGE

The political changes and orientations noted above were more than matched by economic, demographic, and institutional shifts. In East Los Angeles particularly, but also in the suburban area examined, a major economic restructuring affected job opportunities and social habits (Moore and Pinderhughes-Rivera 1993). Many small industries moved either to outlying suburban environs or foreign nations, which decimated the economic base of the area. A statewide recession that had begun years earlier was most intensely felt in Los Angeles County and further damaged the economic base. The repercussions are still being felt and documented, but overall it has severely diminished economic opportunities for much of the populace.

From the 1970s to the 1990s an equally significant factor was the tremendous increase in immigration and the diversification of the greater Los Angeles area population. Mexicans, Central Americans, other Latinos and Caribbeans, along with an especially heavy influx of Asians, made this region truly a world city. Coming on the heels of the civil rights objective of respect for cultural differences, this influx meant that a critical mass of practitioners in the form of newcomers, have emboldened and strengthened "political" objectives based on cultural criteria. It is not only cultural infusion that characterizes this change, however, for there is the additional ingredient that large numbers of these people are economic and political refugees. In certain sections of Los Angeles, this handicap of being "disconnected" and marginal to social and economic institutions and influences became glaringly obvious, and publicized, in the upheavals of 1992 that followed the acquittal of the police officers who engaged in the beating of Rodney King (Vigil 1992b).

Moreover, poverty also increased in response to funding cutbacks and the government's blind eye to persistent socioeconomic problems. Researchers and policy makers have hotly debated the existence of an "underclass"—urban enclaves that experience persistent and concentrated poverty (Wilson 1987; Jencks and Peterson 1991)—and its effects on educational performance. The dispute in some ways echoes the culture of poverty controversy of the 1960s and 1970s (Valentine 1968; Leacock 1971). Latino immigrants are an especially vulnerable group, made so by their marginal status in their homelands, coupled with their low station as an unskilled, cheap reservoir of expendable labor in the United States. Indeed, to cope with this plight, Mexican and other Latino immigrants have introduced interesting entrepreneurial activities to maintain a "working poor" connection to society (Moore and Pinderhughes-Rivera 1993). Examples include the street-based informal economy adaptation of fruit, vegetable, flower, ice cream, and candy and gum vendors. In effect, there has been continuity in the transference and transition of immigrants' economic hardship from one nation to another, but today's immigrants are resilient and creative in their readaptations.

Businesses and government agencies also underwent their own transformations during this time. Political pressure and involvement eventually resulted in greater numbers of elected and appointed officials advocating for Mexican-American interests and concerns. High on the agendas of these leaders have been jobs and better public services, particularly schools. In both areas where the sample high schools are located, local leaders and activists were able to receive a better hearing, even though it was often the critical mass of demographics that pushed those who held the purse strings to the hearings. Heretofore, city councilpersons only listened politely, but now institutional support became attainable.

ACCULTURATION MODES AND STRATEGIES

Mexican Americans are poised for major contributions to the United States in the twenty-first century. In particular, the example of a bilingual-bicultural identity as American citizens will help steer the United States away from a monolithic-centered language and cultural orientation to one that connects Americans to the rest of the world (Arvizu and Snyder 1977; Gibson and Arvizu 1977). Acculturation paths have changed so that even those *Chic-Anglos* (Mexican and Chicanos who have assimilated) are more aware of their Mexican roots. Demographic realities have shifted significantly with large-scale immigration. Immigrant students' academic success has shown marked improvements partly related to the success of learning programs such as *ESL* (English as a second language), *transition* programs (starting school in Spanish and gradually but ultimately moving completely into English) or bilingual-bicultural *maintenance* programs (parity and facility in both languages throughout schooling) that are culture sensitive and have softened "cultural shock." Nevertheless, major, but surmountable, problems still exist (Laskin 1994). Among them are the persistence of mental health stressors and problems associated with acculturation and especially with assimilation (Rogler, Cortes, and Malgady 1991). Added to that is the complexity of politics among proponents of bilingual-bicultural education, with some people accepting the need for bilingual goals but not bicultural ones, and a host of other contentious details and programmatic disagreements.

In short, Mexicanization now guides the ethnic self-identification process among adolescents and youth. The large numbers of Mexicans and Latinos are creating a critical mass to affirm and further invigorate political and cultural awareness efforts. This presence has made it more palatable and acceptable to be "Mexican" in one form or another (Martinez 1994). Immigration and Mexicanization have also contributed to the creation and permutation of new personal and cultural expressions. For example, the more recently emerging styles include the *Chachas,* who are Mexican immigrant youth partially Anglicized in a "mod" style (Santana 1986). Chachas reflect the influence of American television and radio in their music and dress—an "electronic" Anglicization, so to speak, fashionable in the middle and late 1980s but still recalled with great fondness by its adherents, some of whom are graduate students today.

During the same time period, many older barrios with *cholos* (Chicanos who are marginal to both Anglo-American and Mexican cultures) and gang members saw a somewhat similar electronic cultural shift when, for a short time, the "Stoners" style temporarily drew many youths toward music and dress (with occasional satanic overtones) associated with "heavy metal" and "punk rock" music fans and a decidedly more Anglo way of speaking English and acting American; now the cholos and gang members are back in the traditional street mode, khakis and tee shirts.

Further permutations based on the immigrant reality include the *Norteno* (northern Mexican, cowboy style), and the *Banda* (Mexican-German polka music with syncretic Mexican-Anglo developments), and even a new phenomenon known as the "1.5 generation" (immigrants who were born in Mexico but came to America when they were four to six years old) (see Buriel and Cardoza 1993, for ethnic labeling factors).

In the time of cultural diversity, or, perhaps, the expediter of same, the personas mexicanas phenomenon (the mestizo heritage that draws from and reflects many racial and cultural heritages) takes on new dimensions and importance (Vigil 1993b). The ability to perceive oneself as multifaceted linguistically and culturally and to function in a resilient and adaptable way to a complex world directly contradicts the rigid, dichotomous construction of traditional Anglo-American culture that dictates "become like me or become the other." It is now appropriate and necessary to think, "I am this and that and that and that . . ."

In this modern world, which the United States epitomizes in a smaller scale, the improvements of cross-cultural understanding and interaction will result in a better world, particularly in terms of commerce and trade. Indeed, viable participation in a global economy implies some degree of global cultural understanding and exchange. In such a world, ethnic identity no longer needs to be a fixed, irreversible niche that impedes movement, but can become a reflexive, flexible orientation that borrows, changes, adapts, renews, synthesizes, and constantly reevaluates the social and human surroundings (Arvizu 1974).

SCHOOLS AND SCHOOLING

The significant changes in school and schooling must also be acknowledged. The evidence strongly suggests that despite the rhetoric of conservative cultural assimilationists, ESL/bilingual education is successful. Along with the Head Start program, whose naysayers were eventually disproved, bilingual education has made a difference to Mexican-American students. This is confirmed with the outstanding improvements that have resulted in this study's urban high school population. Most of the students there have benefited from early ESL or bilingual efforts, and display a marked confidence in expanding their ethnic identity, also described as "nativist" acculturation (Vigil and Long 1981), to also include facility and competence in the dominant Anglo-American culture.

An example of this process was provided during the spring of 1988, when my wife (an alumnus of this study's urban high school) and I rode one of forty buses the city school district hired for the preview opening of a film based on the urban high school and one of its math teachers. (This teacher had, according to the film's plot, turned the school and students around almost single-handedly, in an epitome of the Hollywood "John Wayne Thesis of Educational Change.") My wife and I were struck with the ease and facility with which the students communicated and joked with each other in the Spanish language, as well as in English when the need arose. What we noted was later affirmed by two of my students at USC (both outstanding premedicine majors) who had attended the same high school and film event (personal communication). According to these students, student repartee and interaction at the urban high school, sometimes including many new Chicano or Latino teachers, provided them with ample opportunities to think and speak in Spanish and act in ways that were Mexican without fear of retribution. They also confirmed that their early education and continuing familiarity and dexterity with Mexican culture and the Spanish language had facilitated their acquisition and use of English and knowledge of Anglo-American culture.

However, it must be noted that both the urban and suburban high schools in this study have failed in one important area: developing effective interventions for cholo, marginalized students who often belong to a gang. Unlike the 1974 study, the 1988 restudy found *no* cholos or gang members in its sample at either school. Yet, in comparison to the 1970s, the street gang activities and acts of violence in both areas had mushroomed in the 1980s. Thus, it is clear that both schools had found more or less subtle ways to push out or otherwise discourage the cholo segment of the Chicano student population, a group already greatly at risk for dropping out (Rumberger 1991). Elsewhere (Vigil 1983, 1988, 1990a, 1993a), I have documented that gaps in home or school socialization for many youths lead inexorably to street socialization. To some degree, the proliferation of street gangs in the last decade can be traced to the failure of schools to reach out and address the special circumstances and learning difficulties of choloized youth (multiply marginality; see Vigil 1988; Trueba 1991).

THE RESEARCH SITES

The interaction of factors that affect school performance, and the contrasts among them, are often compounded by so-called when, where, and who influences: *time* and *place,* as well as the *inherent variations among peoples.* Accounting for macro-historical forces is important, as entrenched racial barriers and structural impediments persist in influencing Mexican-American educational success. Moreover, these forces have affected the dynamics of Chicano acculturation and adaptation differently over time periods and environmental settings.

These environmental constraints, which occur on many levels, determine the access, exposure, and identification (Graves 1967) immigrants have to Anglo-American culture and thus, as the inferred association goes, to socioeconomic mobility and opportunities. For example, federal housing policy created low-income housing projects in many urban areas, including Los Angeles, that also served as an environmental constraint that restricted access to the mainstream culture and even to more mundane things, such as shopping malls and grocery stores. Parents and grandparents of youth in this study's samples have spoken in interviews about the Mexican school being on the "other side of the tracks," having one's "mouth washed out with soap" for speaking Spanish at school and other incidents in their youth that occurred in the days before the 1960s civil rights movement. These experiences served as environmental constraints restricting the ability of Mexican immigrants to identify with the Anglo culture, at least before television and other media brought the culture into their homes.

Equally noteworthy are the segregation and discriminatory practices institutionalized in rural California, which created misery for settled farm laborers and migrant workers (Menchaca 1989). There is an often told story of the teacher in Watsonville, for instance, who always made sure that the farmowners' children took leadership roles over the children of the farmworkers, so as to prepare them for their future relationship based on class, status, and, of course, race (Parsons 1965).

Still, conditions have changed. For this reason, the research for this volume was conducted in high schools in two different environments: An urban community in East Los Angeles and a suburban tract division located about fourteen miles from Los Angeles, during two different time periods (1974 and 1988). The many differences between the two communities enable us to appreciate the extent of the cultural and attitudinal variability of the Mexican and Mexican-American population in the Greater Los Angeles area. Interviews and observations of the youths and the adults of these communities as they carry out their daily activities provide a deeper understanding of what motivates and guides their ambitions and goals. Anthropologists have traditionally been intrigued by the *behavioral environment* (Hallowell 1955; Rodgers and Long 1968) of the peoples they have observed and interviewed. Observing and recording details of the setting and identifying the key players provide a good "snapshot" of the realities of that time and place. With a combination of prolonged stays and periodic visits at that site, the observer can produce a longitudinal, somewhat cinematic image of the place that describes the major and more subtle transformations over time.

The urban community population in this study has long been overwhelmingly composed of Mexican immigrants and Mexican Americans. During the initial study in 1974, the urban barrio had a population of more than 102,000, of whom 85 percent were of Mexican descent. Residents were generally poor: The average annual household income was only $7,526, and 18 percent of the households were receiving some sort of public assistance. Adults in the urban barrio had an average of 8.8 years of education, and 7.4 percent had no formal education whatsoever.

In contrast, the suburban area at that time had a population of approximately 15,500, 48 percent of whom were of Mexican descent. The suburban residents were generally middle and lower class with household heads in blue-collar occupations: The average annual income was $11,478, and only 4 percent of the households received public assistance. Adults in the suburban area had an average of twelve years of education, and only 1.5 percent had no formal education whatsoever (see Table 1-1).

Table 1-1   CHANGES IN THE HIGH SCHOOLS' NEIGHBORHOODS

	URBAN 1974	1988	SUBURBAN 1974	1988
Population of Area	102,000	126,379	15,500	15,520
% Mexicans in Area	85%	91%	48%	67%
Average Yearly Income	$7,526	$22,937	$11,478	$33,313
% of Population on AFDC	18%	24%	4%	20%
Education Completed	8.8 years average	66% have 8 years or less	12 years average	60% completed high school, 7% completed college
No Education	7.4%	N/A	1.5%	N/A

The high schools in 1974 reflected their respective environments. The urban high school was built in the 1920s and sits on relatively little acreage; the suburban school, built in 1955, sits on a sprawling, green campus. The urban high school's population primarily included students of Mexican descent: 32 percent of the students were born in Mexico, and 92 percent of the students were of Mexican heritage. In the suburban high school, 35 percent of the students were Mexican American, and only 5 percent had been born in Mexico. Despite having a similar total number of students and average schoolwide grade point average (GPA), the urban high school had a significantly higher percentage of dropouts than the suburban school—official rates of 24 percent versus 14 percent, respectively (see Table 1-2). Actually, the urban dropout rate was probably higher, as teachers generally suggested it approximated half of the students (see Trueba, Spindler, and Spindler 1989 for a discussion of school dropouts).

Some noteworthy differences became apparent after a series of initial visits to these schools in 1974. In the urban high school, turmoil was common on campus, in contrast to the relative tranquility of the suburban school. Many of the difficulties were related to a power struggle between the Chicano principal of the high school and its older, more entrenched Anglo faculty members. The principal had originally been appointed in the aftermath of student and community protests several years before over the unequal and ethnocentric policies of the school district and faculty. He was an able and proven innovator who created many programs, but his eventual dismissal

Table 1-2   CHANGES IN THE HIGH SCHOOLS

	URBAN 1974	1988	SUBURBAN 1974	1988
School Population	92% Mexican	99% Mexican	35% Mexican	71% Mexican
Born Mexico	32%	63%	5%	23%
Total School Population	2,210	3,402	2,420	1,172
Average GPA for School	2.4	2.51	2.7	2.6
Approximate Dropout Rate	24%	N/A	14%	28%

was brought about by a large number of intransigent teachers who rejected the introduction of his educational experiments. The students' education suffered as a result of this in-fighting. The teachers expended valuable energy on thwarting the principal's culturally based goals (for example, more Chicano faculty, curriculum changes to incorporate Mexican content and contributions, and bilingual education), and students were aware of this.

Gang activity, especially, was more predominant in the urban high school in 1974. The high school student body included members from at least twelve gangs who engaged in frequent, violent conflicts, occasionally on campus, but more frequently in their respective neighborhoods. At the time of the 1974 study, two youths had been killed in such gang violence, one of them on campus. As a result, students in the urban high school were constantly aware of the aura of aggression on campus.

In contrast, although the suburban school included students from two Mexican-American gangs, these gangs were neither as active nor as violent as their urban counterparts. The suburban gangs derived from the older *colonias* (nineteenth-century rural enclaves of Mexican settlers or part of the immigrant waves in the early twentieth century) that were engulfed by the post–World War II suburban sprawl in the 1950s. Moreover, the suburban high school had instituted programs designed to meet the culturally different needs of the adolescent Mexican American and thus alleviate gang problems among them. One program, Expanded Horizons, offered students counseling and cultural enrichment outings and also served as a sounding board or buffer among students, parents, and school personnel. Because the suburban school was dominated by Anglos, the Expanded Horizons effort had only to deal with a small portion of the student body; thus, the campus was relatively peaceful.

It is fairly obvious that in 1974 these two communities and high schools re-flected contrasting populations in terms of cultural, class, and social issues. There-fore, place clearly plays an important role in this study, but the dynamic of time is also significant. By 1988, when I decided to reexamine the high schools, the changes in the interim years had been astounding. Demographic shifts showed an increase in poverty in general, with an alarming emphasis on the feminization of this poverty. An erosion of the economic infrastructure had also occurred, as well as a steady rise in crime and related street gang behavior that was to continue well into the 1990s.

One of the most significant changes, however, has been the mass Mexicaniza-tion of both the urban and the suburban fieldsites, which is producing a new genera-tion of youth and families proud of their cultural background. For example, the urban fieldsite experienced a large influx of Mexican immigrants (as well as other Latinos, especially Central Americans). Although there is also heavy immigration into the suburban fieldsite, here the immigrants include many more 1.5-generation immigrants (that is, immigrants who came to America as young children). Reared mostly in the United States, but Mexican nationals by birth and asserting a cultural allegiance to the "home country," these are unlike either first- or second-generation immigrants of the past, but somewhere in between. As a result of these immigration patterns, the cultural (or acculturation) spectrum of the student bodies is shifting significantly.

In addition, there is a Mexicanization of the political and academic landscape. In 1974, there were no Latinos on the school board of the suburban school and only one Latino on the school board of the urban school's unified district. The faculty and administrators at both schools were predominantly white; school meetings with parents were conducted in English. By 1988, this had changed and the conditions that prevail today were already present. There are now several Latinos on the school boards of both schools, and the number of Latinos in the faculty and admin-istration has also increased. Even school-parent meetings are now often conducted in Spanish.

The U.S. Census of 1990 documents some of the fieldsite changes occurring in the past twenty years. The urban barrio has grown in population, as has the propor-tion of residents of Mexican descent. The residents are still generally poor. The total population in the suburban area has not changed significantly, but the popu-lace is much more Mexicanized. The suburban residents are still generally blue-collar middle and lower class, but approximately 20 percent of the households receive public assistance. Compared to the urban barrio, the suburban population is relatively well educated. (See Table 1-1, page 12 for the statistics describing these changes.)

The high schools have also experienced dramatic changes. The urban high school student body is now composed almost entirely of students of Mexican and other Latino descent, and it has grown by more than 50 percent. In the suburban high school, the proportion of Mexican-American students in the total student popu-lation has nearly doubled. In contrast to the urban high school population, however, the number of students at the suburban high school declined sharply. These changes are summarized in Table 1-2 (page 13).

Another important change has been in the practice (perhaps an unwritten agreement among teachers and administrators) of the high schools towards gangs. Although there are many more gangs today in the streets of Los Angeles than in 1974, in 1988 both the suburban and urban high school appeared to be "gang free." In fact, both campuses, especially the urban school (which had become a so-called magnet school) resembled prep schools, and gang activity was minimal. This was, in part, a result of the schools "discouraging" gang members and other undesirables.

In fact, when I picked the urban sample in 1974, I had to reselect several participants because the original selections had been expelled from school or were facing disciplinary action. In 1988, this problem never arose. The only students allowed in school were those with clean records and "images." Cholo or gang dress was not allowed, although heavy metal or "punk rocker" dress was. All gang members had already been discouraged from going to school by the time I drew my random sample.

In addition, institutional changes in the two high schools and the evolving awareness of gender-based tensions in how males and females receive their education (see Pitman and Eisenhart 1988 for a special issue on women) need to be accounted for in our scenario. School officials, for example, have initiated new approaches to boost the performance of female students. Many teachers, especially female teachers, have also coordinated their efforts to follow a concerted plan to meet the needs of female students.

STUDY DESIGN AND METHODS

In 1974, a semistructured sample of students was chosen from each of the two schools by randomly drawing equal numbers of students of Mexican descent at each grade level (tenth, eleventh, and twelfth). As noted above, replacement drawings were required at the urban school because the original sample included students—mostly gang-affiliated youths—who had recently dropped out or been expelled. A final 1974 sample consisted of thirty-nine urban and forty-one suburban students, evenly divided by gender. These students were questioned in questionnaire-guided interviews covering their language skills, cultural backgrounds, and school behavior, performance, and attitudes. Their responses were tabulated and analyzed statistically. In addition, using an acculturation scale constructed from students' responses about language and culture practices, six students were selected for more in-depth, repeated interviews and observations, at home as well as at school. Two students were chosen with low-scale scores, two with high-scale scores, and two with intermediate scores. Data from interviews with these students and their families were used to inform and illustrate the statistical analyses. Results of the 1974 analyses have been reported by Vigil (1976, 1979, 1982, 1987) and Vigil and Long (1981).

In 1988, a similar design was employed. However, because of time restrictions imposed by the school administration, a smaller sample of students was drawn from the suburban high school. Thus, the 1988 sample included thirty-nine urban students and thirty-one suburban students, about equally divided by gender, who were administered a questionnaire constructed in a manner similar to that used in 1974.

ACCULTURATION SPECTRUM PLACEMENT OF SELECTED INFORMANTS, 1974 AND 1988

← ———— Mexican-Oriented   Intermediate   Anglo-Oriented ————→

1974 **Urban**	Hortensia Matilda	Cecilia Eduardo			Vicente Alberto
1988	Jacinto Lidia Norma Hector	Jorge Daniel	Diana Georgina	Martha Marcia Jose Pascual	

-2 • • • -1 • • • • 0 • • • • +1 • • • • +2

1974 **Suburban**	Carlos Sara		Veronica Juan	Jeffrey Valerie
1988	Fernando Henry Teresa Efrain		Gloria Ryan Leticia Randy Armando	Cynthia Caroline Christine

The average acculturation scale score for each year's sample is indicated by point 0—thus, students whose names are to the right of point 0 had higher-than-average acculturation scale scores and those whose names are to the left had lower-than-average scores (than their respective cohorts).

Using an acculturation scale from this instrument, a larger number of students— twelve from each school—was selected for in-depth interviews and observation. As in the earlier study, these students represented both extremes as well as the middle level of the acculturation score spectrum. (See Figure 1-1 for the distribution of selected students and Appendix 1 for a discussion of quantitative and qualitative research methods for both time periods).

2 / Where Goes Minority Student Achievement: Culture or Class?

For more than a half century researchers have grappled with the effect of acculturation on education. Great strides have been made in coming close to a comprehensive interpretation that at least better documents the problem sources of minority student performance (Neisser 1986; Macias and Garcia Ramos 1995). Simply stated, researchers have focused on either structural or cultural foundations as the causes for poor student performance. According to the structural theorists, it is America's long history of economic dislocation and oppression that creates a "caste" educational system that works to exclude ethnic minority children. According to these same theorists, this exclusion has created a countercultural reaction, an "oppositional" culture (Willis 1977) of distrust and suspicion of dominant institutions and authorities—a sort of turning off to a social system that has traditionally and historically oppressed them. Other theorists argue that cultural barriers or acculturation strains, either language difficulties or a conflict in values, serve as the primary problem source. The cultural difference, or culturalist, viewpoint takes a bottom-up (micro) perspective while the societal, or structuralist, viewpoint prefers a top-down (macro) assessment.

The debate for too long has been cast into an either-or framework between the culturalists and the structuralists (Foley 1990). A more holistic model, one that integrates both the culturalist and structuralist viewpoints, is needed to explain the complex relationship between ethnicity and academic performance. Previous studies have too often neglected the tremendous variability found among Mexican Americans in the largest urban setting in the nation, a region undergoing rapid cultural changes even now. Previous researchers have conducted investigations in intermediate-sized towns or small villages, sometimes rendering their findings less clearly applicable to larger, more diverse populations such as in Los Angeles. Individual character is also an important factor, and limiting the debate to either a cultural or a structural explanation ignores the significance of an individual's persona and motivation.

This investigation is also of long duration and samples a much more heterogeneous population. It encompasses a great amount of variability and focuses specifically on acculturation and school performance relationships. This difference in scope will often make it difficult to directly apply other researchers' findings to key points of my argument.

Anthropologists long ago noted that minority groups, natives and immigrants alike, often fashioned strategies of acculturation that entailed retaining the original culture while learning the new one (Spindler 1970). Researchers have also noted that school success could result with individuals or groups who took that path of biculturalism (Long and Padilla 1971). Even with the debate between the "structuralists" and the "culturalists" sometimes taking center stage, the overwhelming evidence compiled in the last two decades supports the idea that an expansionary rather than contracting acculturation pathway results in successful school performance. Gibson and Ogbu (1991) refer to these concepts as "additive" and "subtractive" acculturation. The expansionary adaptive strategy was discussed earlier by McFee (1968), who coined the phrase "150 percent acculturation" for it. The case for an expansionary mode of acculturation can be found in the academic success of many immigrants, including Mexicans and Cubans (Portes and Bach 1985), Punjabis (Gibson 1988), and Koreans (Hurh and Kim 1984).

However, although there may be general agreement on the value of 150 percent acculturation, the clash between structuralists and culturalists continues to drive much of the literature. One key element in the continuing debate on this issue is the strength of the theoretical framework of John Ogbu, an educational anthropologist at the University of California at Berkeley who belongs to the structuralist school of thought. According to Ogbu and some of his close disciples (Ogbu 1987, 1989, 1991; Gibson 1988; Gibson and Ogbu 1991; Matute-Bianchi 1991), the most fruitful and parsimonious explanation results when we distinguish between primary and secondary cultural discontinuities (Obgu 1982) among minority children. Ogbu's theory, referred to as cultural ecology, postulates that structural and institutional oppression have created a caste system and counterculture among indigenous minorities. According to Ogbu, recent voluntary immigrants are not subject to this caste system and therefore have not developed a counterculture. Separating children on the basis of immigrant versus indigenous backgrounds, or voluntary versus involuntary, Ogbu argues that primary cultural discontinuities occur among immigrants (the "voluntaries") because of the obvious language and cultural differences and barriers that interfere with schooling, but that they are able to overcome these obstacles; whereas the indigenous children (the "involuntaries") suffer from secondary cultural discontinuities that stem from historically racist attitudes and caste-like experiences that have ingrained mistrust and suspicion. Such developments have forged and affirmed a "cultural resistance" stance among these populations.

Many detractors to this model challenge its general applicability. Among the leading critics of this schema are Henry Trueba, an educational anthropologist (Delgado-Gaitan 1991a; Moll 1987), and George and Louise Spindler, pioneers in this field of research. As part of my efforts to refine my skills and insights to further understand this issue, I spent a year at the University of California, Santa Barbara, with Trueba under a Ford Postdoctoral Fellowship in 1987 to 1988.

Trueba (1993a) maintains in his scathing critique of cultural ecology, that this approach tends to over-rely on the influence of a single factor. Specifically, Trueba argues that the following characteristics of Ogbu's model are too rigid and dogmatic (pp. 27–29):

1. Caste-like minorities are here against their will,
2. They fail in schools because they feel and are incompetent,
3. They are incompetent because they develop oppositional identities in opposition to the white mainstream population, and
4. School success is perceived as a white cultural trait.

Further, Trueba states that, "The most interesting feature of the most recent studies purported to support (Ogbu's) cultural ecology is that indeed the data argue against the dominant rigidity of any theoretical dichotomy (voluntary versus involuntary, immigrant versus nonimmigrant) or against any rigid typology" (p. 30). In addition, in concurring with Ramirez and with my early work (Vigil 1979; Vigil and Long 1981), Trueba argues that, "Mexicans are not only highly diversified in their prearrival experiences and socioeconomic background, but also in their differential coping strategies with demands for adaptation in this country" (p. 30). I add that they also vary in their measure of affluence and poverty. Finally, Trueba notes:

> Cultural ecology, in its present form of a dichotomy between voluntary and involuntary minorities, may not explain either success or failure without additional evidence of important functional intervention of other agencies affecting minority communities. Determinism (biological, psychological or cultural) oversimplifies behavioral phenomena and offers reductionistic explanations of complex processes (especially in the learning environments where intellectual functions and learning outcomes are embedded in power relationships,) (1993: 33).

In a seminal issue of the *Anthropology and Education Quarterly* (Jacob and Jordan 1987), these diverse ideas were debated by scholars who presented their views on the subject of school performance of minority students. The scholars were generally divided into the culturalist and the structuralist camps. Yet, according to the editors, the two theories need not conflict or be mutually exclusive; rather "a movement toward synthesis" seems to be more appropriate. I believe that these two perspectives should be considered as different colored pieces of the same cloth, which enables us to understand intergroup variation (societal forces) and factors particular and specific to the classroom and group (cultural differences). Even with social status (for example, low income) and cultural orientation (for example, immigrant) held constant, personal and individual quirks and motivation must be taken into account (Spindler and Spindler 1987, 1991).

In my earlier discussions of this issue (Vigil 1976, 1979; Vigil and Long 1981; Vigil 1982, 1987), I have long argued that both perspectives must be integrated into a broader approach to assess the question of minority student school achievement and performance. Excluding either the structuralist or the culturalist viewpoint would be foolish. Thus, it is still plain to me that one must heed the advice of Manuel Ramirez who stated:

> Specifically there is need for extensive studies of how milieu and socioeconomic class interact with acculturation (read broadly as cultural barriers—Au.) to affect personality and education. The Chicano is now socioeconomically diverse, and is found in so many different milieus that it will be necessary to do studies in rural and urban areas and in different states of the Southwest and Midwest. Who can deny that conditions for acculturation in Texas differ from those in California, or those in East Los Angeles differ from those in Chicago? (1971, 407).

This advice seems to have mustered the support of most researchers on this issue, as they seek to balance structural and economic forces with cultural patterns and adaptations;

a few have looked at "voluntary" versus "involuntary" students within the same family (Hayes 1992). In the case of the Mexican-American population, there is a need to examine them within any given context both as natives and immigrants.

CULTURE CHANGE AND ACCULTURATION

Mexicans are natives of the American Southwest; they began to settle there in 1598. Nearly two and a half centuries later, the Mexican-American War broke out in 1846 and the natives experienced the onslaught of the Anglo-American peoples. Intense economic competition and exploitation dominated as frontier wars and border fili-bustering flared for decades in the aftermath of the war (Acuna 1988). Even though the 1848 Treaty of Guadalupe Hidalgo ended the military engagement and ad-dressed the cultural rights of the vanquished Mexican peoples (Griswold del Castillo 1990), tremendous cultural imperialism resulted as the language practices and values of the Mexican people were demeaned (Monroy 1990; Montejano 1987).

In the nineteenth century, Mexican integration into the United States in this volatile, frictional manner set the tone for future Anglo-American and Mexican re-lations and interactions. In the twentieth century, when immigration from Mexico brought millions of settlers to what was becoming known as the Southwest, sim-mering economic battles and cultural conflicts again erupted. This time the immi-grants were treated outright as aliens who did not belong, as the coloring of cultural subjugation and racial discrimination of the earlier milieu had made its imprint on the Anglo-American mind.

The stream of immigrants intensified in the 1920s, after the Revolution of 1910, and has continued to the present. This prolonged immigration revolves around economic imperatives, where the *pull* of jobs and cheap labor in the United States is matched by the *push* from poverty and job scarcity in Mexico. Thus, an analysis of acculturation and adaptation to American institutions must also think about economic considerations (Bowles and Gintis 1976). If we are to understand educational performance and achievement as the take-off point to socioeconomic mobility, Ramirez's words take on even more importance.

When immigrants leave Mexico they usually are seeking better life opportuni-ties. Immediate jobs and places to live capture their first energies. However, this na-tion's historically rooted practices toward aliens soon make it obvious that many opportunities are closed to Mexicans. The upshot is that Mexicans must acculturate to Anglo-American standards of speaking and behaving if they are to enhance their social mobility. As a result, culture change and acculturation become part of the drive for socioeconomic mobility. If earning a low income and living in a poor, run-down neighborhood characterize the immigrant population, then distancing oneself from that characterization in order to get ahead becomes part and parcel of a strat-egy of acculturation, and even assimilation. After all, if remaining Mexican also meant being poor, why would anyone want to be Mexican (Moore and Pachon 1985)? This belief is typical among many suburban Mexican Americans who now have difficulty resolving their ethnic identity as a result of painful experiences asso-ciated with early poverty.

Thus, the issue of educational performance and achievement is complex; structural considerations, culture change, and acculturation dynamics must be considered in the equation. Categorizing Chicanos as "caste" (involuntary) or "immigrant" (voluntary) minorities is a good starting point, as the above historical summary suggests, but the variability and heterogeneity of the population must be accounted for in ways that show the full range of thinking and acting in the population. Until we address and unravel the many facets of their ethnic experience, the differences based on regional contrasts, ethnic identity, *mestizaje* (race and cultural mixture), and, in particular, the class variations, we must make more modest and guarded claims on whether we have adequately investigated and understood what minority student achievement is, at least among Mexican Americans.

A closer look at the contemporary variability would aid our appreciation of the complexity of the problem. At least 15 million Mexicans now live in the United States, mostly concentrated in the Southwest and Midwest. This figure does not include the estimated 6 to 10 million undocumented Mexican immigrants who reside in these areas and who also send children to the schools. There are also seven million other Latinos, mainly Puerto Ricans, Cubans, and Central Americans who live in particular cities and regions; of these, Central Americans are most common in southern California. During the 1980s, the Latino population grew at a rate more than four times faster than the general population in the United States (Valencia 1991b).

Los Angeles holds the largest concentration of Latinos in the United States. When Central Americans, mainly Salvadorans, Guatemaltecos, Nicaraguans, and Hondurans, are included with the Mexicans, we are talking about a tremendously diverse and complex population in Southern California. Latino children make up more than 60 percent of the Los Angeles public school students, even though Latinos comprise only 40 percent of the total population in Los Angeles. Despite the sheer size of the Latino population in Los Angeles, few studies in the field of educational anthropology have examined students in Los Angeles, and for that matter, students in large urban areas. My goal in this study was not only to outline a more holistic theoretical framework to examine this issue, but also to provide a longitudinal study in a large urban area. The expected result is a more comprehensive and representative understanding of the Mexican population's schooling experiences.

Latino cultural variability is definitely reflected in one's generation in the United States. Before this occurs, however, distinct regional differences from the native country affect the tone and rate of acculturation. To compound matters, acculturation is also affected by socioeconomic status and experience before and after entrance into the United States. For example, some of the immigrants come from fairly affluent and educated backgrounds and do well in the United States either immediately or within a few years. Mexican political refugees and middle-class merchants and professionals who came to the United States in large numbers, especially in the 1920s, following the 1910 Mexican Revolution, are examples of this pattern (Suárez-Orozco 1989). Others might come to this country with modest resources and training but are able to become members of the working, and eventually, middle class.

In recent years, the rise of the middle class within the Mexican population in this country has been considerable in numbers even though the percentage is low by other national standards. This rise in status is often accompanied by cultural changes—the higher the income, the more suburban and white the neighborhood, and the less likely the affiliation with Mexican cultural practices.

There has also been a slight increase in the number of families and children living below poverty levels, with more and more households headed by a single mother. This phenomenon, referred to as the *underclass* (to describe those who experience persistent and concentrated poverty), does not necessarily translate into retention and identification of Mexican culture (Chapa 1988). Instead, there is "cultural loss without cultural replacement," as Anglo-American culture is only filtered into the underclass through the media and mostly negative contacts and interactions with schools, law enforcement, and other public institutions of authority.

It is clear that cultural variations are greatly exacerbated by structural forces and socioeconomic conditions. The past twenty years of demographic and political changes have created this circumstance in the Mexican immigrant and Mexican-American indigenous communities, for now there are obvious and serious splits between the two, based on cultural (mostly generational) and structural (mostly socioeconomic status) differences.

3 / "Coming to America is the Best Thing That Has Happened to Me": The Urban 1974 Informants

The late 1960s and early 1970s were a tumultuous time for Chicanos. It was during this period that Chicanos became more demonstrative in their battle against discrimination and stretched their ethnic muscles. Rallies, protests, and even riots were a common part of the street scene and all together represented an angry challenge to the orthodoxy of the established, Anglo-dominated system. However, after the Chicano Moratorium riot on August 29, 1970 (and a series of similar incidents for a few months thereafter), the situation in East Los Angeles quieted down, and ethnic activism began to wane. Nevertheless, the protests had shaken the status quo. For example, from 1968 onward Los Angeles school district officials rushed to placate walkout activists and other pressure groups by adopting various educational and curriculum reforms. These reforms led to bilingual education and learning and staffing practices that reflected a Mexican-American presence. It has already been noted that these initiatives were quick-fix measures with hazily defined goals, but they were nonetheless moves in the right direction of seeking new cultural solutions to persistent cultural and linguistic barriers and problems.

At the same time, the changes during this era also had a tremendous influence on communities and high schools, as the young people were wracked by the reverberating effects of social and political upheavals that strongly colored the acculturation and ethnic identification processes, and, most importantly, their performance in school.

The upshot was that many students, particularly from the more Anglo-oriented third and fourth generations, found themselves in a quandary. Just when these young people were seeking Anglo lifeways and customs, they found that the cultural rules in their neighborhoods were reversed in a Mexican direction. As more and more whites in the area left for the suburbs and elsewhere, they became isolated. At a time in life when the relationships formed, the friends met, and the people seen on a daily basis all affect the formation of identity, the shrinking presence of whites in the neighborhoods provided them with fewer opportunities to interact with Anglos as a source of identification.

ESL students getting together on a weekend.

Simultaneously, there was pressure on barrio youth to *not* assimilate (that is, kowtow, idolize, copy, and so on), as exemplified in the 1968 Blowouts, which encouraged a philosophy of "no assimilation at any cost," regardless of one's generation or cultural orientation. This was a dramatic reversal; even up to the mid-1960s, it was still common for Chicano students to degrade Spanish-speaking students as "T.J.s" (Tijuaneros, a derogatory slang term for new immigrants from Mexico, or more specifically, Tijuana), even if they were born in the United States.

The dynamic process between Anglo-American and Mexican cultures affects academic performance, resulting in a wide range of variability in acculturation and academic achievement. These differences are directly related to the different degrees of access and exposure that individuals have to a culture, and each individual, of course, will differ in how he or she identifies with the culture. Thus, the roles of access, exposure, and identification with Anglo-American culture and society are also significant.

Unfortunately, however, it is not easy to measure the effects of access, exposure, and identification on academic performance. In particular, during the contentious period of the late 1960s and early 1970s, for both contemporary and historical reasons, school performance was not carefully gauged. The 1968 Blowouts had created fear among school administrators, who spent more time trying to ward off further student protests than in monitoring academic performance. Change and divisiveness were consistent confounding factors: The curriculum was constantly revamped, school teachers were threatened for their somewhat aloof attitudes, and the schools themselves were under constant pressure to correct deficiencies or risk losing their accreditation. Discord was common as macropolitical forces placed the principal, school board, and teachers, separately and collectively, at odds. Under these circumstances, if culture is a barrier, then how do we gauge academic and intellectual progress?

College-bound students, band and drill team members.

On a national level, schools were also under attack in minority communities for failing to educate the youth in inner-city schools. For example, according to school officials, the urban high school in this study had a dropout rate of approximately 50 percent. Despite the vigorous efforts of its first Chicano principal, the high school was unable to retain students, including many children involved in street gangs. The students at risk also created additional stress for the already over-burdened teachers, who unsuccessfully tried to integrate such students. Of course, students who dropped out of school also created significant amounts of stress on themselves and their families—for example, students who received Aid For Dependent Children (AFDC) funds often lost their family's benefits after dropping out.

Amidst all the changes, the only students who seemed to have benefited were the recent Mexican immigrants, especially those in the ESL bilingual programs. This was one of the first significant, but largely unnoticed, improvements at that time (Stanton-Salazar 1995; Garcia 1991).

In addition to environment, however, we must also consider the structure and organization of the family unit, gender differences, socioeconomic factors, and the nature of the educational institution. In short, we need to draw our generalized conclusions by using a multivariate analysis, yet at the same time, we must trace how patterns unfold for each person, changing the contours and nuances in each instance. Though a difficult task, it will become apparent that some general themes can be identified. Overall, the evidence suggests that the students (and their families) have been affected by second-class membership in American society; and the selection and adoption of individual cultural lifestyles reflect each student's socioeconomic and ethnic (racial and cultural) experiences.

These characteristics can be fully grasped by studying the life histories of the students in this study. The life histories were helpful in reflecting and representing the variation within the acculturation scale, but they also provide a valuable intimate,

ACCULTURATION SPECTRUM PLACEMENT OF SELECTED INFORMANTS, 1974 AND 1988

←——— Mexican-Oriented   Intermediate   Anglo-Oriented ———→

1974 **Urban**	Hortensia Matilda	Cecilia Eduardo			Vicente Alberto
1988		Jacinto Lidia Norma Hector	Jorge Daniel	Diana Georgina	Martha Marcia Jose Pascual

-2 • • • • -1 • • • • 0 • • • • +1 • • • • +2

1974 **Suburban**	Carlos Sara		Veronica Juan	Jeffrey Valerie
1988	Fernando Henry Teresa Efrain		Gloria Ryan Leticia Randy Armando	Cynthia Caroline Christine

contextual look into the lives of these students and their ethnic roots, cultural orientations, and social background. These life histories were synthesized from a variety of
sources: extensive interviews with the students and their families and teachers, report
cards, and school records.

I have condensed the life histories into what I call thumbnail ethnographies, or
"thumbnographies" to simplify for illustration the real-life key acculturation issues
and strategies of these students (see Vigil, 1976, Ph.D. dissertation for fuller ethnographic descriptions). These thumbnographies provide us with an intimate, close-up
snapshot picture of the sociocultural forces that affect each student's academic performance. Each of these should be read as part of a panorama of personal cultural
styles and other biographical social events. These developments and events shed
light on the education and academic accomplishments of each student. Within this
broad generational sweep, each case contributes a piece of the cultural mosaic required for understanding how multiple factors affect schooling and learning.

The sequence is also important because the stories begin with the persons closest to the Mexican culture (scaled by birthplace, language use and fluency, cultural
practices, and ethnic labels). By moving through the cultural (or acculturation)
spectrum, we can then examine the interplay between different cultural styles (from
Mexican to intermediate to Anglo) and educational performance. At the same time,
we can also examine how personal habits, social status, environment, and family
matters change for each case. The acculturation spectrum above, with the student
names underlined, will show which thumbnographies are to be discussed.

For comparison purposes, I have classified these students into three categories:
Mexican-, Chicano-, and Anglo-orientation. These categories are based on where
the students placed on the acculturation spectrum. The spectrum, as noted previously, is based on the students' responses to a survey that examined their language
skills, generational background, and cultural preferences. Although labels and categories are always imprecise and general, the three categories I have created are

designed to act as markers to help guide the reader through the students' stories and the acculturation spectrum.

MEXICAN-ORIENTED LIFESTYLES: MATILDA AND HORTENSIA

Matilda and Hortensia are good examples of the Mexican-oriented lifestyle. Both are proud of their native culture and express little eagerness to assimilate. For example, Matilda refers to herself as *morena* (dark-skinned), and the tone of her words implies that her skin color distinctively sets her apart from Anglos. Hortensia responds to discrimination by "becoming more proud of being Mexican, and when the [Mexican] flag is shown, I almost cry from this feeling."

Matilda and Hortensia are relatively recent immigrants, and they have retained strong emotional, cultural, and linguistic ties to their native land. As recent immigrants, they entered the United States at the bottom of the socioeconomic ladder, but they also brought with them a strong immigrant ethic that espouses the value of the family and hard work. As urbanites, they are more Mexican-oriented than their suburban counterparts, as they have less exposure to the Anglo mainstream in the barrio. Thus, they both manifest a definite identification with Mexican cultural traits and customs; they are much more fluent in Spanish than English; they listen to Mexican music, view Mexican films, and follow Mexican traditions on a regular basis.

From their interviews and their life histories, the Mexican-oriented students impart a stable ethnic identity, which has removed a potential source of identity conflict for them. Their ethnic identity is further stabilized by the English as a Second Language program in their school. ESL has softened the culture shock by presenting academic subjects in Spanish until the students can master English. As a result, learning proceeds without interruption, and social and psychological stresses are minimized.

A second key point that emerges from the thumbnographies of the Mexican-oriented students is their strong family support system. Regular family (or guardian) involvement assures them of guidance and direction. Every minute of their day is tracked, even for Hortensia who is separated hundreds of miles away from her parents. Such long-distance bonding underscores the strength of the family's dedication in the lives of the Mexican-oriented students.

Overall, the Mexican-oriented students have excelled in school. Matilda and Hortensia have a combined GPA of 3.1, while the intermediate (Chicano)-oriented and Anglo-oriented students have combined GPAs of 2.6 and 2.3, respectively. (The grade point averages of the students were obtained from school records, based on a standard scale of A = 4.0, B = 3.0, and so on.) It is always difficult to compare GPAs of different students, because students take different classes and are graded by different teachers. I include GPAs here to make crude comparisons, but obviously, because of the small sample size, I attach no statistical significance to differences in the grade point averages. Previous studies done on the 1974 student sample (n = 80), however, revealed a statistically significant inverse correlation between acculturation and school performance (Vigil 1982). Despite their many obstacles, the Mexican-oriented students are doing relatively well. A brief glimpse into their lives will help explain why.

Matilda: From an Ejido in Mexicali to East Los Angeles:
Places so Near, but Cultures so Far

Matilda is usually easy going and relaxed, with little teenage angst evident in her demeanor. She is not one to complain, but because someone has asked her about her new home, she will answer. She tilts her head to the side. "America . . . here, every-thing is too fast." Her round face is expressionless, but her eyes are alive, faraway. It is almost as if she, for her whole life, has visited America in her mind. Now she is here, but the America of her mind is not. "It's not how I thought . . ." These are not surprising words, coming from a fifteen-year-old girl born in an ejido (communal farm) on the outskirts of Mexicali.

Matilda had lived in Mexicali with her father and mother in a one-story adobe structure with no hot water and an outhouse. There are seven children. The three el-dest children are currently receiving their education away from home, paid for by the father on an income of five thousand dollars per year. Two daughters, Matilda and her sister, are in high school in California. A son is studying civil engineering in Mexico City.

Matilda and her older sister arrived in California in 1973 when Matilda was fourteen years old, and she immediately entered the ninth grade of junior high school. Originally, she came only to accompany her sister, who had high ambitions and wanted a new life in America. Matilda doesn't share that ambition with her sis-ter. "It sounded exciting to come, you know, an adventure. But my father is the one who really wanted us both here, together." Her father has stated that, "education is important in getting a better job that pays well." So important, in fact, that the father "ordered" Matilda and her sister to live and learn in this country. On numerous oc-casions the father said that "learning English will get them a better job when they return home, and when they seek a job, this knowledge would aid them." Despite her father's concern, Matilda shows a lackluster academic record.

Matilda and her sister share a small bedroom in a small, old clapboard home with a friend of the family, who acts as their guardian. It is in a poor area, and their tiny, dark bedroom cannot substitute for the lively family life they left behind. Matilda makes the best of the situation, mindful that, ". . . at least we see our par-ents now and then. They come up here to buy different things and then we all get to-gether at my uncle's." This uncle's home appears to be the center of family activities in Los Angeles.

Matilda is an ESL student; most of her courses are in Spanish, with English in-troduced from time to time as a second language. This has eliminated or reduced in-dividual culture shock. Even so, she says, shaking her long hair and letting out a puff of air, "Mexican schools are easier, for sure. I know I'm losing a lot of time because I don't know English. Just learning basic things, basic knowledge, takes so long."

The school is highly esteemed for its material resources, but, "The teachers don't have much discipline, and cannot control the classes. There is too much disor-der here. Writings on the walls, drinking and drugs and gangs all over."

Back at the clapboard house, no such chaos occurs. Reared in a strict Mexican household, Matilda is still admonished by her guardian "Dona" when she misbe-haves or is late from school. She walks a straight line at all times in the home setting.

Matilda's acculturation to the Anglo world is minimal. She is proud to be Mexican and unabashedly refers to herself as "morena" (dark racially). "I'm not going to hide what I am." All of her friends are monolingual recent Mexican immigrants who find succor and comfort in association. They perceive the urban Anglo-dominated greater Los Angeles as harsh, cold, and without sympathy. "A person can tell when someone's looking down at them. I see that look a lot." The treatment meted out to them by the native Chicanos adds further to their plight. Matilda's attitude toward *pochos* (derogatory label for anglicized Mexican Americans) and cholos is as equally stern and rebuking as theirs towards the T.J.s or "ESLs": "They look down on me because I speak Spanish and don't wear the right clothes. They like to make oneself better than another, that's why they speak English all the time." Matilda keeps away from them, doesn't learn English or Anglo cultural traits, and remains Mexican.

Hortensia: Here without Papers, but Here to Stay

Like an anchor in a rough sea, Hortensia remains steadfast and doggedly determined to get an education. Born in Mexico, she came to the United States in 1973 in search of a better life. But her life in America has not been easy. Cast as a foreigner in the eyes of Anglos, and even by other Mexican Americans, the petite teenager remembers the pain of being rejected and teased. Even her clothes became subject to ridicule. "Once," she recalls, "I came to school and the Chicanos stared at me because I wore striped pants and a flowered blouse." She laughs when she says this, clearly expecting no pity at the recollection of this painful episode. Her laughter appears to veil the sense of rejection that the memory stirs; for her eyes, above her smile, look moist. Nevertheless, Hortensia remains persistently optimistic. As she says, "There is no bad that good doesn't come from."

Hortensia's parents and other family members migrated to this country from Guadalajara in various stages, some probably without legal documents. Eight children and two grandchildren live in the household with the father and mother. They earn sixteen thousand dollars annually. It is a collective and united family. Hortensia's mother says, "We came here to keep our older sons out of trouble, for they were drinking too much and not doing anything with their lives. In the United States, I know there is work, and if some of my children want an education, this is a good place to get it." This is not the first time they've moved to find a better life. In Mexico, they hopped from town to town several times hoping to improve matters. Los Angeles is simply the next stop on their journey of hope. They are beginning, however, to have misgivings as to the benefits of living in the United States. The mother explains, "We have always been hopeful. It's easy to lose the hope when there is so much struggle, but it is worse to quit and lose all."

Both of Hortensia's parents have had little education and financial security. The East Los Angeles house they now live in is old, small, and rundown. Paint is peeling, inside and out. A folded ironing board shares wall space with a sofa and a plastic-framed picture of the Madonna. It is also crowded. Twelve people live in the small two-bedroom house. This doesn't bother Hortensia: "It doesn't make any difference where you live if you want to study, or who you hang around with, if you want an education." Straightening her books on the counter, Hortensia continues,

"It is very important how a person acts, not how a house looks." Hortensia remains consistently undaunted in the face of challenges.

Although she refuses to let it discourage her, she still laments the intra- (between Mexicans and Chicanos) and interethnic (between Mexicans and Anglos, or *gavachos*) friction and conflicts that sap her energies. "All the names, the looks, it's all racism." She places herself above the fray. "I know that the *pochos* think we have no intelligence and that we are dumb, but if someone tries to look down on me, I feel superior to them. So it's not going to touch me, see?"

Hortensia says, "Getting an education in Los Angeles is the most important thing that has happened to me up to this day." This statement captures her positive attitude toward school and life in the United States, although it is an experience marred by difficulties. She is a pretty, slim young woman with thick, wavy hair and is undoubtedly considered attractive. Her many Spanish-speaking friends and potential suitors have undoubtedly nurtured her personal stability. A regular participant in Mexican sociocultural activities, she still identifies strongly with Mexico and its traditions. "When the Mexican flag is shown, I almost cry from this feeling."

Hortensia spends a great deal of time doing her school work (she received four A's and two C's in an ESL program) and is quite dedicated to learning the English language, as she is quite anxious to become fluent. Her face shows regret, but her words are hopeful. "If I knew English I could advance more; Spanish hurts my studies." She wants to master English not only to acquire a better paying job, but also to obtain a better education. But Hortensia, even after one year of school in an English-speaking context, still relies on Spanish as her dominant language. Her friends and family members speak only Spanish, which has not aided her acculturation. Nevertheless, her English has improved and she understands it better than she can speak it. As she is intent on pursuing an education, only time will tell if this language barrier will become a serious problem. One potential hindrance may be her attitude toward her teachers. She is so anxious to learn that she sometimes gets impatient with teachers she thinks are too slow. "In all my classes I want to act with civility, but there are teachers who make you feel bad because of their ways, and this causes me to yell back or get impatient."

But Hortensia aims high—she wants to be a lawyer—and her motivation appears unassailable. Her parents support her goal. "They're always showing me, talking about different places where work was hard and pay was cheap to show me why I should get an education." The avoidance of hardship can be a great motivation.

INTERMEDIATE CHICANO-ORIENTED LIFESTYLES: CECILIA AND EDUARDO

Ethnic identity is the central problematic issue for Chicano-oriented students. They are familiar with both Anglo and Mexican cultures, but they cannot bring themselves to intimately embrace either. Instead, they have incompletely amalgamated and blended the two cultures. Confused and ambivalent about their personal identity in this context of change, in which their enduring and situated selves are endangered, other areas of their lives, such as school, are also affected.

ACCULTURATION SPECTRUM PLACEMENT OF SELECTED INFORMANTS, 1974 AND 1988

←——— Mexican-Oriented	Intermediate		Anglo-Oriented ——→
1974 Urban Hortensia Matilda	Cecilia Eduardo		Vicente Alberto
1988 Jacinto Lidia Norma Hector	Jorge Daniel	Diana Georgina	Martha Marcia Jose Pascual

-2 • • • • -1 • • • • 0 • • • • +1 • • • • +2

1974 Suburban Carlos Sara		Veronica Juan	Jeffrey Valerie
1988 Fernando Henry Teresa Efrain		Gloria Leticia Randy Armando	Ryan Cynthia Caroline Christine

Cecilia and Eduardo fit this betwixt-and-between characterization. Neither Cecilia nor Eduardo were born in Mexico, although they both have Mexican-born parents or grandparents, and their parents are now living or have lived in the urban barrio. The parents' experiences of living in East Los Angeles have somewhat soured them toward Anglos, thus Cecilia and Eduardo have learned from them to resent Anglos and dominant institutions.

The parents have sent mixed messages about acculturation, and, as a result, Cecilia and Eduardo are transfixed in the intermediate range of the acculturation spectrum, between Mexican and Anglo cultures. They both display definitive signs of cultural conflict and confusion. Although they are casually bilingual and bicultural, this is more by default rather than by choice, and so their ethnic identity is ambiguous and in flux. Indeed, they have felt more comfortable adopting several ethnic labels. (In contrast, students in the other categories usually selected only one label.) Early educational programs for them largely ignored their linguistic and cultural background, and, as was common to many children during the "Americanization" learning era, they got lost in the shuffle.

Unlike the Mexican-oriented students who have stable, traditional family backgrounds, these two have little familial support. They are also affected by unstable economic backgrounds; Eduardo particularly has had a life of poverty and limited opportunities. Unattached and uncommitted to family and school, both have been members of street gangs, especially Eduardo who lives in a public housing project that is strongly influenced by street life.

In sum, their lives are characterized by marginality, instability, and uncertainty.

Cecilia: Chola or Feminist...Any Way to Fight the "System"

Seventeen-year-old Cecilia has a dream. The tall, shapely girl also has a major case of teenage rebellion. In her early teens, she joined the East Los Angeles Marianna

Monas (Dolls, a female auxiliary to the more common male clique, apparently derived from the Spanish word for monkey) and once bragged that she could consume
a whole fifth of liquor in an afternoon ditch party. Most teenagers emerge unscathed
from these minirevolutions of youth. Some do not. However, dreams die hard and
despite all her rebelliousness, Cecilia still dreams of becoming a child psychologist
and living in a five-bedroom home in the suburbs.

Cecilia was born in the United States, as were both her parents. However, both
parents spent a significant part of their lives in Mexico, where they stake their ethnic identity. Both parents are unskilled, low-paid workers; the father is a machine
operator, the mother a factory worker. The family annual income is fourteen thousand dollars, which supports Cecilia, her brother, and her three sisters. Her mother
began working four years ago, which enhanced their socioeconomic condition
greatly.

Cecilia's primary conflict stems from her patriarchal family arrangement. Her
father is a complete authoritarian in all family matters and demands that Cecilia
adopt the traditional, Mexican, subservient female role. Cecilia will not accept
this role and has strongly articulated her objections to this male-female code of
ethics. "My mother never, never complains: It's like she is programmed to take
anything from my father, who gives her back nothing but trouble. That's not for
me, for sure."

Following a quarrel with her boyfriend, she also stated that, "Men are always
concerned with proving they are *macho,* but at our expense. Lots of times I think
my boyfriend just uses me to get me in bed." She particularly resents her father's re-
fusal to permit her to see friends after school. "He just wants me home all the time,
no hanging out, not even school activities—nothing. Yeah, that would make him
happy—me doing nothing!" She smiles, signaling that no way will this girl settle
for doing nothing. In response to her father's authoritarian style, Cecilia has acquired an assertive and independent personality.

The urban environment offers her many opportunities to express her rebellion.
Barrio life is a key influence. From fifth to eighth grade, she became choloized, that
is, she was exposed to and involved in the subcultural East Los Angeles *chola* behavioral lifestyle. Counting off on her fingers, Cecilia lists her past activities. "Let's
see, what did I do? Ditch school, drink, some drugs." When asked, she also admits
to having cholo boyfriends during this time. Cecilia jumped into this subculture
with full force, donning the chola dress and makeup. She even joined the gang as
one of the monas (young dolls). Her first chola friend's father was a drug pusher, so
drugs were available—pills of all colors and types. Later, an older cholo cousin, a
heroin addict, introduced her to LSD and mescaline. School grades, academics, and
behavior took a predictable turn for the worse.

In addition to the pressures of barrio life, Cecilia also had difficulty in grade
school because family problems caused her to miss a significant amount of school.
Teachers reported that she was an unusually bright girl, yet she was absent many
times and needed remedial help.

Her situation wasn't helped when Cecilia's father discovered she had an eighteen-year-old boyfriend. "That was a real bad time. I hated going home. My father,
he's the type that will never give up. I just said, forget it." Conflict between father

and daughter led to Cecilia running away, and subsequently she spent two days in a juvenile detention center.

The following summer after being put in detention, Cecilia visited her cousin in San Luis Obispo, a small city in the central, coastal region of California. During her three months there, she found the homes, schools, and lifestyle attractive. "It was very nice there—real green, lots of room, more quiet and clean than L.A." After returning to her own home, she began to reevaluate her plans for her future. She realized that people looked down on cholos because of their dress and lifestyle, and even noted that, "Because I am from East Los Angeles, people up north expected me to act rowdy." Entering the ninth grade, she threw herself into her studies, and with the strong assistance of a good teacher, she earned all A's and B's that year. She continued this pattern of success in tenth grade.

In the eleventh grade, her successful streak of good grades ended when Cecilia fell in love. "What my father did is try to keep me away from my boyfriend. He could make me stay home at night. But it didn't work, 'cause I just ditched and dropped classes and I saw him in the daytime instead. My dad didn't know, but his way messed me up. I don't think he cares as long as he's in charge."

During this time, despite the alarming and sudden shift in her school performance, none of her teachers attempted to intervene. Cecilia declares, "Teachers don't give a damn about you, and are boring because they don't care if you're there or not."

She has also had linguistic difficulties. Her parents speak Spanish at home, and the children respond to them in a mixture of English and Spanish. At her school, however, English dominates in the absence of bilingual programs. As a result, her English skills have improved while her Spanish language skills have diminished. She is still able to speak Spanish well but is notably weak in reading or writing the language. "It would be better, you know, if I had both Spanish and English. I understand Spanish, but I just can't say everything I want."

Her linguistic difficulties reflect the difficulty she has had in formulating her own ethnic identity. She wishes her Spanish were better, yet she believes her friends would put her down for speaking too much Spanish. She is proud of her Mexican cultural heritage, but would not want to be known as a Mexican. It would be even worse to her to be called a T.J. or an ESL, other terms for Mexican nationals. She doesn't go out of her way to speak a lot of Spanish or associate with Mexican nationals, for, as she says, "If my friends saw me doing so, it would be a burn." When asked to state her ethnicity, she claims she is an American of Mexican descent.

In sum, Cecilia is experiencing difficulty with her education because of sociocultural problems. Because she is no longer a Mexican and has only partially integrated an Anglo mode of behavior, the obvious assumption is that the transition is creating self-identification conflicts. In the home, personal conflicts and rebellion are part of the power struggle over gender issues. She has an above-average socioeconomic condition compared to others living in the same area. Nevertheless, the subcultural lifestyle and less-than-satisfactory educational climate add to the hurdles Cecilia must clear to achieve her dream. "I know one thing. I don't want to end up like my mother. I know I could get good grades, get better. I did it before."

Eduardo: Every Gang Member Is a Cholo, but Not Every Cholo Is a Gang Member

Most people fight to establish control over their lives. Yet Eduardo is a particularly poignant example. He is five feet, eight inches tall and weighs 140 pounds, is muscular, and moves with an athlete's controlled grace. He is struggling between a cholo identity and one found through his new-found faith in Pentecostal Christianity.

A native of Los Angeles, Eduardo lives with his family in the new two-story Maravilla housing projects. His mother was born in El Paso, Texas. She is a Pentecostal Christian and holds frequent prayer and worship meetings in her home. (Eduardo appeared embarrassed when a visitor surprised him at his home during one of these tambourine and guitar services.) His father was born in Chihuahua, Mexico. It is interesting to note that Eduardo's father wears turbans, rather than hats, which is certainly not a traditional Mexican look. Both parents consider themselves Mexicans. With little formal education, they have had only low-skilled, low-wage jobs. When Eduardo was sixteen, his parents divorced. Before his parents split, however, Eduardo reports that his family was close. These days, his mother is on welfare, he has no male role models, and he is struggling. The family breakup has left its mark on Eduardo.

Perhaps because of his vulnerability, Eduardo was indoctrinated into cholo life in elementary school. He was already an at-risk child. School records from this time reveal his below-average grades, language difficulty, absenteeism related to family problems, and poor study skills.

When his family ruptured, he began to experiment with drugs—"downers," such as "reds." He also started sniffing spray paint in brown paper bags. In his father's absence, and consequently with much less parental supervision, drugs became a major part of his life during his junior high school years. Eventually, crime entered the scene as well. Eduardo committed many acts of vandalism and burglary during these early years. In the eighth grade, he was convicted of a felony and remanded to a juvenile facility, a special live-in school for "incorrigibles."

After his year in detention, Eduardo returned to junior high. His grades, previously D's and F's, shot upward, to almost a B average. Today, he looks back at his troublesome early teen years and recalls that those behaviors were "not really me, I wasn't myself then." He was on a Pop Warner football team for a time but was embarrassed to see his visiting father making obscene hand gestures at him from the stands, apparently to signal his displeasure at Eduardo being a "bench-warmer." As he related this incident, his normally poker-faced expression dissolved into self-conscious laughter. He now belongs to the school gymnastics team and the Movimiento Estudiantil Chicano de Aztlan (MEChA) organization. "I'm not blowing it no more. I'm doing work, keeping cool."

Eduardo has just joined a fundamentalist Protestant sect. He says he has now publicly committed his whole life before Christ for direction. He spends most of his waking hours reading the Bible, praying, and proselytizing others. Yet Eduardo knows that the battle for control rages on within him. He tries and sometimes succeeds in saying no to his cholo friends: "No more drugs, drinking, sniffing and hanging . . . with the vatos." He wants to stop these activities, yet it is clear that, on one level at least, he desires to keep up appearances. His dress and carriage are still pure cholo. He still finds it difficult to avoid the temptation of the streets: "I want God to use me, but sometimes I slip back to what I was before, and don't know what to do."

He also struggles in conceptualizing his ethnic identity, and he has a considerable amount of adolescent angst in asserting his self-identity. He lives in a large ethnic enclave that hinders individual and group acculturation. Consequently, he is not sure of who he is, and he experiences profound identity swings. At times, especially when he is conversing in Spanish with ESL students, he is a Mexican. At other times, he is an American of Mexican descent and like a pocho. He sometimes believes he should use the term *Azteca* because his father told him he was Indian. After vacillating, when pressed, Eduardo blurts out in frustration, "Okay, one word—I'm Mexican, then."

Eduardo's recent report card and teacher evaluation comments demonstrate that he is doing average work in his classes. He performs adequately because he is a well-behaved, likable person who gets along well with other students. However, his school performance tends to falter when family stresses erupt. He is a determined young man, who with the force of willpower and God, desires to redeem his life.

ANGLO-ORIENTED LIFESTYLES: ALBERTO AND VICENTE

The Anglo-oriented informants are third- or fourth-generation Mexican Americans, whose parents are also relatively Americanized. Many of these students, like the Mexican-oriented students, migrated to California recently (but from elsewhere in the United States rather than from Mexico). In contrast to the Mexican-oriented students, however, migration to California was less motivated by perceived socioeconomic advantage, for the families of the Anglo-oriented students are considerably more secure economically than those of the Mexican-oriented and Chicano-oriented students. Nevertheless, the parents of the Anglo-oriented students still have high aspirations for them. They hope that their children will climb to an even higher socioeconomic level.

As Anglo-oriented students, Alberto and Vicente both have distanced themselves from their status as ethnic minorities. For example, both boys stress the term "American" in describing themselves as American of Mexican descent and Mexican American, respectively. Yet, they both know they cannot distance themselves completely, as they are both dark-skinned, and they are embarrassed by their inability to speak Spanish.

Their parents' experiences have had a major role in shaping their acculturation strategies of child-rearing toward an Anglo side of the spectrum. However, the lack of a strong Anglo presence in East Los Angeles has limited their access and exposure to these influences.

Alberto: To Assimilate in East Los Angeles Means Stepping Off One Culture and Slipping Away

Alberto is an intriguing young man. The lean, five-foot-nine-inch-tall teenager likes to present himself as a self-confident achiever, hindered only by his inferior education and surroundings. In his words, "These things are out of my control." He is earnest and shrugs his shoulders while expressing this conviction. On further investigation, it becomes clear that the hindrances facing Alberto are much more complex. Alberto is far from achieving his potential and is comfortable with neither Chicano nor Anglo culture.

ACCULTURATION SPECTRUM PLACEMENT OF SELECTED INFORMANTS, 1974 AND 1988

◄────── Mexican-Oriented	Intermediate	Anglo-Oriented ──────►
1974 Hortensia Matilda **Urban**	Cecilia Eduardo	Vicente Alberto
1988	Jacinto Lidia Norma Hector	Jorge Daniel · Diana Georgina · Martha Marcia Jose Pascual

-2 • • • -1 • • • • 0 • • • • +1 • • • • +2

| **1974** **Suburban** | Carlos Sara | Veronica Juan · Jeffrey Valerie |
| **1988** | Fernando Henry Teresa Efrain | Gloria Leticia Randy Armando · Ryan Cynthia Caroline Christine |

Alberto's family has an adaptive strategy that is based, in part, on the educational level and birthplace of his parents. His father was born and reared in East Los Angeles and finished the eleventh grade. His mother completed the ninth grade in her home state of Indiana. Together the parents earn about eighteen thousand dollars a year working as a skilled factory worker and a hospital nurse assistant. They have a stable home, which they own, where Alberto lives with his two siblings. Their solid middle-class status, combined with their education and familiarity with Anglo culture are the key factors that have guided the parents' child-rearing patterns.

Growing up in Indiana, Alberto's mother experienced an upbringing free from strident anti-Mexican attitudes. "It was boring there," she explains, "but I didn't have problems with the people." Consequently, her ethnic identity and self-image remained intact. Alberto's father grew up in East Los Angeles. Because both parents are Mexican Americans reared in Anglo environments, they have made a conscious effort to acculturate their children so that they would not experience difficulty in the Anglo world. Alberto's parents, and in particular the father, have been instrumental in his socialization to this mode. As his father said, "I'm sorry I didn't emphasize speaking Spanish more at home so the kids could learn the language, but they were always told to be proud of their Mexican ancestry." Therefore, the father's adaptive strategies have nurtured a "fighting" instinct that he has passed on to his offspring: Demand your rights if they are not given; and the way to beat the Anglo is to learn his game.

As a result of his parents' efforts, Alberto strives for a college education and a future high-salaried professional occupation. His aspiration: "not be a laborer, like my father, but to work with my mind and have others under me."

Although he was reared to succeed in an English-speaking world dominated by Anglo cultural traits, Alberto has not ignored or neglected his Mexican cultural roots. "Once in a while I act reserved and proud like a Mexican does; sometimes I open up a lot, but most the time I'm in between." His adaptation to Anglo society has not entailed a negative rejection of being a Mexican. His philosophy is that "It's not that Mexican culture isn't any good but the times are different today and this requires a newer, younger approach to life . . . to a wider life."

His educational performance has not been stellar, but he also has been affected by several mitigating factors. He has had poor health originating from infancy—he once was on the verge of dying from pneumonia. More recently, sinus problems keep him awake at night. Therefore, he is frequently absent from school or tardy. He also does not like his school environment. In his own words, "The school caters to the gangs and neglects the good students . . . and the teachers and classes are boring . . . here the teachers are not that educated, and we don't get a higher-rated staff. It's not that we're lower class, but the school and teachers are lower educated." Since elementary school, beginning in the sixth grade, he believes "The schools have not been fulfilling me." His first year in high school, the tenth grade, his grades were, except for basketball, all D's and F's. These grades belie the early expectations elementary teachers had of him as "outstanding and full of potential." They also conflict with his own description of himself and his friends as students who "have school pride and work hard toward a college education."

The evidence clearly supports a poor assessment of his academic performance, for Alberto "has not learned and developed to the best of his ability," according to his most recent instructors. The schools have also failed Alberto, as his own habits and interests reflect a creative, inquisitive mind. He has read many books on his own, taken up social protest music while learning to play the guitar, studied poetry, written many poems, and immersed himself in the sports-minded community as an active basketball player who spent one week at a John Wooden (famed UCLA coach) player camp for adolescents. Opinionated on a number of topics, including Vietnam, U.S. society, and ethnic relationships, he reveals himself to be knowledgeable and relatively sophisticated in his outlook.

With college looming on the horizon, however, Alberto has started to apply himself in school. His most recent grade and teacher reports show a marked transformation, as he received mostly B's and positive teacher comments of "competent, intelligent, good insightful participation in class discussion, and very gifted in poetry." He makes a revealing statement when he describes himself as being "above all my schoolmates intellectually, and if I were in Beverly Hills or Westwood, I would get a better education and work like hell if given the opportunity to do so." He is certainly applying himself now, as high school graduation nears, and he realizes that time is running out.

Vicente: A Son of Midwestern Parents: The Migrant Stream Ends in the Lake of East Los Angeles

Vicente saunters through the common area at his high school. He is about five feet, four inches tall, but carries every inch with pride. Reserved, but not shy, he looks a person straight in the eyes during conversations. He gestures toward the row of lockers. "This place stinks, look at this crap!" There are junk-food wrappers littering the floor. Nearby, a teenage boy and girl are entwined in a kiss. It is unclear which disgusts him, the trash or the public display of affection.

Vicente's parents were born in the United States, his father in Texas. Later, at age eleven, Vicente's father moved to St. Paul, Minnesota, where Vicente's mother was born and reared. Vicente's father reached the sixth grade, and his mother attended school up to the tenth grade. Only after they married did his mother (who is Mexican) learn Spanish from her bilingual husband.

The experiences of his parents in the Midwest have clearly shaped their child-rearing philosophy. They do not perceive Anglos as threats, and they believe assimilation is a necessary requisite to attaining a higher status in life. In fact, when the parents migrated to Los Angeles in 1966, they were surprised at the negative Anglo attitudes toward Mexicans. Vicente's father recalls, "The joke was that we were with a lot of our own people for the first time in our lives, and here is where we had to deal with racists." Unbowed, the father instilled in his children a certain amount of pride in being capable humans who could and should compete with anyone, including Anglos. In Vicente's own words, "It doesn't matter if you're Mexican or American, it's the brains that count."

Vicente's home situation is extremely stable. He shares a three-bedroom house with his parents, two brothers, and two sisters in a neatly tended neighborhood that is a buffer zone between semisuburbia and the urban East Los Angeles barrio. There are nice lawns and gardens. His home has several well-tended fruit trees in the backyard and a basketball hoop on the garage. This is definitely a neighborhood with pride of ownership. Vicente shows pride in his socioeconomic condition by stating, "We go out almost every weekend." His father exerts tight discipline by acting as a traditional patriarch, and no one dares challenge his authority. Vicente says, "You try to take him on, it'll be one time only. You won't want to come back." He works as an aircraft spray painter and earns thirteen thousand dollars a year. The mother is a hardworking housewife who caters to her husband. Overall, Vicente considers his family to be upper middle class.

Vicente clearly identifies with the Anglo world, and he shuns Mexican traits that would hinder his acculturation. Indian in his features, he is clean-cut Anglo in his dress. Button-down shirts are a large part of his wardrobe. For example, he understands some Spanish, but speaks only a few words. When someone speaks to him in Spanish and assumes that he knows the language, he replies, "We're in America, and here we speak English!" His father supports his philosophy, as he emphasizes that learning English would make it easier for the children in school. "They wouldn't have to experience the problems me and other Mexicans had in school."

Vicente does not actually deny that he is Mexican, but states that he is an American of Mexican descent, with an emphasis on "American." He describes Mexican nationals as being high and mighty and boisterous, and Chicanos as rioters who believe in Chicano Power. He defines the term *Chicano* as "militant revolutionary Mexican American." With disdain, he says, "That kind of guy makes me sick—the 'lost cholo' who joins gangs because he is ashamed of being Mexican." In disassociating himself from these groups he has experienced problems in peer group social relationships. Moreover, he is reserved, and yet has a self-admitted feeling of superiority over his ethnic peers. "I've got more going for me than most."

Vicente is currently doing adequately well in high school, as grades and teacher reports attest, but he has slipped considerably from the record he accomplished in elementary school, where he was listed as "gifted," and junior high school. He used to get mostly A's and B's in junior high school, but now he is only getting C's in his

Finding thier spot, away from the crowd.

classes. No doubt this is due in part to his full-time job, which takes up evenings and weekends. Most of the sixty dollars he earns per week goes to the family.

Vicente doesn't complain, though. He still finds time to participate in the school marching band as a French horn musician. He doesn't have many friends, but this doesn't seem to concern him. Sustained by the inspirational guidance of his father, Vicente aspires to earn fifty-thousand dollars per year "as a professional—either a lawyer or accountant." In spite of his average grades at this time, he is intent on continuing his education in college.

SUMMARY

The ethnic climate of the barrio strongly affects urban students in both positive and negative ways. The Mexican culture and the Spanish language are constant presences, and this creates a favorable environment for the students to retain their native heritage. However, the barrio environment also creates personal conflicts in the students if they try to move away from Mexican influences. For example, both of the urban Chicano-oriented students, Cecilia and Eduardo, are partially fluent in Spanish but express feelings of ethnic ambiguity. The Chicano- and Anglo-oriented students also generally exhibited more signs of stress; the former through gang-related activities, and the latter as a result of their inability to fully acculturate. In comparison, the Mexican-oriented students demonstrated more confidence in their ethnic identification. This sense of allegiance, together with consistent and stable familial support, has resulted in a better educational record. In addition, the ESL program was crucial in helping the

Graffiti galore in the school's hallways.

Mexican-oriented students ease their acquisition of English and prevented the students from experiencing serious identity anxiety and delays in their education.

Preacculturation experiences are also important in the life history of these students, especially as reflected in the lives of the Mexican-oriented students. Immigrants who had a pro-American attitude in Mexico come to America willing to work and sacrifice to attain their American dream. These students also had stable families, another important factor that helped them link their career aspirations to educational achievement. Students who had low aspirations and whose families were unstable showed poor academic performance.

In addition, most of the students who had performed poorly in school also had significant difficulty in formulating their acculturation strategy. They were not comfortable with either the Mexican or Anglo cultural tradition and turned to subcultural lifestyles to find their sense of place and identity. The Anglo-oriented students particularly were set adrift because potential Anglo-American friends and associations were lacking in the barrio community. The Chicanos, too, experienced intense confusion over their identity. For example, Eduardo stated that he was an American of Mexican descent and like a *pocho* (Anglicized Mexican), but he felt that he was *Azteca* because his father told him he was Indian. Nevertheless, when asked, he usually told people he was a Mexican. Confusion about ethnic labels is only a symbolic facet of this marginal dilemma, as many other social and cultural strains emerged in his as well as others' lives.

4 / The 1.5 Generation, "Those Who Came as Children": The 1988 Urban Informants

With the passage of time, the urban neighborhood and school have changed. Demographic realities for both show more of a Mexican-born population, ushering in a variety of transformations. For example, some sections of the area have been neglected and show deterioration, and the number of lower middle-class households appears to have declined. Instead, a working class or working poor ethos defines the area today. Underclass sections are less obvious, but still constitute a presence, especially on the streets in nearby barrios (more than a dozen are close by) where the choloization (marginalization) process continues to produce street gang members. The proliferation of this subcultural style and population stands in marked contrast and competes with the business and cultural revitalization brought by the steady stream of Mexicans and their families. These newcomers have helped remake the human landscape in their own image, contributing to a mosaic of social statuses and cultural styles.

The nearby shopping and commercial strip on Whittier Boulevard, the heart of East Los Angeles, has undergone a renewal, as have other Latino business districts in Los Angeles (Diaz 1993; Roseman and Vigil 1993). As a reflection of the working poor ethic, small entrepreneurial enterprises have been added to by individuals who have started their own self-made street businesses. *Paleta* (popsicle), *elote* (corn on the cob), fruit and vegetable carts and vendors are now part of the landscape, as people doggedly strive to eke out an existence. Pride in ownership and human productivity characterize the place, echoing a spirit that held sway in earlier immigrant eras. Unlike some of the 1970s youths, the young people of the 1980s need not worry about lack of access, exposure, and identification to the dominant culture, as the Spanish language and Mexican culture prevail among most of them.

Educational changes through the years have stabilized since the 1970s and provided a solid base for the intellectual growth and refinement of *personas mexicanas*. This development is in part a response to the challenges presented by the demographic and cultural changes already under way. With the increased Mexican and Latino presence, school officials in the urban locale made progressive changes to meet the demands of their student population. For example, the school has a much stronger and more regulated bilingual education approach that has generally softened the worst effects of culture shock for children from immigrant or Spanish-speaking backgrounds. Moreover, the recruitment of more sensitive and culturally aware teachers, adding to the core of those from the 1970s, and an increase in a significant number of Latino and Latina instructors has contributed to a positive learning climate.

Other counterdevelopments temper these advancements, however. The school district undertook a "return to the basics" education curriculum while continuing to address cultural and language needs of the student population. This entailed the appointment of school principals who took a no-nonsense, quasi-military approach to campus life and operations. Formalizing the school in this manner to match the upbeat, eager-to-learn-and-follow-instructions immigrant attitude, required that something be done with the hard to reach marginal students, especially those who were cholos or street gang members. An already historically common but simplistic solution was to push out and reject those students who came dressed as cholos or in garb that signalled street gang membership. What resulted from this unofficial practice was that the school began to concentrate on school children who conformed to their standards, and the cholos and gang members were left out in the street. Ironically, it was the latter group that had traditionally suffered the worst learning problems, and actually needed the most attention and remediation.

In addition to these changes, the acculturation shift during the past twenty years has produced a different variety of cultural lifestyles. It would be difficult to utilize the same 1974 spectrum for 1988, but we will attempt to approximate it. In 1974, we had three categories, which were drawn statistically but ascribed a label that more or less reflects each of the students' self-chosen ethnic identity: Mexican, Chicano (intermediate), and Anglo. However, in 1988, we found that because of large-scale immigration, bilingual education programs, a continuing and persistent cultural nationalist consciousness, and a critical mass of 1.5 immigrants (those persons who immigrated as children), we had many more "shades" of cultural styles. Nevertheless, for the sake of uniformity and comparisons, we have retained the same three lifestyle labels: Mexican, Chicano, and Anglo. On a cautionary note, this spectrum serves more to represent niches on the spectrum rather than self-described or exact ethnic identity categories. In effect, the diversity in cultural styles demonstrates the subtle nuances in the acculturation spectrum that exist in the "grey" areas between the three categories of Anglo, intermediate (Chicano) and Mexican.

New subcultural innovations also surfaced, as we shall see in the case of Daniel, who is a member of the *Cha-Chas*. This group has some superficial similarities to the gang subculture in that youths organize themselves into groups with monikers and such. However, unlike the gang subculture, which carries with it criminal and conflict activity, the Cha-Cha lifestyle focuses on dancing and is generally nonviolent. Also, the Cha-Cha lifestyle is mostly a first or 1.5 generation phenomenon; and this too has evolved, as Ruben Martinez has so expertly pointed out with the *banda* music generation of the 1990s (Martinez 1994).

As in 1974, several important factors appear to affect educational performance: socioeconomic status, family unit, and preacculturation experiences, along with cultural ambiguity (meaning unstable identity status and clouded cultural orientation). However, in order to fully understand the context of these factors and

Listening close to High Energy music.

Getting ready for a party.

Waving good-bye to the football team.

their influence on educational performance, we turn once again to the thumbnail ethnographies. This time we have selected both good and average-fair-poor student informants within the same cultural realm.

Always time for a smile in between studying.

Crypto-Cholos blend in with the new school ambience.

MEXICAN-ORIENTED LIFESTYLES:
JACINTO, LIDIA, NORMA, AND HECTOR

Both Jacinto and Lidia are first-generation immigrants, and although they have been here for several years, their English is still poor. They are in the initial phase of adaptation and acculturation to America, and they still need to stabilize their strategies for

Contrasting styles make for variety.

Heavy metal comes to East L.A.

self-identification. In large part this uncertainty stems from several other structural
and social situations and conditions. Unstable families and lifestyles characterize the
lives of our urban Mexican students, as poverty and family strain are reflected in
their home and neighborhood. Shy and unsure of themselves as a result, they feel
that the ground has been pulled out from under them. In Lidia's case, it has been a
constant, nagging part of her life since childhood, when she and her family lived in
one of the *vecindades* (poor barrios) in Mexico City.

Both Jacinto and Lidia are also experiencing attenuated parental supervision and
thus lack clear and careful direction and guidance. Striving for success and excelling
in school are outside the realm of their lives, as they both work long hours to support
themselves and contribute to the family household. A constant threat are immigration
authorities (La Migra), which figure much more prominently in this time period, especially in the case of Jacinto, who is in constant fear of detection and apprehension.

Jacinto, however, has still been somewhat successful in school (he has a B average). But it must be underscored that he is two years older than students in the
same grade level, and his course of work revolves around ROTC training. Lidia is
doing poorly and for a variety of reasons is struggling in school and, indeed, with
the whole idea of education.

Generally, the Mexican immigrants of this era are much more troubled person-
ally and socially. They are less well off socioeconomically, surviving rather than
striving, and their academic performance and interest is generally mediocre, as the
other thumbnographies show.

Coming to the United States when they were quite young, Norma (at age
eight) and Hector (at age seven) qualify as 1.5-generation immigrants, and they
fare a little better than the two above. As immigrants lodged between generations,

they have retained significant ties with their native culture, but with plenty of time to acculturate to American life. For example, they both speak English, but are much more comfortable with Spanish, and their families observe traditional Mexican customs. In Hector's family, a sharp contrast appears between the older siblings who are considerably more "Mexican" and Spanish-speaking than the younger children. In short, there is a generation gap within one generation, and it shows in how Hector deals with the world.

Norma's older siblings have all done well in school and paved a path for her to follow. Hector has received little support from anyone in his family and still has no plans for the future. Much of this uncertainty stems from whether the family members, especially the parents, will decide to naturalize and stay in the United States, adding a new element to the generation strain noted above.

Nevertheless, an intact and supportive family situation characterizes their homes, even, as in the case of Norma, where a low-income life has made her family readjust. As 1.5-generation immigrants, they exhibit signs of conflict and confusion as their identities and habits shift from one style to another, but they remain Mexican-oriented. Thus, we have classified them as "Mexican/Chicano-oriented" because they are in the gray area between the Mexican and intermediate (Chicano) places on the spectrum.

Jacinto: A Working Poor Undocumented: To Struggle Is to Overcome

Jacinto reveals, in his life and his words, an interesting conflict. He wants to be respected and he wants to achieve. Unfortunately, as an undocumented immigrant, he also wishes to remain, to a great degree, invisible. Reconciling these mutually exclusive desires creates enormous stress.

Jacinto is seventeen years old and came to the United States when he was fourteen. He lives with his two brothers, their mother, and her live-in boyfriend, and— as is historically typical of poor American immigrant abodes—theirs is ramshackle, crammed into one of the most run-down sections in East Los Angeles, surrounded by other recent immigrant families.

Jacinto was abandoned by his father when quite young. In 1984, he undertook the migrant ordeal of crossing into the United States in the dead of night with the aid of a "coyote" (a person who, for a fee, aids in the clandestine passage of Mexicans into the United States), but arrived in America after the deadline set by IRCA for amnesty. So, without much hope of ever becoming a legal resident, he moves around the city in constant fear of being discovered, knowing that on any day he could be seized and deported by the authorities. In the United States, his material life (the surrogate father is not particularly close to him or his brothers) is bland and mundane.

Although many people would find such an atmosphere depressing, Jacinto makes the most of this stressful situation by accepting the inevitability of his fortunes. Economic circumstances being what they are, it is a common sight to see two or more families living together in one house. Nevertheless, most families keep to themselves because of the ever-present fear of being apprehended by the police and the Immigration and Naturalization Service (INS). The sense of community is not enhanced by the gangs cruising around causing trouble for the new kids on the block.

ACCULTURATION SPECTRUM PLACEMENT OF SELECTED INFORMANTS, 1974 AND 1988

◄──────── Mexican-Oriented	Intermediate		Anglo-Oriented ──────►
1974 Hortensia Matilda	Cecilia Eduardo		Vicente Alberto
Urban			
1988	Jacinto Lidia Norma Hector	Jorge Daniel	Diana Georgina	Martha Marcia Jose Pascual

-2 •   •   •   • -1 •   •   •   • 0 •   •   •   • +1 •   •   •   • +2

	Mexican-Oriented	Intermediate	Anglo-Oriented
1974	Carlos Sara	Veronica Juan	Jeffrey Valerie
Suburban			
1988	Fernando Henry Teresa Efrain	Gloria Leticia Armando Ryan Randy	Cynthia Caroline Christine

For Jacinto and his family, everyone contributes to family well-being. His mother does not work, but her boyfriend has a good job as a carpenter and his paycheck goes a long way in providing for the family. Jacinto works, too, as a sweeper and handyman in a gas station, and his brother sometimes helps him out. Recently, his eldest brother had decided to return to Mexico to fetch his wife and baby, whom he had temporarily left behind because of lack of money when he immigrated. Yet when he arrived at his former home, he found out that his wife had taken the child and left him. After some time, he returned to the United States upset and confused about the lifestyle of poor people like himself. Lamenting this, he exclaims, "So much can be lost when you try to get a better way of life."

Jacinto prefers to hang out with kids that treat him well. He explains, "Who are you going to go with? Not the ones who make *menos* of [belittle] you, that's for sure." His friends are mostly Mexicans and celebrate most of the Mexican traditions and customs. For entertainment, they usually go to church-sponsored dances and often attend many of the social activities sponsored by the school. His plan after graduation from high school is to secure an immediate job where he can work "discreetly" without fear of detection. Jacinto's mother and sister have residence permits and have applied under the Amnesty Law, but he and his brother do not qualify.

Jacinto delayed going to school and entered the United States school system in the ninth grade. He has little motivation and attends only half-heartedly. Often he sits at his desk, arms crossed, leaning back, his attention obviously elsewhere. At present he is in the tenth grade, two years older than most tenth graders. Adjusting to the school environment has been difficult. Proud of being Mexican, he is well-versed in the Spanish language, with minimal English language skills. His mother never attended school, but desires that her children will do so and take advantage of the opportunities here. However, Jacinto's aspirations for the American Dream were not reflected by his performance in class last semester. He received a D average in ESL courses, but considers the grades adequate (and keeps his 3.0 average).

His mother is delighted to discover that he is accomplishing something in learning English and going to school. As an ROTC major he has plenty of time to read (having just finished his first novel in English) and think of a military career.

Although primarily placed in ESL classes, Jacinto has had a difficult time. Placed in the class of a non-Spanish speaking teacher, he grew anxious and was afraid for many different reasons. First of all, the language barrier causes him to complain, "Right away, you're trying to learn but you look real stupid." Additionally, lack of friends and uneasiness characterized his first months in school, but matters have gradually improved. His homeroom contains a mixture of both Mexicans and Chicanos, but he regards the Chicano students as being Americans. *"Se creen mucho* (they think they're better), because they were born here or came over very young, and can speak English well." How Jacinto regards himself will greatly affect his future success.

Lidia: Poverty Follows You Wherever You Go

Lidia has delicate features and is quiet. Her hair swept back in a smooth ponytail, her posture tenuous, she carries herself with great hesitation and great reserve. When one is welcomed into her unassuming home, the invitation also becomes an opportunity to meet the real Lidia. Here she can be herself. Born in an extremely poor barrio in Mexico, Lidia immigrated to Los Angeles at the age of ten. Her family history is complex and extensive on both sides, representing several generations and waves of migration from the rural areas of Mexico to the crowded confines of Mexico City. The momentous decision to move to the United States is the latest tale in this multigenerational saga of migration. Her parents had never proceeded far in education, Lidia states matter-of-factly. "My mother hates school, she only completed one half of the first grade. My father finished fourth grade."

This nomadic lifestyle has left her family in a state of constant change and readjustment, and striving for stability of some kind. Her father died some time ago and her mother remarried, which has left parental directives to help the children adjust to the new environment jumbled and uneven. Lidia's stepfather technically has taken over the responsibility of rearing the family. In reality, he appears to have little interest in his stepchildren. Lidia's mother, with her marriage and workload, has little time or energy for comforting or encouraging her children so that they might deal with the loss of their father and the many changes in their family. Lidia's household also includes two older brothers, a half-brother, and a maternal grandmother—a total of seven people living in a run-down three-bedroom rental home in a poor "working class" neighborhood. Unfortunately, the family is struggling economically. Having to work long, hard hours leaves the members with little energy for other things. The parents are often silent and exhausted during their time at home, even during mealtimes.

Her parents earn together less than three hundred dollars a week. Her mother's work situation is analogous to the harsh sweatshop conditions that were so common for earlier generations of immigrants. She works at two jobs, one as a factory packer eight hours a day and the other at night, sewing pieces of cloth at home that a friend brings her from a factory. According to Lidia, her proverbial wicked stepfather helps support the family but only favors his own son with money and gifts.

Lidia shares a small bedroom with her old, almost ancient grandmother. In the double bed, Lidia and her grandmother have late-night talks. "My grandmother and I talk at night when we go to bed, about dating, boys, and life. She tells me about her life. Even though she is old, I am closer to her than anyone."

Lidia's shyness and insecurity outside her home largely stems from her weak command of the English language and inability to adapt easily to school. This is reflected by the friends she has selected. All share a similar background in language and cultural traditions.

Mexican traditions are always celebrated by her family and relatives. "Sometime we celebrate Thanksgiving and cook a turkey, but usually we just get together with cousins and eat Mexican foods, and at Christmas the relatives come over to the house and help out, too, and eat, too!" Christmas is always honored on Christmas Eve.

As with many immigrant Mexican families, the Catholic church is the hub of most social activities for Lidia's family. Going to church socials with her aunt and uncle is generally considered a safe outing that her parents allow. "Now that I can date, my mother lets me go to my aunt's house and stay overnight." Her aunt is active in the neighborhood church and in many ways is pivotal and seems to direct the family's social outings. Lidia finds that she is comforted and relieved whenever they do things together. "I am more myself with my family. I don't have to try to fit in."

Lidia is shy and reticent, and is dominant in Spanish but nevertheless considers herself bilingual. "Maybe I don't speak English a lot but I still speak it." She has been in the American school system for eight years. Her school performance is low primarily from high absenteeism, which stems from helping out on a regular basis at her uncle's restaurant late into the night. Consequently, she is too exhausted when it comes time to get up and go to school, and has to splash a lot of cold water on her face just to get going. She still aspires to be a nurse, although she is uninformed as to how to apply and what to study. For three generations the family has shown patterns of instability because of migration and poverty, with an accompanying low education experience and outlook. For a variety of reasons, Lidia feels somewhat alienated at home and believes that she will be able to learn from her aunt how to be more successful in adapting to a new environment. "My uncle and aunt have a good business (the restaurant). My aunt's a smart lady, and I watch how she does things."

Her stepfather has a positive attitude toward school but only shows it when directing his son, Victor. Lidia is bitter about that, and wishes she had a little parental interaction and direction, too. She grumbles, "Victor does good in school. His father always makes sure he does his homework and helps him all the time with it."

Although she claims to like school, her grades are abysmally low. Aspirations of being a nurse notwithstanding, she has a gut-level feeling that she will end up in a personal service occupation. Some friends have tried to influence and motivate her, but: "I don't know, I guess they talk about going (to college) and tell me to go. It'll be great fun to go together. Sometimes I do want to go to college. To be a nurse you have to go to college, right?" This question shows that she is unclear about the future. She lacks direction from school staff, and has been unable to enlist a teacher as a mentor.

Her last report card showed a D average. She states, "My mother gets mad at me when I miss school, she says I'll be a dumb donkey." Even with the positive role model provided by her aunt, the mother is the only one who demonstrates consistent interest. "Mother tells me to go to school so I can get a good paying job with good working conditions."

Norma: Measuring Up Against All Odds: Using a Chair as a Desk to Study

"Sometimes I feel sick in my stomach. It's when I know people are looking at me and thinking things. I don't know English well, but I tell myself someday I'll be stronger because of this. I'm weaker now, but one day I'll know both. I don't feel sorry for myself because I know I'm going to learn." Norma's foot is tapping as she speaks. She looks and sounds like a coiled spring, ready to fly.

Norma is a sixteen-year-old eleventh grader. Born in Zacatecas, Mexico, she came to the United States when she was eight years old in 1979. At that time she was at the third-grade level in her education. When she first arrived in the United States she resided in La Puente, but later her family moved to East Los Angeles. She attended Eastman Elementary, then Stevenson Jr. High (both schools are in the East L.A. area). She currently lives in a rented three-bedroom house, crowded in with her parents and eight siblings. Norma's description of her family as lower middle class, whether based on pride or relative perceptions, belies the reality of the family's situation. All of the children are going to school, though, including two older brothers who have graduated from high school and now attend college. Because her father's annual income of nineteen thousand dollars would hardly pay for a semester's tuition at some universities, the older sons, by necessity, have to help out around the house and work part time to contribute. However, the luxury of receiving an education is a reflection of their improved conditions; in Mexico, Norma's father was only able to complete up to the third grade. Her mother did little better, finishing her education at the fourth grade.

Norma lives in a predominantly Mexican neighborhood, and as such, she speaks mostly Spanish at home. She claims she gets nervous speaking English because "sometimes the words don't come out." Her parents speak only Spanish. Subsequently, she has a strong Mexican identity and is proud of it. Her parents support this attitude by emphasizing Mexican traditions. She is also a devout Catholic and celebrates Christmas in a typical Mexican style. "We always make tamales and *atole* and we always celebrate *Posadas*."

Interestingly, the American Dream is very much alive in this family. Her parents are constantly emphasizing the importance of learning English and how to be "American," all with the intention of getting ahead. Yet, in spite of her intention to do well the American way, Norma shows no interest in any political issues, and her parents never go out to vote. When it comes to dating and going out with friends, her parents advise her in the traditional way: "Be very careful of men and do not hide anything from your parents." Although her mastery of the Spanish language has faltered, she still prefers to use Spanish over English. This lack of confidence in using English is exacerbated by her friends, who speak English better than she does. "Maybe they speak better, but they mix Spanish and English together, which sounds strange."

Norma belongs to the 1.5 generation, but she appears to be assimilating fairly well. When she first arrived in the United States she was placed in ESL classes in the third and fourth grades. When they had put her in ESL for the fifth grade, her mother forced a change to a regular English class.

Reticent and somewhat shy, she nevertheless accomplishes what she aims for in a way that shows disciplined determination. For example, Norma is moderately involved in various school activities, yet she still finds time to complete her daily homework assignments. As a clarinetist, she is a member of the school marching band and was also member of the computer club. Studying history, trigonometry, biology, American literature, and Spanish, she appears college bound.

She hopes to work with computers after college, although at present she has lowered her aspirations to what college to attend—daunted perhaps by the prospect of not being accepted by some of the better—known universities. Parental support is strong, and they constantly encourage her to attend college and try her best. Her father even promises to shoulder the financial burden and send her to any college she desires, even if it means working that much harder to get the money.

Even now, school is often a struggle. Norma says, "I feel like pulling my hair out when it comes to my American literature class because I read slower than everyone in the class." This drawback does not prevent her from constantly volunteering to read stories out loud so that she can practice her reading and improve her English. At home, her parents have designated a table where Norma and her siblings can all study. But they all do so in different rooms, and sometimes Norma uses the seat of a chair as a desk. She averages respectable B's and C's in her high school classes.

Hector: A "Split" Generation: An Acculturation Spectrum in One Family

Hector kisses his mother good-bye and slips out the front door. "Good-bye, mother. Have a good day." Even though Los Angeles weather is generally mild, it is uncharacteristically cool this morning. Hector pulls his thin jacket tighter. "I know because I'm the last child, my mother is close to me and has a lot of hope for me. I also know my brothers had it harder than me."

Hector, a quiet sixteen-year-old, is the youngest of nine siblings, all of whom were born in Hermosillo, Mexico. When he was young, his father and two oldest brothers immigrated to Los Angeles to find work. Several years later, when Hector was seven, they had somewhat established themselves and the rest of the family gathered up their meager possessions and followed. Today, Hector lives in a rented one-bedroom house in East Los Angeles with his parents, a brother two years his senior, and his oldest brother, who is thirty-eight. All six of Hector's older sisters have married or otherwise left the house. Not much has changed for Hector, for while one brother shares the bedroom with his parents, Hector and his other brother have to sleep in the living room.

Despite having to crowd in, Hector confidently labels his family as upper middle class because "my brothers are very true," that is, they help to support the parents. It helps that his father receives a disability payment caused by an injury suffered when he was accidentally hit by a tractor while working on a farm in

Bakersfield. The oldest brother works, along with three of the brothers living elsewhere, in a carburetor repair shop in Santa Fe Springs.

Hector and his eighteen-year-old brother are the only family members who can speak English on a day-to-day basis. The others received what limited schooling they had in Mexico and have picked up little English since settling in America. Hector and his brother sometime serve as translators for other family members, but lack strong Spanish language reading or writing skills. Hector says, "My mother regrets dropping out of school, and she wanted us to learn both English and Spanish and to do well in school." His mother also stresses that they should be proud of their Mexican heritage, a feeling she shares with her husband. Although Hector and his siblings have begun the laborious process of applying for legal resident status under the immigration amnesty law, his parents decided not to apply. They intend, instead, to return to Mexico after Hector has completed high school.

Hector began his schooling in the United States as a second-grader. He and his brother were both assigned to ESL classes until they started going to junior high school. The transition was problematic initially. Hector, for example, failed a science class and had difficulty in several other classes as well. He is now in the tenth grade and has built his grade point average back to a respectable 2.0 average, doing best in English and, interestingly, physical science class. "I don't like science, but I'm doing good . . . I got an A." Hector likes school, "'cause you meet more people and make friends; and they give you a good education." He also pitches for the school's baseball team.

Despite his appreciation of school, Hector has not matched the attitude with practical plans for the future. One thing he is quite sure of, however, and that is, "No matter what I decide to do, it will have nothing to do with science."

CHICANO-ORIENTED LIFESTYLES:
DIANA, DANIEL, GEORGINA, AND JORGE

Unlike their 1974 counterparts, there is no gang activity among the Chicano-oriented students. As mentioned previously, this largely reflects the high school's policy of weeding out gang members. Daniel is part of a subcultural set, but this group focuses on dancing, not criminal activity.

Diana and Georgina are both second-generation Mexican Americans. Daniel is more of the 1.5 generation, having immigrated to America when he was seven years old. Jorge was quite young when he immigrated, and so we will classify him as a 1.75 generation immigrant. Although their cultural orientation is intermediate or Chicano, all four are strong bilingual speakers who favor Spanish. Except for Jorge, they all have strong Mexican identities as well. This reflects the mass Mexicanization referred to earlier. Indeed, most of the students in the 1988 study have retained or regained strong Mexican-oriented identities.

Academic performance, in this case, can be separated along gender lines. Daniel and Jorge have both struggled in school, whereas Diana and Georgina have done relatively well.

Diana: Breaking Through Tradition: Gendering Your Social World

Diana moves gracefully through the living room, picking up and stacking the schoolbooks she and her siblings have deposited there. She shakes her head in anger. Explaining herself, she speaks quietly, so as not to be heard by anyone else. "I always have to pick up the house before my father comes home. He doesn't like anything out."

Diana, seventeen years old, is the second of her parents' seven children to be born in the United States. She and four of her siblings—an older and a younger sister, and two younger brothers—live in a rented three-bedroom house in a neighborhood Diane characterizes simply as "poor." The houses are old, yet many of the yards are well-kept. Two older brothers are away at college, but also stay with the family during school vacations. Her father's disability insurance payments allow the family to eke out a livelihood, with the older children working during school break. Diana worked full time in a low-salary clerical job last summer. Diana's mother, who was born in Mexico and left school early to help operate her grandparents' small ranch, has been a full-time housewife since she married.

Diana's parents speak only Spanish at home. They met in Los Angeles, and when her mother returned to Mexico, her father, a Guatemalan, followed. They were married there, " . . . in the Catholic church. She wouldn't have married my dad if she knew he was Mormon." Nevertheless, the children were reared in the Mormon religion, and the traditions of the faith have helped to reinforce a traditional Latino family organization with a patriarchal head of the household and female deference to male privileges. Diana resents this, saying, "Me and my sisters always have to do anything that needs to be done." She blames these gender roles for leading her brothers into "putting us (her and her sisters) down." This, in turn, led her older sister to "not do anything else," that is, seek additional training, after completing high school. Despite these antitraditional feelings, Diana continues to be active in the Church of Latter Day Saints. "I'm the young women's first counselor and a teacher." Indeed, she credits her church activities with inspiring her to do well in school and to go on to college and a career, and she presently carries a strong B average.

Diana is now a senior and has already applied for admission to Columbia University, from which she is also requesting a full scholarship. Her older brothers preceded her and are now enrolled, respectively, in mechanical engineering at MIT and electrical engineering at Yale. Despite her aspirations, Diana admits she is "kind of lazy when it comes to homework," with a curriculum that has included at least one advanced placement course each semester.

She has also been active in extracurricular activities at school and is now the student body president. Her victory in the student election inspired her junior-high school sister to run for vice president, which she won. Diana now hopes for a high-profile career: "My goal is to be a TV anchor. Second choice, I'd go into advertising business."

Daniel: Caught in the "Fluid" Culture: 1.5, Cha-Cha, Cholo, or Jock?

Daniel lingers outside the school gym. His two younger brothers are inside, practicing with the basketball team. He comments on the irony of his situation. "Shoot,

ACCULTURATION SPECTRUM PLACEMENT OF SELECTED INFORMANTS, 1974 AND 1988

←——— Mexican-Oriented	Intermediate	Anglo-Oriented ——→
1974 **Urban** Hortensia Matilda	Cecilia Eduardo	Vicente Alberto

| **1988** | Jacinto
Lidia
Norma
Hector | Jorge
Daniel | Diana
Georgina | Martha
Marcia Jose
Pascual |

-2 • • • -1 • • • • 0 • • • • +1 • • • • +2

| **1974**
Suburban | Carlos
Sara | Veronica
Juan | Jeffrey
Valerie |

| **1988** | Fernando Henry
Teresa
Efrain | Gloria
Leticia Randy
Armando | Ryan | Cynthia Caroline
Christine |

you know, I'm a really good basketball player. Maybe it's the only thing I'm good at and I can't even play because of grades. My brothers know it bugs me and they don't say anything."

Daniel, who is eighteen years old, was born in a small town near Guadalajara. He is the second of five brothers, all but the oldest of whom live with their parents in a two-bedroom house in a neighborhood populated mostly by immigrant Mexicans. His father works as an unlicensed construction contractor or at various tasks for other contractors. He has experience in masonry, stonecutting, and carpentry, and thus is usually employed. Daniel's older brother is now apprenticing with his father. His mother does daycare work for an elderly neighbor woman.

Daniel views his neighborhood as a community in which "everybody gets together . . . they'll go help us or we'll help them." He concedes, however, the existence of an incipient gang of local youths who "rob, do drugs and everything." Three brothers from a family whose father deserted them form the core of this group.

Daniel's parents speak Spanish most of the time, although they understand English to a limited degree. Daniel and his older brother are bilingual, but have poor reading skills in both English and Spanish. In speaking with his friends, Daniel notes, "I actually speak the two of them . . . part English and part Spanish." Most of his friends are also children of immigrants. They dress and behave in a style they call "disco," because of the music they prefer. Daniel says, "Sure, I have some cholo friends but I don't spend much time with them."

The family also observes traditional Mexican holidays at home, or get together at the park with relatives living nearby. Neither parent went far in school; both quit to work for their own parents, but they have been supportive of their sons' schooling. "My mother," he says, "always has insisted that we work on our homework before going to play or watching television. We try to reward our youngest brother. When he brings good grades, we buy him small gifts"

Daniel, however, has not done well at school. He was held back a year in the fourth, with his mother's consent, but despite doing better covering the same material that year, he has continued to struggle. A high school junior now, he is "trying right now to get a C average" in order to make the school's basketball team. Two of his brothers, tenth-graders (one was promoted ahead of his class because of his scholarship), play on the team now. Daniel's aspiration will not be easily attained, however; last semester, he failed a science class, got a C in basic math and D's in his other classes. Unlike his younger brothers, Daniel has no intentions of going to college. "I just want to get the grades to graduate."

Georgina: Comadres Make It Work: Gender Networking and Social Success

Georgina laughs as she describes her omnipotent, omniscient mother. "She knows when I'm not telling her everything. Her eyes, man, they can cut you. Part of me hates it, but the other part thinks it's funny—my short little mother is like Superman with x-ray eyes. You know what? It works and she knows it."

Georgina, fifteen years old, stays with her mother's *comadre,* whom she calls her aunt, during the school week, so that she can attend high school in East Los Angeles. However, her mother drives her to and from school every day, and keeps a tight rein on her over the weekend. When her mother drops her off at school and Georgina says hello to the boys who greet her, her mother demands to know who they are. "She drives me nuts. . . . Her friends started saying that I was with guys here and with guys there and that I would ditch. . . . She's heard so many things about me, she doesn't know what to believe." Georgina denies having done anything to justify these suspicions and says she regularly suggests to her mother that she call the principal about her attendance. Nevertheless, she is usually restricted to going out only with relatives and old friends of the family. The latter includes a boy her age whom she met years ago in Catholic school; he helps her with her math homework.

Georgina was reared in the Boyle Heights neighborhood, where her mother now lives in a two-bedroom home. She is the younger of two sisters, but her sister grew up with her maternal grandmother in Mexico and only came to the United States as a young adult, after the grandmother died. "I didn't even know I had a sister until then," Georgina says. The sister married a Mexican-American marine; now separated, she lives alone with her two children. Georgina's "aunt" has a four-bedroom home which she shares with her grown-up son and a niece.

Georgina's mother is pressing a wrongful injury lawsuit against her former employer; she was injured in a fall. The suit precludes her receiving worker's compensation, so she receives only welfare for her income. Georgina is looking for a job to supplement the household income and to save money for her own needs. She sometimes gets financial help from her "grandmother"—actually an older woman who befriended her mother while Georgina was still in preschool and baby sat for her for many years.

Georgina speaks English and Spanish with equal facility and identifies herself as Mexican American. Her mother speaks to her mostly in Spanish, as does her "aunt." Her adoptive grandmother, however, speaks "more English than Spanish." Georgina began learning to speak and read English in Project Head Start classes and, a few years later, on her own learned to read Spanish from comic books at home.

Much of her home life, including speaking Spanish and strict maternal oversight, reflects traditional Mexican culture. Her family is involved in traditional Catholic church holiday celebrations. Holiday meals tend to feature such dishes as tamales and enchiladas, although she says day-to-day fare is "all mixed up," that is, hot dogs one day, *menudo* (tripe soup) the next. Georgina recalls, "I didn't have a *quinceañera* (fifteen–year–old coming out—a religious event, a traditional Mexican equivalent to the debutante rite of passage), only because it would be too expensive. A lot of people cannot afford them."

Georgina, now in the tenth grade, went to kindergarten and the first eight years of school at a local Catholic school. She transferred to a public junior high school for the ninth grade, after some resistance from her mother. She is enrolled in enrichment classes designed to prepare the students for college, and is maintaining a C average. She does well in both English and Spanish language studies, as well as French, but has difficulty with mathematics. Her mother reluctantly agreed, only recently, to let her attend afterschool tutoring sessions in math.

Because of her mother's restrictions, Georgina is unable to participate in most extracurricular activities at school. She says she has always liked school, although she thought "the nuns were too strict." She expresses some disdain for her current French teacher, who "doesn't even know what today is—Mardi Gras, a French holiday." Georgina aspires to a career as a computer technician and plans to attend college after completing high school.

Jorge: "Being Mexican Is a Disability": School Stereotyping and Cultural Conflict

Jorge walks confidently with an even stride and a ruler-straight posture. "As much as my parents love me, they can't be everywhere. I take their words with me but I'm on my own a lot. I've got to know what I want and what I'm going to do. I think about it a lot. You can't depend on others—you have to do for yourself."

Jorge was born eighteen years ago in a small town near Guadalajara, Mexico. He is the fourth of six siblings. He lives with his parents in their rented three-bedroom home in East Los Angeles, along with his brothers and sisters and an older sister's husband and baby. Both parents work for modest wages, his father in a sofa factory and his mother as a seamstress; another older sister recently completed a job-training course and obtained a part-time bank teller position. An older brother attending California State University, Los Angeles, also works part time.

Jorge describes himself as being proud of his Mexican heritage, but he vehemently rejects the label Chicano. He feels the term is associated with the "stereotype . . . that Chicanos are failures." He is fully bilingual, despite his parents' limited English. He was enrolled in ESL classes in the first and second grade, after which "it only took half a year to catch up to the grade level." He soon transferred to a different elementary school (when the family moved) and he remains bitter today about being "automatically put back in ESL . . . until they tested me." He also believed he was discriminated against by junior high school counselors. "They used to put me in all the lower-skill classes. I saw myself like one of the guys; they saw me as Mexican." Because of that, he says, "I started thinking being Mexican was a disability. But after a while I stopped believing that and I realized I was intelligent. My parents always believed in me, and they wanted me to go to college and get a good job."

Jorge notes that his parents, who did not finish grammar school, are enrolled in high school English classes (apparently in connection with provisions of the immigration amnesty).

Jorge is now in the eleventh grade in high school. He has had average grades, despite his continuing difficulties with English spelling. He still expresses antipathy toward school counselors who have steered him away from certain classes he would have preferred, despite his recognition of overcrowding at the school. He says it is "like a lottery—you're lucky if you get your class." He is also uneasy with some teachers. He explains, "I've got this rookie teacher who is disorganized and doesn't know what he's doing. I know my grade in English could have been higher if I had a different teacher." He does best in chemistry and history classes. Politics and history are his favorite subjects. Jorge hopes, in fact, to become a history teacher.

Unlike most of his peers and teachers, and unlike his father as well, Jorge says he is a supporter of Republicans Ronald Reagan and George Deukmejian. Although his political views seemingly distance him from the predominately Democratic Mexican-American community, his views on other matters reflect loyalty to the community. He is somewhat disdainful, for example, of his younger sister's decision not to attend his high school. Apparently, she is afraid because she heard the "stereotype of us being rough." His sister, who has the fairest complexion among his siblings—she "is all white . . . has blonder hair"—instead attends a predominantly Anglo high school. She dresses "like in the '60s, while all of us at public school dress to make the statement, 'I want to be American.'"

ANGLO-ORIENTED LIFESTYLE:
MARTHA, MARCIA, JOSE, AND PASCUAL

Martha and Marcia are both second-generation Chicanas, and they are moderately bilingual. They still retain a strong identity with their Mexican heritage, and both are comfortable with Mexican customs and tradition. However, they are more comfortable speaking English, and they are both capable of moving into the dominant Anglo culture.

Martha's family has a strong educational background, and this is reflected in the educational success of Martha and her older siblings. Marcia has not done quite as well, and has had some brushes with drugs and the street subculture.

The two male students, Jose and Pascual, speak some Spanish, but they are English dominant and are considerably assimilated. However, they both still retain a relatively strong pride and identification with their Mexican heritage. This again is a reflection of the mass Mexicanization of their environment.

Jose's family life has been characterized by instability, and he lacks strong role models. In contrast, Pascual's family is stable, and his parents are retired and so they have the time to direct Pascual's efforts. It is not surprising then, that of the two students, Pascual has performed better in school.

Martha: A Second-Generation Success: Acculturating with Family Support

Martha yawns and rubs her eyes. "I'm really tired today. I usually have more energy. My brothers always tease me and say I'm like a nervous bird. Actually, I think I'm normal. They're the weird ones. They love to nag me and watch out for me. I ask them, 'Don't you have anything else to do?'" She laughs. "Really, I like it—most of the time."

Martha, seventeen years old, is quiet, yet seemingly sure of herself. Born in Los Angeles to Mexican-born parents, she is their only daughter. She has four older brothers, the oldest of whom is twenty-six. The family is completely bilingual; Martha reads and speaks Spanish well, although she is more fluent in English. She regards herself as Mexican American though her family has seldom celebrated traditional Mexican holidays. "But my mother usually points out Cinco de Mayo and Mexican Independence Day and reminds us what they mean." When the family gathers for Christmas or other holidays, the menu is likely to feature both traditional Mexican and Anglo-American dishes, for example, tamales and a Christmas goose. She says her mother "prefers it that way because sometimes she makes a type of food and we don't even like it. And my brothers are, like, 'where's the hamburgers?'"

Martha and three of her brothers live with their parents; the oldest brother, an electrical engineer, has his own apartment. The family resides in both two-bedroom apartments of a duplex, where an enclosed front porch serves as a corridor from one side to the other. In the future, when the boys have married, her parents plan to rent out the apartments and buy more real estate. Her father is a self-employed real estate broker working out of an office he shares with several others. Martha's mother does not work outside the home except to occasionally help her husband.

Martha's parents married and came to the United States before having children. They are naturalized citizens who tend to vote Democratic, and they vote in every election. They disdain Mexican politics as "corrupt." Despite the degree to which they have assimilated, however, they retain many traditional family values. For instance, Martha explains that her parents selected the duplex when they bought a home so that her brothers "still have their privacy (in one of the apartments) and are not far from home, in case of an emergency." However, they watch more closely over her. "I never dated, to tell you the truth. I have a lot of friends that are guys and my parents don't say anything. They say that's okay."

Martha, now a senior, maintains a B average in her courses and has generally favorable feelings about school. However, she is critical of her teachers for not helping students plan for their futures. "All they talk about is the subject of their class." Instead, she turns to her parents and brothers for advice on what classes to enroll in and how to prepare for college. Her two oldest brothers graduated from the University of California at Irvine, and the others are now attending California State, Northridge, which she is also considering. She is active in the California

ACCULTURATION SPECTRUM PLACEMENT OF SELECTED INFORMANTS, 1974 AND 1988

← Mexican-Oriented	Intermediate	Anglo-Oriented →

1974 Urban	Hortensia Matilda	Cecilia Eduardo	Vicente Alberto

| 1988 | Jacinto Lidia Norma Hector | Jorge Daniel | Diana Georgina | Martha Marcia Jose Pascual |

-2 • • • • -1 • • • • 0 • • • • +1 • • • • +2

1974 Suburban	Carlos Sara	Veronica Juan	Jeffrey Valerie

| 1988 | Fernando Henry Teresa Efrain | Gloria Leticia Randy Armando | Ryan Cynthia Caroline Christine |

Scholarship Federation at school, and hopes to parlay that participation into financial assistance for college. She enjoys learning about computers. Martha is interested in a career in business and she expects to become an accountant.

Marcia: Economic and Family Instability Spells Trouble for the Second Generation

Marcia misses her first appointment for this interview. At her rescheduled second interview the wavy-haired, slim teen explained, "Usually, I'm here (in East Los Angeles) all week and I only go home on weekends. Well, this week my mom was sick with flu so I had to go home to help. That's why I had to miss." It's difficult to tell whether she is telling the truth about her mother's illness. Yet it is certain throughout the interview that Marcia deeply respects her mother and is torn between wanting to please her and wanting to satisfy her own desire for independence.

Marcia, seventeen years old, was born and reared in East Los Angeles, the youngest of five siblings. When she was fifteen, just after she completed junior high school, her parents moved the family (Marcia and one brother were still living with them) to Inglewood. Marcia spent most of that summer riding the bus or hitching rides with her uncle to East Los Angeles to be with her friends. When school started in the fall, she moved in with her grandparents in East Los Angeles so that she could attend school there. She has continued this pattern. During the school year, she goes by bus each Saturday to visit with her mother in Inglewood.

Marcia's parents met in Mexico when her mother was a teenager. Her father was much older and was already married. He left his wife behind and, soon after, accompanied Marcia's mother and grandparents to California. Marcia's father worked in a succession of unskilled and semiskilled jobs, most recently trucking, until he was injured on the job several years ago. His worker's compensation is now the principal source of the family's income. Between babies, her mother also worked at a succession of low-paying jobs, but, "She hasn't been working in a long time."

Marcia describes her family as lower middle class because "we don't have much money." She worked full time last summer to contribute to the household and to save a little for school. Her brother at home also shares his earnings when he can find a job.

Marcia's maternal grandparents are Evangelical Protestants and reared her mother accordingly. Her father, however, is Catholic and celebrates major holidays in traditional Mexican fashion, with large, lively parties. Marcia seldom attends church, as is the case with most of her family; her grandparents are the exception. When asked about her ethnic identification, she replies, "Latina, Mexican American, Mexican." She says, "I'm proud of my identity. I have my mother to thank for this." Although she sees her father as somewhat aloof, she feels close to her mother. She also fondly remembers her third-grade teacher, a Mexican-American woman who taught the class to sing Spanish songs and converse in Spanish. "She'd say not to lose our Mexican power."

Marcia is now in the eleventh grade, and she intends to be the first in her family to complete high school. One brother made it to the twelfth grade before quitting; the others dropped out much earlier. "My mother was so disappointed. To her, school in Mexico cannot compare to the schooling here. You have fees to pay and books to buy there. She cannot understand why they wouldn't take advantage of their opportunity." Marcia shakes her head and continues, "I got to do it for my Mom. She expects something from me. I want to graduate."

Nevertheless, her school performance has been erratic. She is often absent and once was arrested with some friends for truancy. She has experimented with drugs at times when skipping school. Her grades are mixed: B's and A's in Spanish, history, and science classes (which she likes), C's in English, and poor grades in mathematics. She is now repeating algebra after failing it the first time through. Still, her determination to complete high school is evident in the fact that she attends night school to take a civics course that is required for graduation.

Marcia is vague about her plans after high school. "I'm just trying to finish here first." She thinks her mother would like her to go to college, although she has not pressed the issue. Marcia expects to someday have a career as a salesperson.

Pascual: "We Have a Very Good Home:" Parents' Encouragement and Guidance Equals School Success

Pascual is one of those rare teenagers who already reveal a semblance of the middle-aged person they will become. To be sure, his physical appearance contributes to this perception. He has wavy hair beaten down into submission, wire-rimmed glasses, and a grave, earnest expression. He takes his studies, his sports, and his future quite seriously. His mother says, "I've always called him my little old man."

Pascual is a scholarly-looking seventeen-year-old. Born in the United States to parents who immigrated from Mexico, he and three siblings reside in a neighborhood he describes as lower middle class. It has clean streets, nice yards, and diminutive houses.

Although his parents speak Spanish at home, they have always insisted that the children learn English as well. Pascual identifies himself as Mexican American, and although he is oriented to American ways, he also engages in several traditional Mexican activities. He attends mass regularly at a local Catholic church with a predominantly Mexican congregation.

At his parents' insistence, he has always devoted adequate time to his homework; both his mother (who attended but did not complete college) and his father (who had seven years of school) involve themselves in the children's school activities. Pascual also receives encouragement from his older sister, whose employment is a major resource for the family.

The family lives in a three-bedroom house. His parents are retired, the father a former meat packer and the mother a former seamstress. His father, age sixty-five, receives about fifteen hundred dollars monthly in pension benefits, which is supplemented by Pascual's sister's contribution to family finances. These resources and the apparent sense of family unity in the household lead Pascual to conclude, "We have a very good home."

Pascual is now in the eleventh grade at the urban high school that he chose to attend in order to major in computer science. He is a well-organized student, a fact reflected in his 3.2 grade point average. He reports with pride that he is "getting an A in Spanish." He participates in an advanced-studies program, conducted at East Los Angeles College, which is a joint project of the college and his high school. He has maintained a 2.5 GPA in that program. He also involves himself in extracurricular activities at school, including sports. He denies ever experimenting with drugs and reports that he has never had any problems with the police. Pascual plans to attend college and aspires to a career in public service.

Jose: Marginally Poor: High Aspirations, Low Directions

Most adults remember the guys from high school days who had the height and bulk to intimidate. Rarely called upon to prove their strength, the mental image of the damage they could inflict was enough to gain instant respect. Jose is an exception to the rule. He is broad-chested, tall, and could be quite the tough guy. Yet in conversation, his eyes reveal insecurity and a desire to impress that is at odds with his towering physical presence.

Jose was born eighteen years ago at Los Angeles County General Hospital. He is the youngest of seven siblings, with brothers and sisters ranging in age up to thirty-four. Jose's parents divorced when he was a young boy, and he has rarely seen his father (who has remarried) since. "I wouldn't feel right just to go up to him and talk. I wouldn't know what to say." Jose's father was his mother's second husband; only Jose and one sister were born of the second marriage.

Child support and alimony payments initially allowed his mother to quit her job as a seamstress and stay home to care for her younger children. When the payments became irregular after a year or two, she resumed working for a while and then went on welfare. With the children now grown, her principal income comes from county General Relief payments along with occasional monetary gifts from her children.

Jose now lives with his mother in a two-bedroom house located in the middle of unincorporated East Los Angeles. Although the barrio has an active street gang, he says, "I never was into the gang thing, and I hardly ever even hang out with someone who's in one." He prefers the company of "rockers" like himself, that is, youths who are avid rock-and-roll fans.

"I would call myself Mexican American most of the time, but occasionally, when I put on my 'bad' look and attitude, I call myself Chicano." He seldom speaks Spanish, although he understands it well. His father was born in Mexico, and his mother, American-born, mostly speaks English around the house. Jose notes, "My brothers and sisters speak Spanish better, especially my brother who works with a lot of immigrants."

Jose is now a senior in high school. Although he was active in athletics in junior high school, especially with football (he is tall and heavily built), he has participated little in high school athletics. He explains, "I decided to mostly go for academics. I really wanted to get my grades up."

He has followed a general education curriculum and has even completed several college preparatory classes in high school. His overall GPA, however, is only 2.2, and he most often gets C grades. He says his best subjects are history, government, and economics, and his worst is math—he recently received his second D in two semesters of algebra.

Despite his poor grades, Jose plans to go to college and major in business. Asked about the course work required for college, he says, "I'll take those classes at East L.A. (Community College), and then I'll transfer to Cal State (California State University, Los Angeles)." Despite his declared intention, however, Jose exhibits little enthusiasm for school and cannot articulate what sort of business he is interested in.

SUMMARY

Several major themes emerge from these ethnographies. Poverty and lower income status is one theme that can be seen especially clearly in some individual cases. Some of our informants and their families have struggled to escape from poverty, both in Mexico and in America. Yet, they have had little economic success and continue to struggle to survive. This low-income life has especially affected the attitudes of some of the parents, who have neither aspirations nor a strategy for achievement. As a result, the bitterness of poverty has appeared to dampen their hopes, and they do not share the immigrant aspirations we noted in the urban 1974 Mexican-oriented students.

Poverty and economic dislocation, however, have not had the same effect on all the students in this sample. Several students from low-income backgrounds did not see themselves as poor. For them, life in America is still a step up from what they remember about life in Mexico, and so they think of themselves as upper middle class. They still maintain socioeconomic aspirations and are not as cynical about their ability to achieve their goals.

The key to these differences in poverty and socioeconomic aspirations may lie in the preacculturation experiences in Mexico. The level of poverty experienced in

Mexico has a great bearing on how individuals perceive their economic situation in America. To those who are born poor in Mexico and immigrate to America in search of a better life, only to find themselves poor again, their situation must be extremely discouraging. Their background of little or no education and low socioeconomic status hampers them from the beginning. In contrast, there are examples in this sample of students whose parents were socially mobile. They had a strong educational background and relatively high socioeconomic status in Mexico, and thus they have an accelerated headstart. Other parents were preacculturated; that is, they were familiar with and acclimated to American culture, and they were better able to achieve their socioeconomic goals.

Family stability is also another important factor that emerges from the thumbnail ethnographies. An intact, functional family headed by parents with high expectations is clearly associated with academic success. However, family stability is not always associated with a two-parent household. Despite poverty and single parenthood, some students still have a household in which education is highly valued. These parents not only verbally encourage their children, but also take the effort to track their exams and oversee their homework. The parents are able to transmit to their children an ethic of hard work and sacrifice, a belief that education is their way out of poverty.

Finally, the ethnographies of these students illustrate their identity as 1.5-generation Mexican Americans. Neither rooted completely in Mexican traditions of the first-generation group, nor completely assimilated as the second- or third-generation group, they are in between generations and cultures in a way that is resilient and both bilingual and bicultural.

In terms of the acculturation spectrum, there are many grey areas between the Anglo- and Mexican-oriented lifestyles. The Anglo-oriented students are not as Anglo as those in the 1974 sample, nor are the Mexican-oriented students as Mexican as their 1974 counterparts. This can have positive results, as the range of bilingualness is much broader in 1988 than in 1974. However, the marginal status of being "in between" can also create conflict. Although none of the students are involved in street gangs, several of the students are attached to subcultural lifestyles such as dance groups (for example, the Cha-Chas) and moderate drug use.

Chicanas find time for friendship in the Quad.

High sports interest for a school athlete.

A new cultural style emerging.

Getting ready for the bus ride.

5 / "We Knew We Were Mexican, but We Were Told to Say We Were White": The 1974 Suburban Informants

Having examined the urban students in both 1974 and 1988, I now turn to an examination of the suburban students from these two time periods. Location and place are important variables, and it should not be surprising that the suburban area contrasts sharply with the urban environ. Whereas the urban residents are primarily of Mexican background and the infrastructure is older and built more than half a century ago, the suburban community is mostly Anglo, with a sizable minority of Mexican Americans. The homes in this area are mostly post–World War II tract homes, and support services are only a few decades old. Thus, in addition to the time continuum, we must also review and assess location or space in the considerations of change and ethnic identity.

The suburban environment presents a different set of locational and socioeconomic stimuli and influences than the urban environment. Socioeconomic experiences play a particularly important role in determining an individual's access, exposure, and identification to the dominant culture (Graves 1967). Some of the students' families have acquired more material wealth than others, and in doing so have gradually undergone a significant acceleration toward the Anglo side of the acculturation spectrum. This is not surprising, for as a person's socioeconomic status (SES) improves, the tendency is to move from the barrio to more Anglicized neighborhoods. This reduces the likelihood that the person will only have Mexican-American friends and increases access to Anglo peers. Higher SES also tends to increase the chances that relatives or friends will be married to Anglos, further bringing the entire family closer to the dominant culture. Older generations of Mexicans with a higher SES are also less likely to retain use of the Spanish language.

Moreover, the suburban locale is much more tranquil and less congested than the urban fieldsite. There is a centralized city hall surrounded by nearby rows of relatively recent tract home developments. Subcultural street gang activity is relatively minimal; only two gangs exist in the area. One is an older rural colonia, Canta Ranas, that has been engulfed by newer homes, businesses, and developments and

Khakis are in with the Hippie look, the merging of two styles.

which has had a long history of gang activity. In contrast, the other is a recently formed gang in one of the older, cheaper tract home sections of the city.

The school programs in the suburban school also demonstrated a progressive vision and a sense of experimentation. In 1968, before student unrest and the radical push for educational reform enveloped the greater Los Angeles area, the suburban school district had already initiated a cultural and learning enrichment program, Expanded Horizons. Structured to meet the needs of a culturally different population from a lower income background, this prevention and intervention effort has addressed a number of problem issues, as we shall discuss in greater detail.

The cultural transition process characterizes most of the suburban group. Second and third generations of families and students are either in the throes of change or are sifting through the pieces left over from the experience. Generally, each student harbors some inner doubts as to the efficacy of such a cultural shift. For example, the Mexican-oriented students find that the suburban habitat is not really suited for the full anchoring of a retention and practice of their Mexican heritage. Chicano-oriented students lean more towards the Anglo side of the spectrum and participate in some form of gang behavior, although to a less intense degree than is found in the urban environment.

MEXICAN-ORIENTED LIFESTYLES: CARLOS AND SARA

The suburban Mexican-oriented students are more intermediate in their orientation in comparison to their urban counterparts. For example, they are less influenced by the Mexican culture, and are generally content with their school experiences and interaction with Anglos. These factors explain why they are more bilingual and able

Hollywood Swingers out for a ride.

to function in both the Anglo and Mexican cultural worlds with some amount of dexterity. Particularly important, as also noted for the urban Mexican-oriented individuals, these students have benefited from a family support network that has aided their academic careers in positive and constructive ways.

Both students also performed relatively well academically and were aided by the school's Expanded Horizons program. This special program provides students personal counseling and field trips for cultural enrichment and events at nearby campuses. It could be argued that such programs serve to promote the Mexican culture or Mexicanization, especially in helping individuals regain their familiarity with their "native" culture. These students are also less pejorative toward Anglos, which some associate with the greater resources and better material life in the suburban community.

Carlos: Country Living to City Dwelling Without Moving Your Home: Migrant Enclave Enveloped

At first, a new life in the United States left Carlos confused, yet excited. He loved the fast foods, the hypnotic toy commercials, the special closeness he shared with family members in this strange new place. But the sharp-sounding language bewildered him and the people didn't act the same. Above all else, he missed his mother and father, who had stayed behind in Mexico. Since then, much has changed, yet many core issues remain the same.

Carlos came to America as an undocumented immigrant at the age of five and began school as a member of the 1.5 generation in the first grade. As the eldest child, he has been guided by his parents (and grandparents) to receive a proper education, including English language skills, so that when he returns to Mexico he can work as a bilingual interpreter and earn more money.

ACCULTURATION SPECTRUM PLACEMENT OF SELECTED INFORMANTS, 1974 AND 1988

← Mexican-Oriented	Intermediate	Anglo-Oriented →
1974 Hortensia Matilda **Urban**	Cecilia Eduardo	Vicente Alberto
1988 Jacinto / Lidia / Norma / Hector	Jorge Daniel Diana Georgina	Martha Marcia Jose Pascual

-2 • • • • -1 • • • • 0 • • • • +1 • • • • +2

1974 Carlos **Suburban** Sara	Veronica Juan	Jeffrey Valerie
1988 Fernando Henry / Teresa / Efrain	Gloria Ryan Leticia Randy Armando	Cynthia Caroline Christine

Carlos's parents and most members of his extended family are illiterate and unskilled. Those who left Mexico entered the United States without legal documents. When he arrived in the United States, he lived with his grandparents on a migrant ranch in Whittier [a suburb of Los Angeles], which, he says, was like living in "a Mexican community of small houses." Later, the grandparents moved to a suburban barrio just outside the city of Los Angeles. Carlos currently lives in a twenty-year-old tract home with seven other members of his family.

Much of Carlos's activity revolves around the extended family. They are actively helpful to each other on a daily basis, both economically and socially. Carlos is always going to the store, baby-sitting, and helping with chores. "It's the way it is in my family—my family will always be there." They are a traditional Spanish-speaking Mexican family. His family also travels north each summer to work on a farm, picking and drying apricots. Carlos has worked with them and uses the money to help the family.

When Carlos has to switch to the Anglo world outside his home and family, he does so without conflict or guilt: "I want to behave, act, eat, and live like them, but inside I'm Mexican. It's a good opportunity to come to the United States, especially from Mexicali. I like the Anglo way. I'm proud of being a Mexican, but I like Anglo ways, the high standard of living." Unfortunately, he does not have many friends and, despite his approval of the Anglo lifestyle in Los Angeles, he describes it as a lonely town. Carlos enjoys living in his suburban neighborhood and dislikes where his cousins live in East Los Angeles. "If you live in East Los Angeles, live in poor houses, or need money all the time, that might turn you to become a cholo."

His educational performance has been commendable since elementary school. On his last high school report card, he earned five A's and one B in a regular course of study. One of his high school English teachers says, "He is a very bright and aggressive boy who received an A last semester. He never has the high test scores but he always asks for extra credit and gives 110% effort. He is reading at about an eighth grade level."

Thus, the language barrier has been somewhat problematic, but not critical. He became functionally fluent in the fourth grade, but as his English teacher stated, "His 'bilingualness' shows up in his work."

Carlos's innate potential and hard work have brought him academic success. However, he has low aspirations, and is not presently considering pursuing a college education. In fact, Carlos does not even wish to become a translator. He would rather become a truck driver like his father, because he misses his father and respects him deeply. Much of his time is spent gleefully driving the family pickup truck on short errands as he imagines the day "when I'll be doing what my father does." He does believe he should do his best in school: "My parents expect a lot of me, so I try my best." But his grandparents are more ambivalent; they tell Carlos that they never went to school because there was "no need to . . . look at us, we're doing fine." So, Carlos tries to do well in school, but sees little reason to perform well. As one teacher said: "He is just a rather bright boy trying to survive, to plan for the future a little, and have a little fun in the meantime."

Sara: Recapturing Cultural Identity: A Chicana Mediates in a Changing World

One thing Sara, sixteen years old, dislikes is judgmental people. She is quick with a comeback when people use racial slurs, whether against black, brown, or white. She explains, "Some people really are losers and probably deserve to be called names. Just why is it always the skin?"

The youngest of five siblings, Sara lives with her parents, one of her three brothers, a sister, and the sister's husband and son. Her mother says, "I keep my eye on all my kids. It's my job to care for them, watch for them." Her efforts have produced a relatively peaceful and disciplined atmosphere in the small, clapboard house. She also has been supportive and involved in her children's educational pursuits.

Financially, Sara's family is struggling. The mother is currently out of work and on disability, and the father, unemployed, brings in $125 per week. The family somehow is eking out a living, with Sara contributing from her part-time job (full-time during the summer vacation) as a clerical worker at school.

In spite of their economic hardship, Sara's parents moved to the suburbs to raise the children in a better environment that would improve their opportunities. Sara is cognizant of this and states, "If I lived in a poorer area it would bother me, turn me off to school."

Sara is completely comfortable with both the Mexican and Anglo culture, although she refers to herself as a Mexican American. She positively identifies with Mexican traits, in part because of her participation in Expanded Horizons, a special pro-Mexican cultural program for students from that background. This program teaches Sara her ethnic history and linguistic heritage. (She works for this program, also.)

Her parents are supportive of Sara's participation in the Expanded Horizons program, especially so because they believe that Anglos are racist. The father often voices vehemently anti-*gringo* (anti-Anglo) attitudes such as, "Well, the gringos don't let the Mexicans get up there. They keep them down with the blacks." He also declares, "This Anglo culture is down the drain."

Despite her father's comments, Sara keeps an open mind. She explains, "People should not accept you just for what ethnicity you are. They should accept you for what abilities you have." Sara also has a strong sense of her own ethnic identity and capabilities. "A Chicano can be everything—a Mexican American, American of Mexican descent, a militant revolutionary, or Anglo if he wants to." Her statement sums up her expansive approach to life and aids her immensely in gaining acceptance in all social circles, and especially with her Anglo peers.

Sara spends much of her free time with her boyfriend and other young friends in a group known as the "Hollywood Swingers." "My boyfriend is a Hollywood Swinger. He's twenty-five years old. He makes good money . . . why hang around someone that's going to be getting into trouble?" The group engages in Chicano subcultural activity such as cruising, "partying," and light alcohol and drug (marijuana) use. Sara's participation in the Swingers is not intense, however, and she still maintains a good record at school. She's careful to not go too far in her partying; as she says, "Cholos are always getting into trouble and it's fun for them now, but what is it going to get them now and in the future?"

Since elementary school, Sara has been referred to by her teachers as "likable, friendly, cooperative, hard worker, polite, confident, well dressed, socially conscious." She has also joined many extracurricular activities, which have opened many opportunities to her. Teachers have never made a negative statement about her in their reports. She has maintained a B average throughout her educational career, partly because she is well behaved. She is currently taking basic and commercial-oriented courses, such as typing and office work.

After school, she attends two hours of cosmetology classes at a beauty college, hoping to become a beautician. She entertains other career aspirations as well. She might become an airline stewardess. Recently, after canceling her marriage engagement, she has even been thinking about pursuing a college education: "I'm looking forward to attending college and making something out of myself. This coming year (her senior year) I'm going to put all my efforts toward myself and my future."

CHICANO-ORIENTED LIFESTYLES: JUAN AND VERONICA

Like the intermediate Chicano urbanites, Juan and Veronica are members of street gangs, but they also lean closer to the Anglo end of the spectrum. Gang activity is more intense in the urban barrio, but even Veronica was "jumped into" (initiated into) a local gang by being beaten by the older female members. In contrast, none of the selected Mexican-oriented or Anglo-oriented informants in either area belong to gangs, although they do take part in some of the less aggressive activities of gang members. In fact, only eight out of the eighty students surveyed were gang members, and all eight placed in the middle of the acculturation spectrum. (Note, however, that these students were selected because they were in the middle of the acculturation spectrum, not because they were in gangs.)

Removed from their Mexican roots and generally unsocialized by their parents and family in this culture, they speak little Spanish. Thus, their ethnic identification processes were thwarted during the acculturation process. In the absence of a stable ethnic identity, Juan and Veronica joined gangs to create a place where they "belonged." This intermediate, marginal situation of choloization has been a source of conflict and ambivalence. It appears that being in between cultures makes it difficult for Juan and Veronica to claim allegiance to either of the cultures. Rather, they have been attracted to a cultural innovation that bridges the two cultures. This, of course, is not a new phenomenon, and has been present in the Chicano community at least as far back as the 1930s.

Growing up as members of the second generation, Juan and Veronica's parents had experiences in East Los Angeles that shaped their child-rearing practices in different ways. On the one hand, their parents wanted to leave the barrio to provide better opportunities and living conditions for their children, so they moved to suburbia. One of my students, a Mexican American whose parents similarly moved from East Los Angeles to a suburban community located seven miles away, once described the experience in a paper he entitled "From East L.A. to Pico Rivera: Seven Miles to the American Dream." These parents also resented the racist experiences they and their own parents encountered, and passed their resentment on to their children. The fact that these parents and the children were dark, mestizo in racial appearance, adds weight to these beliefs. In short, a double message was given to the children: Move to a better, Anglo area but watch out for white people. A poor, hit-or-miss strategy of acculturation resulted. Coupled with weak support and direction for the discipline and responsibility needed to achieve academically, this hit-or-miss strategy produced, at best, mixed results.

One last issue, an interesting and persisting one in the suburban scene, is the sense of relative affluence that pervades informants in this area. In the 1970s, I referred to it as a "saturation" point, where the children believed they had made it and did not desire to strive much further than what their parents had attained. In some ways, this attitude is a combination of the forces spoken of above, such as a lack of a strategy based on conflicting experiences, and a working-class ethos that finds satisfaction with the basics of life.

Juan, Making a "Barrio" in Suburbia: Ethnic and Socioeconomic Strains

Kicking back on the street corner, it appears Juan knows two out of every three people who pass by name. He greets them all with a smile. "Hey, what's up, Leticia?" Fun for Juan is hanging out—no trouble, no worries.

Juan's family life is stable, but an interesting and new phenomenon has affected him: the recent development of a suburban-based subcultural gang named "Peaceful." His role in the gang is peripheral, for he takes greater pride in riding his motorcycle and lifting weights most of the time than in hard-core gang activity. Partying and drinking are his only pursuits, although he was once arrested outside a party for malicious mischief and public drunkenness and he spent the night in jail. His youngest brother, fourteen, is also a part of the gang and more militant than Juan.

Undoubtedly the greatest influence in keeping Juan from falling completely in the gang is his father. In Juan's words, "I always and still like my father to be proud of myself." Much of the father's spare time is spent in building additions to tract

ACCULTURATION SPECTRUM PLACEMENT OF SELECTED INFORMANTS, 1974 AND 1988

← Mexican-Oriented	Intermediate	Anglo-Oriented →
1974 Hortensia Matilda	Cecilia	Vicente
Urban	Eduardo	Alberto

1988	Jacinto Jorge	Diana Martha
	Lidia Daniel	Georgina Marcia Jose
	Norma	Pascual
	Hector	

-2 • • • • -1 • • • • 0 • • • • +1 • • • • +2

| **1974** | Carlos | Veronica | Jeffrey |
| **Suburban** | Sara | Juan | Valerie |

1988	Fernando Henry	Gloria Ryan Cynthia Caroline
	Teresa	Leticia Randy Christine
	Efrain	Armando

homes. Juan relishes helping him. The male-led family activity has given Juan a good male model to emulate.

The father's own words poignantly highlight why the gang habitat has not captured Juan: "All his friends were hanging around the corner drinking and getting high on weed. All his buddies went to jail or continuation school, but not Juan. Juan seems to be different than his friends. It depends on the parents. If the parents keep pushing them then it's up to the individual."

Both of Juan's parents work and together earn about fifteen thousand dollars per year to care for four children. Their three-bedroom tract home with an added den is functionally furnished. The couch is worn. The beds have no bedspreads. Everything is in place and clean. Although their neighborhood is a working-class tract home area of mostly single-level dwellings, it is uncharacteristically bestowed the label of a "barrio."

Juan's parents had to leave school before high school graduation because of lack of money, and this has affected Juan in two ways: their limited education and subsequent need for both to work to earn a satisfactory living has deprived him of parental guidance and direction that emphasizes the importance of education. It is rare for all members of the family to even be at home at the same time. As a result, Juan does not value educational activities as a means to move up socioeconomically, even though he wishes it could happen. "My social class is all right," Juan says. "I get everything I want, and I want to move up too. I want to make thirty to forty thousand dollars a year. The higher the better. I'd like to be comfortable. Not to worry about bills, children. I don't want to work hard like my father."

Even with this reservation about working hard, however, he worked part time during the school year, fifteen to twenty hours per week, in a graphic arts business (printing)—a subject that he has majored in and enjoyed as a part of his high school training. Despite his talk of moving up, Juan chooses mainly vocational courses.

As a marginal person in the suburban area, Juan reflects an incomplete cultural adaptation. This shows in his ethnic identity fixation experiences. He applies the label Mexican American to himself and wears it proudly. "Hey, I am a Mexican American and I hold my head high about it." He does not identify with Anglos and is embarrassed when people speak Spanish to him, assuming he knows the language. At these times he mentally stammers and stutters, trying to make out what the Spanish-speaker is saying. A third-generation American, he does not speak the tongue of his ancestors, and he seems to be ashamed of this. Claiming the label but not the language leaves him in a predicament. He tries to explain: "I'm Mexican in everything except language—I can't speak Spanish. Maybe that's why I say I'm a little American. I'm not white, that's for sure. I move more in the Mexican side than the white side."

Thus, it is a confusing ethnic identity sense that he imparts. Yet, he shows only superficial psychological conflict over this problem, for his strong macho personality incorporates a philosophy that demands that he treat people the way he wants to be treated "As long as I do my best, people will try to help me out." Nevertheless, others, notably his parents, have recognized on numerous occasions his aversion to the "paddies" (whites) and his feeling of not fitting in with some of the paddie ways. His pride in his Mexican heritage as well as his machismo can be traced to his father's influence. He has a particularly militant Chicano father who regularly lambastes Anglo institutional racism. Juan has been taught that a man has to stand up to anybody for his rights.

Surprisingly, this has not helped his education. For, in addition, there is a common problem in working-class households between stated objectives and actual experiences. What has resulted in Juan's life is a discrepancy between what he would like to do and what he is capable of doing. On the one hand, he talks of striving for more. He is "very egoistic. I build myself up. I'm competitive, I like to show people I'm number one. I like to get ahead. I want the best for myself. My father has helped me here. He says it depends on your determination." On the other hand, however, he is content with his present niche: "I really don't dig geometry and biology. I don't need them in graphic arts." Perhaps he is a late bloomer, and the positive attitude he has will carry him through later. "I wouldn't want to settle for a little job. I guess I'll go get a little more education, like college." But his school record is average because he avoids academic subjects like the plague.

Overall, however, Juan's marginal cultural status has not appreciably affected his educational performance; it is generally good. Teacher reports state that he is "conscientious and productive; associates well with people of all races; does work, but not too involved." Most of his school grades since elementary have been average. In his recent report card he earned an A (physical education), two B's (graphic arts), and one C. It's important to note that, as mentioned earlier, most of his courses are vocational. These are the source of his higher grades, which have tended to bring his GPA up to 2.8, compensating for the C and D grades he receives in regular courses. Juan has the strength of character and discipline to avoid the most serious, dangerous gang activities. He has already proven this. It is entirely possible that those qualities could serve him well in reaching for the future he desires.

Veronica: A Tomboy Takes to the Streets: Redefining Gender Roles

As she opens the door to kick her gym shoes into her bedroom, Veronica briefly reveals a far wall with a ribbon-filled bulletin board and a shelf with several shiny trophies on it. She closes the door, and the silent testimony to her athletic ability is gone, for the moment. It is fascinating that someone so gifted in health-enriching sports could also dabble so freely in life- and soul-threatening activities.

Veronica, a fifteen-year-old athlete, lives in a three-bedroom home in suburbia. She lives with both parents, a sister, and a brother. Her parents decided to move from East Los Angeles to give their children a better environment and socioeconomic improvement. Her mother has worked to supplement the father's income. Together, they earn about eleven thousand dollars a year. All of her grandparents were born in the United States, except for her maternal grandfather, who was born in Puerto Rico.

The guiding force behind Veronica's life is her mother. Her mother encourages her to press on in her studies. Veronica explains, "Well, my mom does not want us to quit school. They want us to get a good job. They want us to have more things than they had." Veronica is not as eager for the extra "luxuries" as her mother. She says, "It don't bother me if I don't wear all the good clothes. I feel that my parents get me everything I want. I live in a tract home, don't I? It's better than my cousins' in East L.A."

Perhaps the influence of her father accounts for her uninspired attitude. He has less than stellar dreams for his children and would be content for them to "not be dumb like me."

Veronica, under the watchful eye of her mother, works hard at household chores. She cooks, cleans, washes, and irons to receive credit for a job well done. If she passes inspection, she may go out on the weekend with a girlfriend, usually to a party or a movie. She laughs, "I usually make it, too, you can bet." No matter what happens, she is at Catholic church every Sunday. Her grandmother visits frequently. The rest of her extended family are active and meet often.

Despite her large family, Veronica is at the age where the pull of peer relationships often outweighs the pull of family. Her closest friends live in the same tract-home development, but belong to and identify with an old and well-established rural barrio, Canta Ranas (translation: Singing Frogs, also known as C.R.), which is several miles away from their homes. Her affiliation with C.R. began in the ninth grade. She was jumped (gang initiation by getting beaten up) into the gang by older female members in the tenth grade. Veronica says, "My house is in the dead part of the barrio. All the real happenings are over where the wall is (a large five-foot-high concrete wall that separates the "real" barrio from a main street). Over there, everybody has their *placas* [graffiti indicating a gang member's name or nickname and barrio affiliation] on the wall, and we cruise by there every chance we get."

Veronica is not a hard-core gang member, yet she participates in quite a few subcultural practices. She spray paints her placas on walls, houses, and buildings. She drinks alcohol occasionally. Less frequently, she also experiments with marijuana, and whites and reds (amphetamines). She reveals, "About two months ago I planted a Mary Jane (marijuana) plant in my backyard, just to see what would happen—kinda' like a science experiment." Her parents, especially her mother, would not tolerate any such experimentation, and she fears their discovery of her behavior. As she told me, "Don't say anything about C.R. My parents don't know I belong to it."

Veronica plays softball, basketball, and girls' football. She takes great pride in mentioning, "I was on a championship softball team in junior high." These sports help to reduce her gang involvement. Her father, a sports enthusiast, trained his daughter at an early age. She shares her father's enthusiasm, and regularly participates in these sports both in and out of school.

Her toughest struggle is reading. Her mother observed this during her elementary years. Seeking to interest and motivate her daughter, she purchased many books for her. Her reading has subsequently improved as a result.

Another problem, although one could hardly say Veronica struggles with it, is her talkativeness. Talking in class sent her to the office several times this year. But since her GPA is 2.5, or a C+ average, these problems are not creating a crisis situation for her education.

In sum, Veronica is an average student with no desire at this time to pursue a college education. Veronica is content; she states, "Material things are not as important as long as you're happy. I just want a nice house and nice car. Something to show for yourself. The level would be like my parents."

ANGLO-ORIENTED LIFESTYLES: JEFF AND VALERIE

Jeffrey and Valerie usually describe themselves simply as "white." Jeffrey even aspires to a different ethnicity, noting that he is often mistaken for an Italian and argues that he might well be, as many *manitos* (New Mexico–born) have Spanish or Latin ancestors. It should also be noted that Jeffrey and Valerie are both light-skinned and Iberian in appearance.

In large part, the adaptation path selected by the families of these students was shaped by their experiences in New Mexico, where incidents of racism had a significant influence on their acculturation strategy. Both students appear to believe in the perceived wisdom that Anglo-oriented acculturation equates with a higher quality of life. In the case of Valerie, whose adaptation and acculturation strategy was a careful, thoughtful process planned by her parents, it seems that the route of assimilation can be smooth and relatively stress free, even if some anti-Mexican sentiments accompany the changes. But acculturation does not always imply educational achievement and performance, for assuming part of the dominant culture sometimes requires accepting the inferiority of the minority culture, which can result in low self-esteem, confusion, and intrapersonal angst. This appears to be the case for Jeff, who despite his parents' efforts, seems to lack a clear sense of direction, identity, and purpose.

Jeff: A Loner from Suburbia: Leaving Our Spanish in New Mexico

As Jeffrey rides his old bike to the beach, his movement mirrors his general approach to life. He cycles in an indolent manner, with just enough momentum to keep himself from wobbling or tipping over. No one would know, by observing his speed, that he's heading out to his favorite activity—fishing.

Jeff's family lives in a well-furnished but slightly worn home. The three eldest children—there are seven in all—have finished college. His parents have a deliberate strategy for acculturating him and his siblings to the Anglo life style. From the outside, this strategy appears to have been successful.

The family has come onto hard times, however, since 1972 when a plant shutdown eliminated Jeffrey's father's job as a tool mechanic (which he had held for twenty-three years and which earned him one thousand dollars per month). Since then, Jeffrey's mother has been forced to seek employment as a department store sales clerk to aid the family income. The father also now works as a janitor for $650 per month. The mother can no longer devote most of her time to the children. Also, the financial resources are not enough to meet the family's necessities. Thus, Jeffrey's recreational interest in fishing has now been turned into a money-making venture as he travels on his rickety bike along the ocean shoreline, selling the day's catch.

Jeffrey's cultural identity and behavior are largely in the Anglo realm as he generally tries to avoid things that are Mexican. However, he states that he doesn't believe that the Mexican culture is inferior. He explains, "It's not a big thing. I don't hate Mexican this or that. I just don't think about it or look for it everywhere." Much of his attitude can be traced back to his parents, especially his father. Both of his parents had numerous experiences with racism, and so they decided to aid their children by teaching them English so that they could avoid the problems they experienced.

This Anglo enculturation coincided with his family migrating from New Mexico to Southern California. As his mother says, "When we left home (New Mexico) we left our Spanish (language) there." The father also stresses why he avoids drawing attention to his ethnicity: "*Gabachos* [whites, generalized from a Spanish derogatory term for the French that became established in Mexican usage during the French intervention of the 1860s] had jobs. They were just better off, not better people. Mexicans worked in low-class jobs, and they brought up their families in barrios and they don't have much. What helped me is that I left and got the heck out of there."

The parents refer to themselves as Spanish, a regular custom in New Mexico, and they have European physical features. This racial card has significantly enhanced the acculturational potential for their children. Jeffrey, for example, often refers to himself as white: "I'm Mexican American, but usually I call myself white." In more serious conversation, however, he states that, "I'm different. A lot of people think I'm Italian. In fact, I wouldn't doubt if maybe I look more Italian than Mexican."

Thus, there is some confusion and conflict in the ethnic labels he embraces—white, Italian, Mexican American—and his parents' preference for the Spanish label. More serious are behavioral traits that depict a personality undergoing a great deal of stress. He is considered shy and reticent by many teachers and observers who believe that he has no friends. Jeffrey says he doesn't have many friends because they are betrayers. Numerous altercations with authority figures

ACCULTURATION SPECTRUM PLACEMENT OF SELECTED INFORMANTS, 1974 AND 1988

◄─────── Mexican-Oriented   Intermediate   Anglo-Oriented ─────►

	Mexican-Oriented	Intermediate		Anglo-Oriented	
1974 Urban	Hortensia Matilda	Cecilia Eduardo		Vicente Alberto	
1988	Jacinto Lidia Norma Hector	Jorge Daniel	Diana Georgina	Martha Marcia Jose Pascual	

-2 • • • • -1 • • • • 0 • • • • +1 • • • • +2

	Mexican-Oriented	Intermediate		Anglo-Oriented	
1974 Suburban	Carlos Sara	Veronica Juan		Jeffrey Valerie	
1988	Fernando Henry Teresa Efrain	Gloria Leticia Randy Armando	Ryan	Cynthia Caroline Christine	

have led to suspensions from school and lectures and citations from law enforcement officers. The citations were for what he calls "squirrelly" things, such as passing red traffic lights on his bicycle as well as breaking curfew at 2:00 a.m. while bicycling to the beach to fish.

His personal life and habits are those of a loner. Most of his time out of school is spent alone. He smokes and drinks alone. His only hobbies are tending to his vegetable garden ("Maybe I'd like to be a farmer," he muses) and fishing off the Seal Beach Pier. Jeffrey also tinkers with bikes and bakes for his family—especially cakes.

School has never been a successful experience for him. Throughout his school career, his behavior has been slightly negative, increasingly so when he did not care for the teacher. His teachers' comments are revealing: "He has no participation, no performance, no friends"; "A self-defeating attitude with no apparent self-motivating desires." One teacher, digging deep for redeeming qualities, comments: "He's good with his pocket knife, but he makes marks in the chair seat."

His GPA is 1.95, in a vocational/basic course of study. When questioned about his lack of effort and performance he merely says, "I goof around a lot and don't do the work and homework. I can get an A in any class I want to, if I put my mind to it. But I guess I'm just plain lazy. As long as I get C's I'm happy, and I do all right to satisfy myself."

As a result of this behavior and performance, most of the school day for him is a boring, drawn-out experience. Once in a while, an altercation with another student rescues him from boredom: "Just another day, like any other—boring. My last class was kind of interesting in a way. That chick I called a whore the day before hit me across the side of the face. It really didn't hurt much, but then she asked me if I wanted to step outside and have a have-it-out routine. But I told her that I didn't hit girls. And she said, 'That statement is saving you from getting hit again on the other side.' If I would've been a bad dude, I could've really left her messed up pretty bad."

At this time, Jeffrey is considering pursuing a welding occupation and he has, unlike his brothers and sisters, no aspirations for attending college. Although he is definitely more Anglo- than Mexican-oriented, especially in language ability and usage, the motivation is missing to ensure his success in school and a better future. In general, this stage of his life is characterized by apathy and angst.

Valerie: We Knew We Were Mexican, but We Were Told to Say We Were "White"

It's only four o'clock in the afternoon, but the dining room table bears pencils, notebooks, and a couple of volumes of the World Book Encyclopedia. The house is quiet as a library. Valerie explains, "I don't like music or anything when I study. This paper's due in three weeks."

Valerie's parents have provided a stable and well-furnished, middle-class home, which they own. They actively participate in their children's education by helping with homework and undertaking regular school visitations for conferences or open houses. This has guided the children in aspiring to a college education. Both parents work, Valerie's father as a partner in a TV repair business and her mother part-time as a sales clerk in a department store. Together they earn more than fifteen thousand dollars per year.

Valerie's daily plans are carefully scheduled and centered on family activities. She says, "I cook and help with chores most days. If there's time, I have a few neighborhood friends." What little social life she has mostly involves idle chatter with class friends. On occasion, she does enjoy attending school sporting events. Her remaining time is spent at school and studying at home, with little TV viewing.

Valerie fits the "ideal" model of an Anglo-oriented Chicana. She states, "I feel that I'm Anglo, not Mexican, and this has helped my education. Some teachers might put you down because you're Mexican. I've never seen it, but I heard it around. We've been brought up to know we are Mexican, but to say we're white." She describes herself as a white Catholic. These words validate her claim to "Anglo-ness," and most of her behavior supports it. Her friends are all Anglo, and she avoids everything that is Mexican; for example, she says, "I don't like Mexican music."

Overall, she was never really socialized within the Mexican culture. Therefore, she hasn't had to forget or slight her original culture. She was raised in suburbia, among mostly Anglos, and told to speak only English (she speaks only the Spanish learned in courses). Along the way, she was molded by parents who had their own reasons for changing cultures.

Indeed, the background and experiences of the parents are important to understand in analyzing Valerie. A Czechoslovakian immigrant, her mother believes that assimilating allows one "to get a better education, and you get a better job. It's not like digging ditches." In contrast to her father, though, the mother is much more relaxed and tolerant when commenting about the Mexican culture. Valerie's father came from a former land owning *rico* (rich) family, and he often denigrates the Mexican culture and the people who epitomize it: "As long as they have a six-pack (of beer) and something to eat, they're happy. They don't care and are only interested in living from day to day." In his native New Mexico it is common to identify one's self as "Spanish." When emphasizing the importance of learning English, Valerie's father states, "It's more of an advantage because you're going to mix more and learn to speak the language of the land instead of speaking the language of the little corner where you hang out."

Valerie's comments when contrasting the cultures are revealing: "When I think of Mexican culture I think of fiestas, mariachis, and dancing. Mexicans are more poor and have a language barrier." She believes that Anglos always tell their children to grow up and settle down with a good job and home: "Go to college. Be a doctor or lawyer. They are trying to get ahead all the time."

Valerie's educational performance is exemplary, and it has been that way since elementary school. In fact, with the graceful prodding of her mother, who would like her to be trilingual, she has taken Spanish language courses and is able to read quite well. She is currently part of an accelerated high school program that places her in college prep courses. Teacher reports state that she is: "Quiet, conscientious, self-disciplined, and responsible; bright, interesting, does work well; achieves above grade level in all areas; and one fantastic girl." Her recent report card was somewhat below her GPA of 3.5, but still strong in the academic areas—3 As, 1 B, and 2 Cs.

Given her background and her grades, she fits quite well into the model of Anglo acculturation and school performance.

SUMMARY

The suburban environment provided better conditions for acculturation. However, it also created a sense of relative affluence, that is, a sense of material comfort, or socioeconomic satisfaction. This sentiment was particularly expressed when some of the students compared their lifestyle to that of their relatives in the urban barrio. The idea expressed is one of, "We've made it. What more is there to achieve?" Thus, the future aspirations of these students are low. They merely want to maintain their current status and are satisfied in living a life of blue-collar complacency.

Residence in the United States for a longer period of time is usually associated with a higher rate of acculturation, as is higher socioeconomic status, but there is no assurance that it guarantees advanced academic performance. The students in each cultural style are affected by cultural changes in different ways. Even if Anglo acculturation is more enhanced in the suburban locale, there are still feelings of anxiety and ambivalence associated with the process. Mexican-oriented students enjoy the opportunities and conveniences in the community, but they also remark that the conditions for retention of the Mexican culture and practice of the Spanish language are limited. Finally, the intermediate, Chicano students might lean more to the Anglo end of the spectrum, but they also tend to identify with the street culture, that is, gang life, in their community.

Nevertheless, if personal sociocultural problems emerge, the suburban environment tends to soften the severity of these conflicts. The students display less deviant behavior and the suburban environment has fewer gangs and a lower level of

Waiting for the baseball game.

violence and aggression. Also important in aiding acculturation is the presence of the Anglo majority that students can emulate and with whom they can interact.

As part of the migratory nature of Mexicans in southern California and the Southwest, beginning with first-generation immigrants in earlier eras, suburban parents of second and third generations pointed out that they left East Los Angeles (or another Southwest state) to provide a better neighborhood and home for their children. It was a spatial and social move that resulted in several of the students (especially those who were Anglo-oriented) feeling no discomfort in denying their ethnic identity. Raised in a suburb that was predominantly Anglo, these students did not have an environment that favored the retention of their ethnic heritage. Moreover, several students had parents who explicitly instructed them to change their ethnicity. Some parents did this to spare their children the racism they experienced when they were young. Other parents' motives were based more on their own prejudice and perhaps even shame of their ethnicity. Regardless of their reasons, these parents' strategies of denial were successful in part because their children were in an Anglo suburban environment.

With the exception of one female Anglo-oriented informant, Valerie, who followed a well-engineered adaptation strategy, the other persons underwent a shaky acculturation journey. Parents in all instances were responsible for fashioning a strategy in the hope of avoiding cultural and linguistic obstacles, especially those based on racism, and thus socialized their children toward the dominant culture in obvious and sometimes subtle ways. "I was told to say I was white" epitomizes this trend at the Anglo end of the spectrum, a perception that surfaced in other cases as well.

It is also interesting to note the role of racial appearance in acculturation. Several of the Anglo-oriented students had light complexions, and actually appeared to be "white." Their racial appearance undoubtedly has helped them adapt to the suburban environment, allowing them to create a new ethnic persona. This

Powder Puff football in the spring.

was especially important for them, as they were somewhat ashamed of being Mexican. In contrast, the darker, mestizo students carried the wary attitude toward Anglos that their parents had instilled in them. Thus, racial appearance is also a mediating factor in acculturation and can affect the direction and rate in changing one's identity.

However, even in an Anglo suburban environment, there is still a great deal of diversity within this sample. Despite the absence of a large Mexican ethnic population base such as East Los Angeles, several students were still strongly Mexican-oriented. For these students, the Expanded Horizons program helped them mediate the acculturation process. The program helped instill a sense of ethnic pride in several students, even if they could not speak Spanish and knew little about their heritage. Thus, the Expanded Horizons program has helped students regain a sense of identity and stability.

6 / "I Can't Speak Spanish, but I'm Mexican and Proud of It": The 1988 Suburban Informants

The suburban locale, which was a working- and lower middle-class enclave in the 1970s, has now become the new suburbia for Mexican Americans looking for a better place to raise their children. Although the locale is only a few miles from East Los Angeles, the suburban area in this study is now perceived as an area of relative affluence and prosperity; hence, the slogan, "From East L.A. to _____, seven miles to the American Dream," an orientation that characterizes the Chicano experience.

The transformation of the suburban locale is directly related to the influx of new immigrants into the Los Angeles area. By 1988, East L.A. and its barrios had

The hallways are outdoors.

The white tee-shirt is always in style.

Coed interests in drafting.

1.5ers in a crowd.

been saturated with new immigrants. Consequently, slightly older immigrants and second- or third-generation families started settling into other areas of Los Angeles, including our suburban fieldsite. This mass Mexicanization has had a striking effect on suburbia and the students in this sample, who are now appreciably comfortable with being identified as Mexican or Mexican American. This is true even of some of the Anglo-oriented students who cannot speak Spanish and who do not follow traditional Mexican customs. These students may only have a symbolic, emotional connection to their ethnic heritage, but it is a connection nonetheless, and it indicates how the cultural climate has changed.

Given the diversity of the students in this group, it is even more remarkable that they have claimed an association to their heritage. Some of the students are third- and fourth-generation Mexican Americans, and several are biracial and part European. Yet, no matter how far removed they may be from their heritage, in at least some form, they still identify themselves as Mexican.

The Anglo residents who have remained in the suburban community have met the Mexicanization phenomenon with some resentment, even hostility. Outnumbered, but clinging to their notion of territorial priority, many Anglos, including teachers and other public employees, have struggled to maintain an aura of control and dominance. For example, the school principal, an Anglo female, reflects this attitude in many overt and covert ways. Denying that gangs exist in the neighborhood or that Mexican students need cultural enrichment and special learning routines, this principal had stubbornly resisted advice and suggestions from the community. She also had made matters difficult for herself by being inconsistent in her policies. Several years later, she was forced out by community activists.

This Anglo resentment is somewhat predictable because of the demographic shifts that have made Mexican Americans a perceived threat. The entrenched

Friendships come in all colors and cultures (and sizes!).

dominant ethnic group, the Anglos, are wary and feel besieged and pressured to readjust against their will. This, coupled with other negative intrusions such as the expansion of street gangs, has exacerbated feelings of hostility, adding to the belief that the neighborhood is a less attractive place.

Nevertheless, the suburban community still has a good, sound industrial and tax base, and the students there enjoy a relatively higher standard of living than their urban counterparts. Following a pattern noted in the 1974 suburban group, this perception of relative affluence has appeared to blunt social mobility aspirations of several students and thus they do not appear to feel as much of a "push" to put forth greater effort in school. In sum, their "comfort zone" has been reached

Gang and subcultural activity has increased, but it is not a predominant theme in this area. Many social and recreational programs have attempted, with some success, to address the youth and gang problem. Neighborhood Watch units and other adult voluntary associations and pressure groups have also been active. The schools have responded to the problem by discouraging gang members and have adopted strict dress codes. Unfortunately, the problems of nearby communities, without the resources to develop similar outreach programs, have tended to spill into the community of this investigation.

MEXICAN-ORIENTED LIFESTYLES:
FERNANDO, HENRY, EFRAIN, AND TERESA

In the years between investigations, certain changes have redefined the Mexican immigrant population. Binationality is much more prevalent, and immigrants are much more likely to keep ties with friends and relatives in the old country. Periodic visits to Mexico for birthdays, weddings, and the like are quite common. Such "geo-movements" help maintain a stable family environment because extended family members are incorporated into this transnational network of social reciprocity.

But there has also been culture strain, especially between the parents and the children. In particular, children who are members of the 1.5 generation, who came to America as children, have been caught in a culture-change dilemma. They are definitely Mexicans and proud of their heritage, but they are also able to speak English and have assimilated to a certain degree, at least much more so than their parents. As a result, they have frequent disagreements with their parents over cultural practices and norms.

A working-class ethic, something rich and deeply rooted in Mexican culture and history, is also representative of this group. Nonetheless, this is a strength that often undermines strivings toward education. Sometimes just having a decent paying job is seen as satisfactory, particularly when Mexicans have historically been barred from higher status jobs. This learned attitude and practice has been around for quite a while and reflects many other working-class populations. Coupled with racial barriers, this orientation has tended to discourage the value of schooling in some segments of the Mexican community, as this old quotation underscores: "Look at Manuel, Miss M. He went to high school, and he works in the brickyard the same as Pedro, who never went to school" (from Bogardus 1926: 107).

Although the school district has been open to innovative and experimental approaches to learning (for example, Advancement Via Individual Determination—AVID, a program that addresses low-achieving but "bright" students), the small immigrant population has been given cursory attention with an ESL program (mostly from their early experiences in Los Angeles schools, prior to resettlement in suburbia) that is more of an Anglo assimilation route. Teachers and administrators in these programs would argue otherwise, but ESL student experiences were more for transition than maintenance. The student in this category, Fernando, suffered from these language and learning inconsistencies, and was more open about his belief that this treatment stemmed from racism.

This group also has some students whose lives contain interesting and complex elements, and a few are almost 1.5 generation by default. In one case, the return to the native land (Colombia, in this instance) was a stay that lasted six years, with the father citing racism as the reason for the return home. In any event, such interactions and exchanges make the Mexican and Latino category fascinating and broadens the concept of *personas mexicanas*. (I've included non-Mexicans as Chicanos because the cauldron that is Los Angeles has tended to make adaptation among them similar.) A sharp and dedicated decision to acculturate to Anglo lifeways, coupled with the philosophical strategy to retain (even regain, in this instance) native culture, shows that ethnic identity strains are not necessarily tied solely to cultural change in the United States.

Stable, traditional families have provided a sound foundation for these individuals. Parents here emphasize that the children must behave, and disobedience is not tolerated. Only one of these students has been notably successful in academic terms. Another, the only girl among these examples, has had an average academic performance caused more by a lack of interest than poor habits. In her case, none of the family members have excelled in school, although the mother, feeling bad about the educational voids in her family, has gone back to adult school to take classes.

ACCULTURATION SPECTRUM PLACEMENT OF SELECTED INFORMANTS, 1974 AND 1988

← Mexican-Oriented		Intermediate		Anglo-Oriented →	
1974 Urban	Hortensia Matilda	Cecilia Eduardo		Vicente Alberto	

| **1988** | Jacinto Lidia Norma Hector | Jorge Daniel | Diana Georgina | Martha Marcia Jose Pascual | |

-2 • • • • -1 • • • • 0 • • • • +1 • • • • +2

| **1974 Suburban** | Carlos Sara | | Veronica Juan | Jeffrey Valerie | |

| **1988** | Fernando Henry Teresa Efrain | | Gloria Leticia Randy Armando | Ryan Cynthia Caroline Christine | |

Fernando: A "Too-Late Mexican": Still in the Acculturation Stream

"This above all: to thine own self be true." Fernando, whether he knows Shake-speare or not, lives by truth. His demeanor and language are not calculated to im-press. He is at peace with the pauses in a conversation, never uncomfortable taking his time to consider his response. Some may even interpret this lack of guile as slowness of thought. His parents' efforts to push him into a quicker acculturation meet with a similar response. He will not be rushed into "faking like I'm an Anglo." It is disingenuous, in Fernando's mind, to pretend.

Born in Mexico, Fernando's parents have gradually familiarized themselves with the English language since their arrival in America. As a homemaker, his mother takes care of the family while his father has to work two jobs—one at a Dodge dealership and the other at a company where he makes parts for turbine en-gines. Both were fortunate enough to graduate from high school, and value this ex-perience highly. Fernando sees his family as being a part of the upper middle class, although his father only takes home about six hundred dollars a month. They live in a seven-bedroom home. It was a four-bedroom home, but Fernando's parents con-verted the porch, den, and garage into needed bedrooms. In addition to the nuclear family of seven, a cousin who arrived from Mexico two years ago lives with them. One of Fernando's older brothers is employed full time, and his sister attends a community college during the day, paying for this by working part time at night. As for himself, Fernando says he only works "so I can earn money for my clothes. I work during summer—last summer I worked with my father's friend fixing cars."

Fernando was born in Mexico City and immigrated with his family to the United States when he was ten years old. Out of necessity he speaks English, but he is also proud of his Mexican roots. His parents would like to become naturalized citizens, but he hotly reminds them, "You are Mexican and should not try to be something you're not." As traditional Mexicans, the family goes through great pains to attend their relatives' *quinceañeras* in Mexico. In fact, family visitation and exchanges are a regular part of their lives. Similarly, as traditional Mexicans, Fernando and his family are devout Roman Catholics, and attend mass at their local church every Sunday.

Fernando is now in the eleventh grade. He is usually a C student, with an overall GPA of 2.6, but recently his grades have fallen somewhat because of his frequent absences. When he first arrived from Mexico, the school officials immediately placed him in an ESL class. However, after only three quick months of language training, his teachers decided to move him into a regular classroom. He recalls, "I knew it was too soon. From that point on it was very, very hard to adjust, ready or not. I was supposed to understand all the English and do my work." Fernando is angry with his school because of numerous incidents of what he perceives as discrimination. For example, as a sophomore, the school did not allow him to take algebra or geometry. Instead he had to take basic math, and wait until "they were ready," he says. "What did they have to get ready for?" he questions angrily. In another incident, Fernando was aware that he needed good grades to play soccer, and because he is a good soccer player, the coach let him play for the last half of the season. When the season had ended, the coach shocked Fernando with the news that he would not be allowed to attend the team banquet or receive a varsity letter because his grade point average was too low. It turned out to be a "grading" mistake, which Fernando hastily tried to correct, but the coach stubbornly refused to take the time to reconsider his pleas. This type of treatment, he believed, would not be tolerated by "gringos."

Fernando's parents are a positive force in his efforts to do well in school. They regularly give him encouragement and exhort him to take advantage of every chance. "You won't have another chance in life if you don't do it right now in school," they tell him. Also, his parents lend him an open ear when it comes to any problems he might be having at school. They tell him he can reach his goals, no matter how lofty they are. At this time, Fernando wants to work on jets as an engine mechanic. He wants to learn the trade by joining the Marines. He is a whiz in his auto mechanics course and is always eager to learn more. His interests germinated in this field when he was first introduced to auto mechanics in Mexico, where he helped his friend in a garage and began learning how to fix engines. He says he definitely plans to pursue this interest. Fernando always means what he says.

Henry: A Binational "Colombian": Drinking from Two Cultural Waters

"Most people think of Colombia and they think of coffee. Other people just lump us in with Chicanos. I sometimes don't even explain." Henry shakes his head, obviously disgusted by the necessity to explain his position as a minority among minorities.

Both of Henry's parents were born in Colombia. His father speaks both English and Spanish and works as a maintenance mechanic, while his mother works part time at a retail store. Together they make about thirty thousand dollars a year. Henry works, too, putting in between eighteen and twenty-four hours a week at a warehouse while attending high school. His brother attends a technical institute and expects to eventually become an electrical engineer.

The term "working class" fully defines Henry's family—everybody in the family works. Furthermore, they manifest a singular trait that many immigrants possess, which is a strong ethic for hard work and the eagerness to do well. Henry and his four other family members live comfortably in a commodious three-bedroom apartment: Sparkling clean, well kept, and presentable as a member of a large village of similar-looking apartments.

Henry was born in Los Angeles, but returned to live in Colombia for six years when he was nine years old. This decision to return "home" was his father's, who was fed up with the constant racial badgering he faced in the Land of Opportunity. But, as his father states, "Once you live in the United States, it's hard to go back." Additionally, the fact that the Colombian army had press gangs sweeping the countryside for young recruits was a further catalyst for returning. In regards to his parents' path of acculturation, the family made great efforts to keep hold of their Colombian customs, but the forces of assimilation were hard to deny, and they gradually started to become more American. Only a few of their relatives live in the United States, and so family gatherings are few and far between. Religion and political discourse play a minimal role in Henry's life, for, in his father's view, "The priests love to get all the details of your sins—they get a kick out of it. As for politicians, they're worse than the priests. At least the priests are truly interested, even if it's in a sick way. In Latin American countries, the politicians are too crazy."

Henry considers himself Colombian, and feels comfortable with his ethnicity. An excellent bilingual, he speaks, reads, and writes both in Spanish and English. Henry says, "I don't mind someone calling me Hispanic or Latino. The only thing I can't relate to is being called Chicano, because that applies to Mexicans, which I'm not." At school, Henry also likes to hang out more with the "Stoners" than he does with any of the cholos.

Henry is an excellent student, with a 3.6 GPA, and is actively involved in sports, where he excels in football and track. He plans to go to California State University, Los Angeles, and major in accounting or law. While in college, Henry also plans to work part time at any job he can get so that he can pay for his tuition, and he has also decided—albeit reluctantly—to put his athletic career on hold for now. Inspired by the flashy stereotype of the Hollywood detective, Henry eventually wants to become an agent for the FBI.

Henry's parents have always been supportive. Henry's father states that in order for kids to do well in life, they have to "start early in the crib." He says his children used to go to sleep at 7:30 p.m. Also, the father says both Henry and his brother were "given hand motion treatment" (spanked) when they were young, and by the time school began, the boys were self-starters. More than anyone else, Henry cites his parents as the primary influence behind his decision to enroll in college.

Efrain: Broken Families, Shifting Social Networks, and Schooling Changes: "Nobody Pushed Me."

Given the chance to warm up to a person, Efrain talks openly and at length about his life. "I look around me and people are going, going, going—to college, to work. Sometimes I want to go, too, but I don't. I wish something would happen to get rid of this lazy part." Efrain is at a loss to explain why, yet he knows something's missing.

Efrain's father was born in Mexico and eventually obtained a college degree there, and his mother was also born in Mexico and was able to finish high school. Born in the United States, Efrain was about seven or eight years old when his parents divorced, leaving the task of raising Efrain and the four other children to his mom.

Early on, Efrain was forced to go to five different schools in five consecutive years. The harsh realities of raising a large family weighed heavily on his mother, so Efrain had to spend a lot of time living with his foster parents. After Efrain graduated from junior high school, his mother decided that the schools in Los Angeles were not doing a good job, so she sent Efrain to live with his father who was able to provide for a better education for Efrain in high school. In spite of his improved conditions, however, Efrain still misses his mother deeply.

Efrain currently lives with his father and stepmother, along with two sisters, one stepsister, and two stepbrothers, all in a five-bedroom house. Efrain's father had returned to college in the United States and studied engineering. However, he works as a production manager and is in sales, and he brings home about sixty-five thousand dollars annually. Efrain says his family is upper middle class because they own three houses and four cars. In reality, the true flavor of the neighborhood is given away by the predominance of working-class people living in quite ordinary-looking, stucco-sided homes. Efrain feels comfortable saying he is a Mexican American, but his heritage is that of Mexico, and this is what he has learned as a bilingual-bicultural. He enjoys Mexican music, a habit he has learned from his father. Efrain has learned much more from his grandmother, who would often take him to see Mexican performers and entertainers. Sometimes, she would even take him on trips to Mexico. Efrain speaks Spanish fluently, unlike his younger brothers, who, their Dad says, speak "Spanglish." Efrain boasts, "I can speak two languages so I've got an advantage here over some people."

His observations of his ESL experience are interesting because it was not the Mexican students who were being ridiculed for not being able to speak Spanish, but the Anglo students. Nevertheless, he has gotten a good whiff of racism at his school. One high school teacher made fun of him. He recalls, "She said, 'You're not a native citizen, right? I can tell you're not from here.'" This dressing down occurred in front of his classmates, most of whom were Anglo.

Efrain is an average student with an overall 2.5 GPA. He says he likes his present high school, especially when compared to the Los Angeles schools. Taking basic courses, he looks at his senior year as the best. Although he never took ESL classes, he had a hard time in kindergarten because he did not understand the language. He said it took him about half a year to get used to it, and that was because his mother, a teacher's aide, helped him. His grades in junior high school were barely adequate, and even now his semester GPA is only 1.8. Efrain reports, "I don't have nobody in my corner pushing me, and I've always had a problem pushing myself to study." He knows he could do well, but just does not make the effort. Even with his father sometimes getting on his case, he still has not shown any major improvements. He is, however, impressed by the nice-looking suburban high school he attends because everyone there wants to learn. In Los Angeles, he says, "only two or three people in my school wanted to learn, and the rest just wanted to get by." He says that that is the same way he was conditioned to behave.

When Efrain graduates from high school he is going to the nearest Navy recruiting office, for he has already signed up with them for four years to learn radio. Eventually, he wishes to become an expert in communications. "It sure beats just bumming around." His father is trying to encourage his other sons to follow Efrain into the armed services, so that they can learn a useful trade or two.

Teresa: Traditional and Unmotivated: Keeping Your Head Above Water the Old Way

Walking slowly by the vice-principal's office, Teresa casts a wary glance at a friend waiting on a chair inside, obviously concerned that a friend may be in trouble. She postulates, "It's probably just for joking too much, or talking." Teresa is a young woman who cares about her friends' reputations, and who honors her parents. Not particularly academically oriented, yet secure with herself, she is gifted in relational, "people" skills.

Teresa's parents were both born in Mexico and received only a minimal education. They immigrated to the United States a few years before Teresa—who now is sixteen—was born. Her father is a masonry contractor, and her mother has never worked outside of the home. Teresa is the youngest of her parents' six children, and she lives with her family in a five-bedroom house. Her family view themselves as middle class, and when she looks out of her bedroom window, she sees a neighborhood that is similar in lifestyle to theirs. The neighborhood is quiet, clean, and relatively free of graffiti and gang activities.

Teresa feels comfortable with her ethnicity. She has a positive self-image and is proud of being Mexican. Her parents reared the family in an environment that espoused the good things in their culture. Her father is bilingual, but her mother does not understand English very well.

Holidays are considered special events, and the family does a lot of celebrating. At Christmas time the family likes to gather up and go to Mexico—but this is only once in a while. Even their religious beliefs and observances reflect what Buriel (1984) has called the "Mexican Catholic ideology": a strict, formal, and profoundly spiritual renewal based on mixed Spanish and indigenous patterns.

Both Teresa and her sister had *quinceañeras,* but even now she is still "under wraps" and not allowed to date until she is at least eighteen years old. Suitors must visit her and solemnly chat at her home, while her parents sit on a sofa and peer at them from across the way. She believes this is old fashioned, but, "In a way, it's good." Dominated by a strong Mexican cultural theme, the family nevertheless has some Anglo cultural appreciations and practices.

Teresa, an eleventh grader, is an average student with a 2.2 GPA. She is not enrolled in college prep classes. She says her parents are always encouraging her to get good grades, and when she has problems with her homework, her parents always try to help. Although she believes she can do better, she says, "I get lazy and most of the time a C is good enough for me." She plans to enroll in a community college and then transfer to a university, but isn't quite sure yet about these plans. Her choice of career is up to her, as her parents do not wish to interfere. Teresa likes working with children, and looks at a career as a social worker with a somewhat brighter perspective.

Proud of her bilingual abilities, she fondly remembers incidents where she had to interpret for newly arrived students from Mexico, whose ability to speak English was nonexistent. "It felt really good to help them. I remember saying they wouldn't need my help very long." Interestingly enough, she noticed that as she moved on into junior high many of those same students were arrogant and looked down on those who could not speak English. However, because of her faith in herself as a Mexican and in her culture, it is a self-fulfilling feeling for her to help those who need it the most.

CHICANO-ORIENTED LIFESTYLES:
GLORIA, ARMANDO, RANDY, AND LETICIA

Although they are theoretically in between cultures for this time period, none of the Chicano-oriented students have problems in articulating their strong Mexican identity. For example, they are all fluent in Spanish, and they and their families still observe traditional Mexican holidays and customs. As intermediates, however, they have also assimilated into their Anglo environment. Thus, they are truly bicultural, but not without some interesting problems and developments.

As members of the second and third generation, they have strong Mexican ties. This is remarkable because some of their parents were 1.5 generation themselves, but still have cultivated connections and associations with families in Mexico and visit there fairly frequently. In a sense, the acculturation spectrum has been tweaked in a Mexican direction. A reflection of the binationality noted earlier, these families and their children are clearly steeped in their Mexican roots but have also somewhat adequately integrated Anglo patterns into their ethnic and cultural repertoire. Cultural adjustments span the gamut of conflict and strain. In one instance of intra- as well intergenerational difficulties, both the parents and siblings shifted back and forth in their attitudes and practices.

Only one of the students is involved in subcultural activity. Of the four, only one has done reasonably well in school. Social issues and forces explain most of these differences. Some have missed connections with Anglo-American society in particular. Family variances and other gaps have also undermined their opportunities to integrate, and thus a certain amount of ambivalence is apparent. Overall, this group shows both the positive and negative dynamics of the second and third generation in transition (with the added complication of their parents coming from a 1.5 generation), even if in a less-receptive Anglo world.

Gloria: Putting It All Together: Solid Home, Secure Bilingual Identity, and Goals to Prove It

"I really look up to my mother," declares Gloria. "I'm proud of how she works at a good job and still takes care of us. If I could be like her, it'd be great." Gloria juggles a lot of activities successfully. The teenager is already showing the same discipline and effort that characterize the life of her mother.

ACCULTURATION SPECTRUM PLACEMENT OF SELECTED INFORMANTS, 1974 AND 1988

◄──────── Mexican-Oriented	Intermediate	Anglo-Oriented ──────►
1974 Hortensia Matilda	Cecilia	Vicente
Urban	Eduardo	Alberto
1988 Jacinto	Jorge Diana	Martha
Lidia	Daniel Georgina	Marcia Jose
Norma		Pascual
Hector		

-2 • • • • -1 • • • • 0 • • • • +1 • • • • +2

| **1974** Carlos | Veronica | Jeffrey |
Suburban Sara	Juan	Valerie
1988 Fernando Henry	Gloria Ryan Cynthia Caroline
Teresa	Leticia Randy Christine
Efrain	Armando

Gloria's parents were born in Mexico, and after immigrating to the United States as teenagers, they eventually became fluent in English. Her father reached the twelfth grade and is currently working as a supervisor for a major company. Her mother finished at the eleventh grade and is now working as a secretary. Their work provides a combined annual income of more than forty-five thousand dollars for the family, not including benefits. Gloria describes her family of two brothers, ages nineteen and twelve, and one sister of twenty months, as upper middle class.

Living fairly comfortably in a three-bedroom house, she describes her neighborhood as peaceful and says her mother works hard to keep the house nicely cleaned and decorated. Currently in the process of moving to Chino, the parents are going to rent out the present house, but Gloria will be staying with an aunt in the suburban area to graduate from what she considers a nice high school.

Gloria is secure and confident with her self-image. Her ethnicity, she says, is Mexican, but sometimes her parents correct her and say she is Hispanic. Gloria is bilingual and bicultural, and has been reared that way. She is proud of being bilingual and knows this will help her employment. Brought up in the traditions of the Mexican culture, she celebrates many personal and family customs throughout the year. For Christmas, Gloria's extended family members come from Mexico and for several days make a celebration of cooking the tamales and *menudo*. Her family also participates in the *Posadas*. Her parents said no to dating, however, not at least until she had had her *quinceañera*. As a nominal Catholic, she mostly attends those church functions that reflect her cultural heritage. However, Gloria views her family and herself as becoming Americanized because they "can't really bring back things from Mexico. We don't talk too much about the olden days." She says this Americanization process shows in many ways, including the fact that her father sometimes lets her go out even if he knows drinking will occur. Her father will also joke with her about being Mexican and tells her "to take her burrito [various foods wrapped in a tortilla] to school."

Gloria has experienced some discrimination from both sides, but this has not shaken her identity. For example, her geometry teacher would often start class by making racial remarks in regards to personal hygiene. He would also make fun of Chinese immigrants and remark that Mexicans make good dishwashers. On the other hand, one of her Mexican-American friends, who looks white, insulted another friend by saying she has a "TJ accent and won't win any student body office." These experiences have tended to make Gloria guarded yet convinced that it is better to be honest about who you are, even though in this school and neighborhood it is not fashionable to speak in Spanish.

Gloria is an above average student with a 3.0 GPA, and active in extracurricular activities. As a senior class officer, head of a class committee, and a member of the soccer team, she has a busy schedule. Gloria would like to attend college and become a business administrator. Her parents share her hopes and show it by providing support when needed. In sum, the assurance and support she receives from her family on all fronts makes for a solid foundation.

Armando: A *Güero* in Rocker's Clothing: Poor, Partying, and Losing Out

Armando, seventeen years old, is one of many youths attracted to the spirit of anarchy espoused in much of the lyrics in heavy metal music. These youths are united in their stand against authority. "We don't need no thought control . . . Hey, Teacher! Leave us kids alone!"* The problem with this worldview arises when one of its youthful proponents, free of all authority, finds himself without personal goals, motivation, or respect for traditional paths to achievement. "Doing things you don't feel like doing is so tiresome," says Armando.

Armando's father is deceased, and he lives with his mother, a homemaker, two siblings, and his stepfather, who is disabled. The family is living on Social Security, which provides just enough to survive. Armando lives with five family members in a three-bedroom house in one of the older tract developments. He describes his family as working class and the neighborhood as middle and working class. Armando assists his brother with cabinetmaking work in order to earn money. "In the summertime, I like to work repairing air conditioners and heaters," he adds.

Armando describes himself as Hispanic and he is bilingual, but also Anglicized. His mother was born in Michoacan and sometimes makes fun of Armando for his *güero* (white, Anglo) ways. "She always says I'm trying to act *güero* or something," reveals Armando. He reluctantly follows some Mexican customs to please his mother. "I do some things to make her happy. I'm not ashamed of the culture or nothing. It's just I get tired of making the effort to go along." Armando is familiar with relatives and customs from Mexico, for he has visited there many times.

Armando is part of a social group called the "Rascals," a group made up of youths from nearby communities. The Rascals' primary goal is to "party." They indulge in some light drinking and provide DJ music. Armando says, "Hey, I'm the organizer. I get the music together." This is, at times, a money-making venture for Armando, for such DJs bring their records and sound systems to many parties for a fee.

*A line from Pink Floyd's song "The Wall".

The Rascals is really the only institution in his life. As an inactive Catholic, he rarely attends church. Armando also believes, "There should be anarchy all over our country, get rid of the government." This comment reflects his media-driven political beliefs and how easily he is influenced by friends and music.

Armando has a 1.52 GPA in high school. He usually gets C's and D's in his classes. Currently, he is making an effort to at least graduate this year. "I'm going to night school right now. I just have to go Thursday, then, I just have to go to school and keep my grades up. From there I want to get a job, get a car, and then go to junior college to go to a better university." He hasn't narrowed his aspirations down. "I like doing architect stuff, but I like working with my hands, too. Maybe I'll be a tool and die mechanic or maybe I'll do dental work." His mother interjects at this point, "He takes apart radios and then puts them back together."

School has never been a strong suit with Armando. He just has never done well there. He does say, "When I was a little kid, my uncle tried to scare me into studying and acting right. It kind of worked. But all of a sudden, he stopped pushing me and I totally stopped trying." Armando faltered and developed school and learning problems. His mother couldn't help him with school because she obtained little formal education in Mexico.

The loss of a father, a nihilistic worldview, and a lukewarm attitude to his culture are all factors in Armando's life. Free of all but peer influence, it is difficult to say how he will find the strength and purpose to forge a path for himself in the future.

Randy: A "Jock" Without a Direction: No Role Model in a Studyless World

Randy is a well-built "jock," or successful athlete. In the many social circles of high school, such a person is often the center of attention. Generally, for the time being, that is enough. The problem with this immensely gratifying identity is that it can sometimes work against you. Stripped of his varsity jacket, the young man underneath is often ill-equipped to compete in the long life that lies ahead of him.

Randy's father, born in Texas, is a bilingual Mexican American. He works in sales and earns about thirty-five thousand dollars per year. Born in New Mexico, Randy's bilingual mother identifies herself as Mexican American. She makes about fifteen thousand dollars a year, working in professional services.

The family's three-bedroom house sits in a neighborhood of well-kept middle-class tract homes. Randy lives with his parents, a brother, and a sister. He describes his neighborhood: "all the houses are nice, with the grass cut." Quite proud, he goes on about his impressive home—the new cabinets and modern furniture. He also brags about the expansive backyard "where the dogs play," in all probability on just-cut grass. Randy describes his family as middle class because they are "average," middle-type people.

Randy describes himself as Mexican, not Mexican American. Because he is a United States citizen, he is referring to his Mexican heritage. In spite of this claim, he is effectively Anglicized. His parents speak to their children in English, even though they speak Spanish with each other. This is not uncommon for parents of the "3.5 generation" in which Randy fits. Still, the family does follow many Mexican traditions for the holidays. The extended family comes over for exchanges of gifts, emotional renewals, and an abundance of food. Revealing their bicultural upbringing, the family also celebrates Thanksgiving by eating turkey. Randy and his family are Catholics, but he is inactive in church.

Randy is an average student, with a low C average. He says that he falters in reading comprehension and memorizing. He blames an experience in elementary school for his academic downfall; he had a neglectful teacher in the fifth grade. "He was a kickback teacher that just liked to mess around." As a result, when Randy entered sixth grade, he was completely lost. He remembers not understanding anything that was going on in the classroom. This lost, wasted year, he claims, was the setback that plagues him to the present.

Randy has played sports since junior high. They have always been a positive element in his life. He peppers his recollections with the comments and teachings of the coaches who have been his role models. They told him about the importance of an education, but "it's just some of the classes are hard and boring." As for his parents, they value education and would like him to attend a four-year college. Still, the decision, he says, is left up to him—verbal support is all he gets from his parents. "Mom," as he calls her, "always talks to me and follows up with encouragement, even if I'm coasting along not doing anything." Knowing that he is highly involved with sports, something she also excelled in when she was young, she would like him to use this athletic ability and pursue a career as a football or baseball player. She also tells him to emphasize academics. His father would like to see Randy succeed but leaves the decision to Randy and takes a detached approach to parenting. Randy would like to go on to college and knows that school counseling and tutoring could help him to get there. Unfortunately, there is a "time" conflict with his sports activities, which seem to take priority over everything else.

Positive home dynamics are a crucial foundation for success in education. Young people need encouragement, a climate conducive to learning, and stimulating discussions of current events, among other requirements. In Randy's case, the home environment seems to fall short. Randy is on his own and, enjoying his time as the center of attention, is playing full time.

Leticia: Doing Poorly, but She Keeps on Trying

"God makes people different." Sipping from her soda, Leticia reflects on her situation. "I don't know if school will ever be easy for me. I wish I could improve so much that my mother and father could be proud of me. I know they want me to keep trying." She doesn't seem sad, merely resigned. She accepts the fact that school has been and will continue, most likely, to be difficult for her. It is frustrating that a person with such a willing attitude must live with such a sense of mediocrity.

Leticia's father was born in Mexico, and her mother was born in Arizona. Both completed the tenth grade. Leticia's father works as a welder, and her mother works in ceramic design, and together they bring in about twenty-eight thousand dollars a year. Leticia, her parents, and her three sisters live in a three-bedroom home. She also works as a baby-sitter to help supplement the family income. "We're definitely middle class. We don't have a lot of money but our life is pretty good."

Speaking both languages, she has been acculturated to this country yet continues to follow Mexican cultural traditions. For example, she celebrates both Mexican and American holidays, has no preference in regards to either Mexican or American music, and equally attends Spanish- and English-language movies. Leticia says, "Most things we do—the holidays, parties, music, are all Mexican things—but I'm Hispanic."

At the present time, religion is the dominant influence in her life and the prime catalyst in the reshaping of her family's life. As a family, they go to church at least four times a week. They used to be Catholic, but that ended when Leticia's father argued heatedly with a priest during mass. She recalls, "I died a thousand deaths. How many people can say they've had this happen—a fight in church—anyway, the priest was hateful and cut down people. We all walked out and that was it." The family has since embraced a fundamentalist, Pentecostal Christian sect whose members are mostly Mexicans. Yet Leticia also has a good friend who is an Anglo. The friendship has survived despite the fact her friend was reared to be atheist. Atheist or not, Leticia was able to convince her friend to join the Pentecostals.

Leticia says that because of her new religion, the family does not celebrate Christmas by throwing parties. "I've got Catholic relatives nearby who throw some good stuff, still. There are no political discussions." In this "new," converted family, political issues are of equal importance as discussions on the different genetic strains of grass.

Leticia has a GPA of only 2.0, but she does say she likes school. She is currently in a "special education" program, a course of study designed to offer assistance to students with learning disabilities. (Neither Leticia nor her parents are able to identify the specific disability she has.) She initially wanted to attend college to become a physical therapist, but she believes she will eventually become a teacher instead. Leticia's parents have been good boosters—verbally supportive—but have not been demonstrative in actually helping in her efforts to do well. On top of school and work, Leticia also plays for the school volleyball team and is a secretary at her church. Although her learning disability presents a daunting challenge, Leticia continually rallies herself to go "once more into the breach."

ANGLO-ORIENTED LIFESTYLES:
RYAN, CHRISTINE, CYNTHIA, AND CAROLINE

Not only are these students Anglo-oriented, some of them are actually part European. Ryan, Caroline, and Cynthia, for example, have mothers who are Anglos. This has no doubt contributed to their assimilation.

None of the four can speak Spanish fluently. Some of them observe Mexican customs, others do not. Yet, most of them express a comfortable satisfaction with their self-selected ethnic identity label and if anything, are not overly concerned about their ethnicity.

Ryan and Cynthia are doing well in school, while Christine and Caroline are faring average.

ACCULTURATION SPECTRUM PLACEMENT OF SELECTED INFORMANTS, 1974 AND 1988

◄──────── Mexican-Oriented   Intermediate   Anglo-Oriented ────────►

	Mexican-Oriented	Intermediate	Anglo-Oriented
1974 **Urban**	Hortensia Matilda	Cecilia Eduardo	Vicente Alberto
1988	Jacinto Lidia Norma Hector	Jorge Diana Daniel Georgina	Martha Marcia Jose Pascual

-2 • • • • -1 • • • • 0 • • • • +1 • • • • +2

	Mexican-Oriented	Intermediate	Anglo-Oriented
1974 **Suburban**	Carlos Sara	Veronica Juan	Jeffrey Valerie
1988	Fernando Henry Teresa Efrain	Gloria Ryan Leticia Randy Armando	Cynthia Caroline Christine

Ryan: "Irish" I Were Mexican: A Mother Directs a Good Son

It is four o'clock in the afternoon. The high school is almost empty, save for the football team, the teachers, and those, such as Ryan, who are in student government. As he hand-stencils a message onto a poster, he explains, "We're always trying to publicize something. This time, it's homecoming. One of my goals is to get all the students interested. You know, people act like they don't care about school. The thing is, they would never make a poster or do what we do. But they want us to keep doing it!"

Ryan's father is Mexican and was born in Texas; his mother is Irish-American and was born in Detroit, Michigan. Both of his parents graduated from high school. His father is bilingual, but his mother speaks only English. When he was four years old, his parents divorced, but the father used his visitation rights and saw his son often. Ryan currently lives with his mother and stepfather, who is Anglo and was born in Colorado. Thus Ryan is in effect a 0.5 (one-half) generation reared by Anglos.

Ryan's mother is a bus driver and his stepfather works in a warehouse. Their annual household income totals about forty thousand dollars a year. Based on the amount of this steady sum, Ryan describes his family as working class. He lives comfortably in a three-bedroom house along with his parents, his older sister who is a senior at the same high school, and his younger stepbrother.

Ryan is comfortable with his ethnicity, and identifies himself as Irish-Mexican. He is Anglicized and monolingual, but does not feel any embarrassment for not being able to speak Spanish. "I don't need Spanish," he shrugs matter-of-factly. There is no extended family network on either of his parents' sides, but his mother knows a little about both Mexican culture and food through her experiences with the Catholic church, and also what she was able to pick up from Ryan's dad when she married him.

Ryan is a Christian, and religion has always been a part of his life. In junior high school, Ryan had a friend who was a devout Christian. It was through him and his family that Ryan chose a Christian life. "Before I was a Christian, I was sorta' wild. I wasn't the school bully or anything. I was just hanging around the wrong people and disrespectful of my mom. Now, my relationship with Christ has shown me what's important." Ryan is part of Young Life, a Christian support group for youths like himself. As a musician of some note (he says), he has played his guitar for the group going on three years now. He also attends Young Life summer camp, where he enjoys the hair-raising excitement of whitewater rafting.

Ryan is an above-average student, who last semester obtained a 3.2 GPA in college prep classes. He is active in student affairs and involved in various sports, and he is planning to go to college and become either a teacher or a physical therapist. Ryan considers himself one of the "Socies" (he is socially active and a student leader). "It's embarrassing to admit I'm in a group, but most people fit into one group at school. Even though I'm really involved in student government, I try not to limit who I can be friends with. I think it's bad to just stick to your group." His mother has been a strong force in his life, making sure he behaves well and encouraging him to always try hard in school. A practitioner of "measured pressure," the mother once pushed him hard, and later relaxed completely. Now, she moves in and out of Ryan's affairs as needed—usually with advice or admonition. As a result, Ryan has learned to show responsibility and has become a self-motivator who needs little external discipline.

Ryan was not always a good student. He places great emphasis on the fact that his religious faith was the initial catalyst that sparked his improvement in this area. In elementary school, he barely got by on passing grades and did not really care too much about school. "I call it my sleepwalking days." Now, he feels good about coming to school, and he has kept his eyes resolutely focused on his goal. His mother, too, says, "You're going to college."

Christine: A Working-Class Dilemma: "If You Want to Spend the Rest of Your Life in It (School), Go Ahead."

Tomorrow is the day many students will take the Standard Achievement Test (SAT) in preparation for college entrance. For Christine, this is just another Friday night. She's not taking the test. When questioned, she shrugs. When pressed for an answer, she explains, "I already take a ton of tests. Then they want you to go on a Saturday for more." She sees the test as an affliction "they" (school authorities) want to visit on her. Nowhere in her words can be found an inkling of understanding that the test may actually benefit her.

Christine's family, whether through attrition or design, has left behind much of the Mexican culture their ancestors embraced. They claim Anglo culture as their own. Having pruned the old away, they graft on the new. Yet it is apparent they have left behind the strength of the old ways to gain only a nominal identity in Anglo culture. This nominal identity may well explain the sense of hopelessness and resignation that Christine's case study reveals.

Both parents were born in the United States; her father in Oklahoma, her mother in Paramount, California. They live with their six children, ages four through twenty-one years, in a three-bedroom home. Christine calls her neighborhood "nice." Actually, the area of tract homes is one of the most rundown in the city. Christine claims her home is middle class "because we have a lot of cars in our driveway." Five cars are parked there, at last count. None of them are recent models.

Christine's father was disabled by an accident on the job, and receives Social Security and disability. Her mother, a beautician, contributes to the combined annual family income of twenty-three thousand dollars. This is barely sufficient to maintain a struggling working-class life. Two of her older brothers have managed to finish high school and obtain working-class occupations. They work in the auto parts and auto paint industries, respectively.

Her parents do not set a tone of ethnic traditions that even remotely resembles Mexican culture. The family speaks English at home. Christmas is a day for turkey, ham, and potatoes. It is strictly a nuclear family affair. Special occasions, such as birthdays, call for eating Mexican food. At these times, a special trip to the "Mexican" store will provide the tamales. The only positive Mexican cultural experience Christine remembers is Cinco de Mayo, in the sixth grade, when all the kids had a feast. Her family, nominal Catholics, attend church infrequently, and shun most church-sponsored activities as well. The family's Anglo cultural style is working class.

Despite their lifestyle, Christine's parents refer to themselves as Mexican Americans. Even though she is third generation and speaks little Spanish, Christine considers herself Mexican. She says, "It's the heritage and not the citizenship that counts." When asked what she means by that, she appears confused and cannot explain her comment.

Christine is an average student. She has a 2.2 GPA and less than average abilities in formal English. She has no school-related involvement in sports or clubs. Her parents seldom, if ever, encourage or entertain education aspirations in their children. She believes this is the main reason her brothers did not go on to college. She explains her father's attitude: "He had to go through it and says, 'If she wants to spend the rest of her life in it—go ahead'." Christine's mother, busy and tired from carrying the family's load, has no time to worry about supporting Christine's education and future. She needs Christine's support in providing child care while she works. Christine baby-sits every day until her mother returns from work at the beauty shop, which can be late when customers make night appointments.

Christine, not surprisingly, has a limited view of education. "I could work in business, but then I would be stuck in one place, and I really, really want to travel. Maybe the Navy would be good. Either way, I don't need to go to college." A high school diploma is more than enough for her.

Christine does harbor dreams for her future children. With her children, she says, she won't be as strict as her father was with her. Christine will influence them to get a better education. She will take the time to help them with their homework, rather than "rob" time away from them. "If they do a good job, even in elementary school, I'm going to give rewards. That way they'll want to keep up." When Christine looks ahead to the time when she will be a parent, she opens a window and perhaps reveals to the world her own longings, the unmet needs in her own life.

Cynthia: A Teen-Age Mother: Knows She's Mexican, Acts Anglo, and Does Well

When the average high school student finishes her laborious Algebra 2 assignment, it's usually time to dial that phone or get those car keys. When Cynthia finishes, it's time to crack open a jar of mashed carrots or mix up a batch of formula. Cynthia is an unmarried teenage mother. In many cases, this situation brings a halt to education or any career plans beyond the need for instant income. Looking at Cynthia's life, one would be foolish to pin that prediction on her. She certainly does not count herself out, not just yet.

Cynthia's parents are both native-born United States citizens. A Mexican American, her father was born in Arizona. He works with rod iron as a welder, making more than thirty thousand dollars per year. Her mother, born in Maine, is French American. She earns seventeen thousand dollars a year as an executive secretary. Cynthia lives with her parents, her baby, two brothers ages sixteen and twelve, and her grandmother in a three-bedroom house. There are potted flowers next to the walkway, and, "My mom and I keep the house clean, and my dad does the yard every week." Their neighborhood is located in one of the better-kept tract home areas, away from major thoroughfares, noise from small industrial plants and congestion.

The father of her baby assumes some of the financial responsibility for their child. His future relationship with Cynthia is uncertain, yet he does pay child support regularly. He works in the sales department of a local do-it-yourself builders' supply store. He attended college for two years. The birth of the baby has affected his educational timetable, slowing it down considerably, but he is saving his money to major in sociology or psychology and plans to resume his education.

Cynthia is Anglicized, and, as a fourth-generation American, does not speak much Spanish. Her mother can speak a little Spanish, and her father is bilingual. However, he never spoke Spanish to his children. Only when his friends came over to the house did he speak Spanish. As he was not brought up in the traditional Mexican culture, he allows Cynthia to pick and choose what she wants. She and her family refrain from participating in most Mexican traditions. For instance, at Christmas, ham and turkey have replaced tamales and sweet bread (although the father laments, "No tamales at Christmas!"). Nevertheless, Cynthia describes herself as Mexican American.

Although they don't force her, her parents do encourage her to learn Spanish. She has taken a couple of classes at school. Her mother instructs her to be "creative" in her cultural attitude and exemplifies this by cooking Mexican, French, and American food. The family has an eclectic taste in music and other customs. The entire family attends Catholic church every Sunday. Their habits could be likened to a smorgasbord—a little of this and a little of that, openly tolerant of other cultural styles and influences, but decidedly Anglo.

When Cynthia was in elementary and junior high school, she lacked motivation. Her grades and reviews were fair to poor. However, upon attending high school, her reading teacher played a large role in turning Cynthia on to school and higher aspirations. Cynthia is certain that encouragement coming from a female made the difference in her development and life. "This teacher took a special interest in developing my self-image and it sparked something within me. It was not a cultural thing."

Cynthia is an above-average student with a 3.0 GPA. She has always been self-assured and goal oriented. Her motivation to succeed has been enhanced since she became a mother. After high school graduation, she plans on attending night school at Cerritos College in order to become an executive secretary. Cynthia believes college is as important as high school, even though she has chosen a two-year vocational program versus a four-year degree. Her parents are supportive and regularly remind her of homework or offer help. They encourage learning during leisure hours. For example, they make sure the family is aware of upcoming educational programs on television. This is just one way a parent can casually push learning.

Discussing the future of her baby, Cynthia says, "I'm going to help her in school by being there to answer questions about homework. I'll make sure she has the books, like an encyclopedia and everything. Probably a computer, too. I'm going to be there for her, but not pushing her." Like Cynthia's parents before her, she wants to give her child options.

Caroline: A Blond Chic-Angla: Comfortable and Waiting for "Something to Happen to Me."

Sitting with her legs crossed, leaning forward, hands gesturing, Caroline is focusing all her attention on the conversation she is having. Though her face is that of a teenager, she has the commanding attentiveness of a mature woman. She seems oblivious to the parade of students marching by her. "What I'm about is, whatever you want to be, it's okay, as long as it's truth, as long as it's you. To me, living like that is real success."

Caroline's father says he is Spanish and was born in Long Beach, California, but he is not conversant with the language at all. Her mother's ethnicity is Czechoslovakian, and she too was born in Long Beach. Both of her parents work hard: Her father has his own business as an auto mechanic, and her mother works as a bookkeeper. Together, their productivity brings in approximately fifty-thousand dollars a year. Her small family, according to Caroline, is upper middle class, mainly because her family has a "little more than anyone else." Carolyn declares ebulliently, "We have horses!"

She is comfortable with the fact that she is the only child. This means she does not have to compete with other siblings for finite family resources. She tosses her blonde hair back and counts off on her fingers, "First, I have my own room. That's a big one. Second, I can't fight with a little brother who doesn't exist. Third, I'm not the lonely type. I've got my friends." Caroline lives in a mostly Anglo neighborhood that is relatively free of crime.

Caroline seems confused about her ethnicity. At first, she describes herself as a Mexican American. When later asked why she identified herself as such, she responds: "Because a lot of people say Spaniards came to Mexico, so they're the same thing as Mexican." Afterwards, Caroline hastily corrects herself and says she is Spanish American. She explains, "I don't know what I was thinking. I just put Mexican American just to put something." When people ask her why she is so white with a name like Garcia, she responds she is Spanish American.

Caroline has also experienced reverse discrimination from her Mexican classmates, who tell her she is a "rat" for denying her heritage. Indeed, she is Anglicized and does not speak any Spanish. Caroline also has many Anglo manners and customs and bleaches her hair with peroxide. She says she does this as a fashion statement, and not because she wants to look white. She has both Mexican and Anglo friends and asserts that race is not important to her in choosing friends.

Caroline is an independent thinker, and she tends to avoid groups that require conformity. "I hate it when people want to look alike, talk alike, eat alike. I avoid all those cliques—forget it." Although a Catholic, she does not attend church regularly, and firmly believes that "it's what's inside you and not just what your parents want you to do that really counts." So she does what she wants and is proud of it.

Caroline has a 2.5 GPA and is taking some college prep courses, but she has often struggled. Her parents have a positive attitude and want Caroline to go to college—they have even offered to assume the full burden of her expenses. She is reluctant about the idea of college right now, but considers it a possibility in the future. Meanwhile, she is taking courses in a nurse's assistant program, where she is, surprisingly, churning out A's. She declares, "I can learn if I really like the subject." Next year, Caroline will begin to take cosmetology classes as a safety net, just in case she can't find a job in nursing. But her ultimate goal is to secure a job of any type. "I'm not picky, as long as I get paid okay." She also talks somewhat wistfully about working with animals, as a veterinarian or as an animal trainer. Undecided about college at the moment, she hopes that "something will happen to me to help me decide."

SUMMARY

It is fairly clear that various types and degrees of strains separate the high and the low achievers, taking into account, of course, the school practice that excluded students involved in gangs. Had these students been included, they probably would have been the true low achievers, as they were in the first survey in 1974.

In any event, the contrast between high and low is steeped in the social milieu of this rapidly changing suburban area. For example, one stark difference in the neighborhood today is the growth of rundown pockets of older tract home sections. These new "suburban barrios" contain all the problems that afflict modern urban society: gangs, crime, and drugs. Indeed, during this period of time neighborhood watch groups and citizen meetings and protest marches have spawned and begun to mark the monthly affairs of the community. In contrast to the urban setting, however, the gap between the middle class and the poor is much wider here.

Yet, as a group, the suburban students are relatively well off economically, especially when compared to their urban counterparts. As I have suggested, relative affluence can also work against educational performance. Several students believe they have already accomplished their goals. In their minds, they have already achieved the American Dream. Thus, although they are not particularly poor students, they seem to lack drive, ambition, and higher aspirations.

Unfortunately, family dynamics and inconsistent parental support is also a recurrent theme in the thumbnographies. Despite the socioeconomic status of the general neighborhood, some of the families are struggling and in at least a couple of instances lack of a father and strong male role model has made a difference.

Last minute changes for the student newspaper.

Several of the students also have parents that simply have no strategy, interest, or aspirations to help their children attain educational success. Their strategy is almost nonexistent and reflects their preoccupation with work and other concerns, thus depriving the children of their time and attention.

This is unfortunate; we have already noted the powerful influence role models can have on educational performance. Several students, despite many obstacles, are successful in school, a success they themselves attribute to the efforts of a teacher or their parents.

Taking a look backward at the homies.

Sweet sixteen bonding.

7 / "Snapshot" and "Cinematic" Views of the Issue

Each of the thumbnographies, as a snapshot of a person in one time and place, provides valuable detailed information on educational performance within the context of many other factors. With the collection of portraits, or snapshots, across an expanse of cultural styles and ethnic identities in that same time period, the thumbnographies also give us an indication of how adolescents are engaged by varied influences and confront different obstacles in acquiring an education.

When we add the dimension of time to the equation—moving through time—even more subtleties of the ethnic and cultural identification processes become apparent (Bernal and Knight 1993, Romanucci-Ross and De Vos 1995). To provide a more dynamic insight into educational performance, we need a collection of views, a cinematic approach that encompasses the big picture to study and contemplate ethnic identity and other cultural change issues over a period of time. With such an approach, we can more fully and broadly contextualize the educational performance of Chicano youth. In this chapter, we will use a cinematic perspective to look at some of the larger issues that surfaced in the ethnographic portraits of the two time periods.

Some of the most important changes that occurred between the two time periods are the demographic transformations that created a more critical mass of Mexicans, which in turn, has resulted in a twofold political adjustment. Mexicans are showing increasing political clout and demands for services under an umbrella of cultural awareness and sensitivity. This mounting pressure and assertiveness has, in turn, created a backlash among entrenched Anglo-Americans used to the privileges of the past (Estrada 1995). As a result, the English-Only movement, anti-immigration sentiments and legislation, and a general mood of antipathy toward Latinos has reached a new height since the 1970s (Gingrich 1995). As noted earlier, the 1970s were a decidedly confrontational time when bilingual programs were first being launched. Some programs often went by the "seat of their pants," but still they indicated that the cultural "Maginot line" had been penetrated. Teachers and school districts began to respond in more sensitive and innovative ways to the learning needs of the population, howsoever grudgingly. Indeed, the advice and suggestions of an activist of that time period, Marcos De Leon, began to be heeded as he outlined them in an influential article, "The Hamburger and the Taco: A Cultural Reality" (De Leon 1970).

In the midst of these shifts, school policies (as well as the changing nature of ethnic identity and cultural styles among the high schoolers) have unfolded in an interesting fashion. Indeed, the passage of time has created quite a different context for acculturation and achievement (Lambert 1990).

IMMIGRATION AND MEXICANIZATION

Clearly, immigration trends and ethnic nationalism have affected the acculturation patterns during the past twenty years. In the early 1970s, both the urban and suburban youths we examined were more likely to express doubt and ambivalence about their ethnic heritage. Most of the youths could not speak Spanish, and few celebrated the traditional ethnic rituals and customs. Witness the cultural intermediates in both settings who joined gangs, and the Anglicized ones who appeared culturally "stretched out" in the 1970s. Cultural and ethnic identification dynamics have been reforged through the heavy immigration from across the Mexican border.

East Los Angeles has always been primarily Mexican, with a distribution of generations from first to third or fourth. Even in 1974 it was already becoming saturated as a port of entry for new immigrants. By the 1980s, the neighborhood and the high school of the study had received a new wave of immigrants. This has stunningly augmented the Mexicanization of the Los Angeles area; and, indeed, "Latinization," as large numbers of Central Americans are a part of it, too. Thus, the students at the high school now were more typically from the 1.5 generation, and the high school had gradually become a magnet school for gifted students within the greater East L.A. area.

The new wave of immigration and Mexicanization of Los Angeles has also spread beyond the borders of East L.A.'s barrios. Ports of entry and dense concentrations of immigrants are now found in south central Los Angeles (traditionally an African American enclave; Boyer 1995), just west of downtown Los Angeles (the Pico Union area), and even in some suburban enclaves.

By the 1980s and on to the 1990s, these demographic shifts and cultural realities had already made strong impressions on the youth culture. Even those students who were Anglo-oriented and could not speak Spanish claimed at least a symbolic emotional attachment to their heritage. Ryan, the "Irish I were Mexican" case, is one of the more glaring examples in suburbia, although his upbringing and lifestyle showed little connection to his Mexican heritage.

Another example, as noted in Chapter 1, occurred when my wife and I rode a school bus with the urban high schoolers to view a movie debut about Mexican Americans. We were amazed at the number of students who conversed easily and comfortably in Spanish. Even minor events in the film that showed the Mexican and Spanish-speaking students in a positive light, for example, the imagery of struggling against all odds and through perseverance conquering all, brought cheers and responses with a pride and certainty we had seldom before witnessed.

Several years later, two of the students who attended this event were college students of mine and shared with me how the high school and classroom climate had bred and encouraged a comfortable sense of ethnic identity. During classroom activities, for instance, teachers would readily keep the learning pace going by allowing students to respond to the lessons bilingually. Similarly, interactions among students in the classrooms, as in the bus experience above, were in both the English and Spanish languages. Without fear of retribution or self-doubt, students cheerfully mastered learning assignments through whatever cultural avenue would expedite the recognition and retention of the material.

Immigrant values to maintain a strong family.

Thus, in the past twenty years, a sense of ethnic pride has blossomed to encourage Chicano youth to reclaim their heritage, if only symbolically. The foods they eat at Christmas (*posadas*) and their celebration of ethnic traditions (for example, *quinceañera*) are tangible examples of this connection. The recent reemergence of Chicano and Chicana activism on high school and college campuses throughout the area, in part, attests to this awareness (del Olmo 1995). As noted, some of this was simply a symbolic reaffirmation of ethnic roots, a type of ethnic reclamation. Nevertheless, it is a reflection of the mass physical and symbolic Mexicanization that has engulfed the suburban environment, both in the critical presence of people of Mexican and Latino origin as well as a heightened awareness in thinking and acting "ethnic" (see Keefe and Padilla, 1987). A look at the placement of the selected students in the acculturation spectrum (see Figure 1-1, page 12) illustrates the narrowing of the spectrum and the crowding of students in the middle of it after two decades of change. A bilingual-bicultural experience and orientation seem to mark the 1990s and, perhaps, the future (Hurtado and Gurin 1995).

The mass Mexicanization of both the urban and suburban locales has also lessened the cultural differences between the students, at least in terms of ethnic identity symbols. They know they are Mexican, and are not ashamed of publicly labeling themselves as Mexican or Chicano. This was even true of some of the students of ethnically mixed backgrounds, and of the third- and fourth-generation students. Unable to speak Spanish, they still sought to affirm their identity by following traditions and customs such as eating Mexican foods, maintaining an interest in their native history, and by associating with other Mexicans. They also welcomed support from ethnic role models and their extended family; several of the Anglicized suburban students in the 1980s sample expressed renewed appreciation for this tradition. In some cases, other factors, such as the church (especially the Catholic church, but also the growing Spanish-language pentecostal Protestant churches that reinforce bilingual maintenance), helped students maintain ties to their ethnicity, as many traditions were centered in the church. Overall, this phenomenon reflects the readier acceptance of Mexican culture in the greater Los Angeles cultural region.

However, mass Mexicanization has not had a uniform effect on all the students, nor has it eliminated discrimination, as several students are still upset by past incidents. Fernando, the 1988 suburban Mexican-oriented student, remains disturbed by the discriminatory treatment he received from his math teachers and soccer coach. Jorge, the 1988 urban Chicano-oriented student, also remembers what he felt was shabby treatment from his grade school ESL teachers and his high school counselors. Jorge feels this treatment has brought him dishonor and tarnished his identity, so that he considers "being Mexican a disability."

INSTITUTIONAL AND OTHER CHANGES: MACRO, MESO, AND MICRO

The mass Mexicanization phenomenon has a leading role in our "movie," but our story contains many other important subplots and characters. For example, there are the *macroinstitutional* changes (for example, in government) that have unfolded in the past twenty years. These broader national and statewide changes set the stage for our longitudinal assessments and shed light on *mesoinstitutional* (school district and community institutions) and *microinstitutional* (classroom and teachers) transformations.

Macro: Governmental and Political Forces

On the macro level, national shifts and trends have affected Chicano youths in school. When I began this study in 1974, government funding for low-income and ethnic minority communities had already dropped significantly from the levels of the Great Society era during the late 1960s (Katz 1986; Quadagno 1994). Special education and learning innovations were particularly hard hit, even though Title I funds maintained some programs. Bilingual education expanded, principally because of lobbying efforts initiated by a coalition of ethnic organizations who championed second-language maintenance and acquisition. Prominent among these was the National Association of Bilingual Education (NABE), with help from a sister unit, the California Association of Bilingual Education (CABE). Various other groups, who did not always cooperate on other issues, coordinated their efforts for bilingual education. Perhaps because of this organizational thrust, the backlash against a bilingual and multicultural education philosophy surfaced and gradually mushroomed. Critics lamented that schools, in their effort to tolerate and encourage linguistic and cultural differences, would, instead, instill confusion and ambivalence in ethnic identity. An ethnic identification process of this type, critics railed, would undermine a person's loyalty and allegiance to the United States. This national debate and struggle also found its way to the community and board of education levels, sometimes making in-novation and experimentation in bilingual curriculum and practices difficult, if not impossible, to initiate and conduct. Lost in the invective and controversy that con-tinue today was the fact that these programs were initially aimed to pragmatically soften cultural shock for newcomers. It is also puzzling, even embarrassing, that so many who value education would nevertheless argue for monolingualism in the global community we live in.

During the Reagan era of the 1980s, a concerted, tight-fisted approach placed a cap on experimental pilot programs and militantly accelerated a "return-to-the-ba-sics" education trend then already underway. In large part, the lack of government support to root out and resolve historically based educational problems forced school districts to provide a bare-bones learning environment—only the present and not the past was to be a part of the equation to address ethnic minority schooling. Worthwhile programs such as Head Start caught the wrath of this counterreaction, as cutbacks kept the program from expanding. This, coupled with the taxpayer re-volt symbolized by the earlier passage of Proposition 13 in 1978 in California, con-tributed to schools catering primarily to students who could be "accountable." As we will discuss, these macro-level forces took their toll in many different ways.

Meso: School District and Community

On the mesoinstitutional level, school practices and community institutions were also dramatically transformed. For example, school practices toward students at risk, for example, potential gang members, were being revamped, as insufficient re-sources placed limits on which students to serve and what learning programs to em-phasize. It is interesting to note that on the whole, students in this study's 1988 sample were not involved with gangs. There was certainly more gang activity in these communities in 1988 than in 1974: Official statistics compiled by the L.A. County Sheriff's Department special gang unit, Operation Safe Streets (OSS), show a marked increase in the number of identified gang members in the area where the urban high school is located, from 3,800 in 1980, when such information began to be recorded, to 10,500 in 1995, even though the population of the area remained about the same. Similar increases in gang-related incidents and homicides hold for the same time period, although gradual decreases in some categories have been noted in 1995. Nevertheless, gang members were absent from the 1988 sample.

The absence of gang members on campus is most likely a result of the high school's practice (an unwritten policy) of discouraging known gang members from attending school. (Detection and identification of those to be turned away some-times simply followed a rule police often employ: if he looks like a duck, walks like a duck, and talks likes a duck, he must be a duck. The public has generally sup-ported this approach by refusing to tolerate gang dress, graffiti, and other gang signs in their neighborhoods.)

By the time of the 1988 survey, the gang members had been effectively "rooted out" of the schools and onto the streets. The socialization process of home, school, and street (thus, law enforcement) for social control was short circuited in the 1980s

Life in the Projects, East of the Los Angeles river.

when youths at risk went from their homes to the streets without spending much time in school. Thus, the problem that began in the streets was returned to the streets. School officials and teachers had by now admitted defeat (Stromquist and Vigil 1996). This was in direct contrast with what had been the school policy and practice during the first study in the 1970s.

With a downturn in school funding (California dropped to forty-second place nationwide in money expended per student by the 1990s), and an escalation in street-gang activities, much more money and resources were budgeted and allocated to law enforcement and the criminal justice system. When ties with parents were loosened, children were subjected to other influences and were at risk to become gang members. Lacking a nurturing home environment, they also had difficulties bonding with their teachers and classmates in school. That left the police as the last bastion of social control. Police are the protectors of society's normative standards and behaviors, and thus are what I refer to as the street social-control specialists.

Ironically, just when more programs to assist troubled youths were needed, and the expansion of programs such as Head Start were making a difference, the government veered off in other directions as it changed its policies about how to address the poor and ethnic minority populations. Instead of ensuring continuity by following Head Start with Getsmart in elementary school and Staysmart in junior high school, we turned our backs on these marginal children and students (Vigil 1993a). What we did not spend on education was allocated to police and a complex social-control apparatus. Specialized law enforcement and criminal justice units and procedures were launched to combat what we had let out into the streets: gang members.

In Los Angeles since the 1970s, we now have OSS (Operation Safe Streets) organized by the L.A. County Sheriff's Department and CRASH (Community Resources Against Street Hoodlums) initiated by the L.A. Police Department. The build–up of similar antigang units throughout California, and the nation for that matter, went hand in hand with cutbacks in programs for minority youth and the gutting of school programs and activities, including even extracurricular activities such as football and band (see Plaschke 1995, for how these programs do so much good, but sparse resources limit their drawing power). Meanwhile, California's jail population has doubled since 1980, and the state pays forty thousand dollars per year to house an inmate. The national annual budget for the criminal justice system is now $650 billion and growing.

In reaction to the rise and proliferation of street-gang influences, and as another means of social control, religious leaders and organizations have also entered the fray. Victory Outreach, based on a fundamentalist type of Protestantism centered in the Assembly of God congregation, has had a modicum of success in attacking the problem at the spiritual and emotional level. Victory Outreach is a grassroots–based effort to turn street gang members and drug addicts around with a "born again" revitalization experience (Vigil 1983). Many of the new street converts have in turn participated in recasting the net to gather and convert more members. This movement has spread to many other barrios as well as other places in the Southwest. The void left by inattentive parents, underfunded schools, and overburdened police demonstrate the importance of these grassroots organizations.

Micro: Classrooms and Teachers

On the microinstitutional level, significant changes have occurred in the classroom and with teachers. During the 1970s study, teachers' racist comments and negative attitudes were more prevalent, and their expectations for student academic achievement also seemed low. For example, one regular teacher, thinking I was a substitute for the day, offhandedly advised me to show a film and not worry about the absent teacher's lesson plan. The Chicano principal at his school (the urban high school in this study) had been appointed as the result of the demands of Chicano movement activists, and many teachers, mostly "McWasp" (middle class, white, Anglo-Saxon, Protestant), resented this outside intrusion. Consequently, a great deal of hostility and animosity contributed to a climate of friction and negativity in the teacher–principal relationship and in the school generally.

Gang graffiti could also be viewed all over the urban school, even on the walls inside the buildings. Twelve known gangs had staked out their schoolyard "turf," and gang fights were routine affairs. Two youths were killed during this year, one of whom died on campus after a knifing incident (Vigil 1976: 28). The suburban school was much more quiet and subdued. As noted, gang activity existed on the streets, but the school of mostly Anglo students appeared to symbolize what one would expect from a "bedroom" community.

Although there had always been a cadre of teachers in the urban school, including several Anglos, who had shown great interest and care in the predominantly Mexican-American student body, a critical mass was needed to turn the school around. After a heated political struggle that included teachers and many community and school officials, the school district replaced the Chicano principal of the urban high school in the mid-1970s and embarked on a path of least resistance. A series of administrators, at the behest of Los Angeles school district officials, began to reintroduce a more traditional educational curriculum, avoiding some of the more culturally experimental or "relevant," as movement activists would say, learning programs. Meanwhile, with the recruitment and hiring of teachers better informed and trained in current issues and the problems of contemporary ethnic minority students, new teachers, many of them Chicanas and Chicanos, joined the faculty. Together with the more established Latino teachers, they collectively make a difference despite the opposition of some top administrators. Interestingly, the increase in Chicano teachers included many former students of the school; the number of past students returning as teachers has reached forty in 1995 (Helfand 1995; see The Tomas Rivera Center 1993, a report noting the crisis in the shortage of Latino school teachers).

The most important part of this reversal is that the student population also changed (especially as a result of the school practice of zero tolerance for the marginal and gang youth). More specifically, however, the demographic shifts and Mexicanization currents noted above accounted for a student body that reflected an achievement orientation that many experts had noted several decades before, except by this time educational programs had changed to take advantage of this attitude, building on it to facilitate learning and higher aspirations.

Immigrants and their children have always come to the United States to participate and partake in the American Dream, but previous barriers and difficulties had weakened this orientation (Myers 1995). Central to this goal is the attainment of an education in order to improve opportunities and prospects. Students of the first and the 1.5 generations in our study were in general much more optimistic and overachieving than the third- and fourth-generation Chicanos who had comprised the student body in the 1970s.

Significantly, this transformation was not heralded or accorded its proper acknowledgment until a commercial film based on a math teacher's accomplishments with these students was released in 1988. The message of the film was that these students were motivated to achieve because one teacher told them to have *ganas* (desire) and they would prevail. No one questions the significant role and contributions this teacher played in helping turn the school around (Lavin 1995), especially by making other teachers realize that these students could study hard, learn, and be competitive. However, this explanation for some impressive student achievements at the urban school ignores other factors by placing responsibility on and giving credit to one individual for the rather radical and rapid improvements. In the best tradition of Hollywood, it is at worst a fabrication and at best an attempt to sell copy, a type of "John Wayne Thesis of Educational Change."

As it is with so much that changes, it was a combination of forces—students, teachers, and other individuals, as well as demographics—that helped make the urban school attractive as a magnet school. For example, administrative changes were made, well-trained teachers were recruited, and the math program developed a city-wide reputation. Moreover, most of these students had already benefited from elementary school bilingual and ESL programs that helped prepare them (Delgado-Gaitan 1994). Thus, without downplaying the role of any one individual in bringing about change, a more equitable assessment suggests spreading the credit around, for the conditions for change (including other persons, who are often unheralded) have to exist before the catalyst of a "person" can actuate it (see White 1949 for an excellent explanation for how inventions and innovations often result through a combination of forces or collection of individuals, not just one factor or person).

Suburban changes in these years also were considerable, principally in that the majority of the neighborhood and student body populations were now composed of Mexicans and other Latinos. School district officials successfully struggled to cope with this radical demographic transformation. Under these new circumstances, curriculum, teacher recruitment and training, learning programs, and established programs such as Expanded Horizons needed to be rethought and reorganized. However, even with this relatively smooth transition, many local citizens and several school board members resented the changed conditions. Mexicans in earlier decades were a minority that received special attention; thus, as noted, Expanded Horizons was launched in the mid-1960s and was considered innovative but somewhat safe. In the late 1970s and 1980s, when the district, school, teachers, and officials began to become increasingly Mexican, some people began to consider programs such as Expanded Horizons a threat. Fortunately, cooler, more rational thinking prevailed, as the school district leaders made adequate adjustments. Nonetheless, these questions remained: Who would control such programming? Where would the power lie?

The principal of the suburban high school in 1988 had worked her way up from the classroom and remembered when the school and the school district were primarily Anglo. In her attempts to adjust to the tide of Mexicanization, she fumbled away opportunities to bring the community closer to the school and learning. Also, adopting a practice similar to the urban school, the suburban principal refused to tolerate any dress and other signs and symbols that suggested gang membership. Certain cholo-style clothing and other aspects of appearance would spark her disapproval, and the student would be removed from school. She even censured the faculty adviser to the school newspaper for allowing a feature article on gangs. Nevertheless, with the persistence and help of certain district officials and a group of committed and dedicated teachers and parents, most of the students were still able to gain a good education and develop a pride in their Mexican heritage. Expanded Horizons had become institutionalized districtwide as New Horizons, and now included many working-class whites in the network and activities. As previously mentioned, other learning plans such as AVID, aimed at underachieving bright students, were also introduced (Mehan et al. 1994).

SUMMARY

Of the many changes that mark this study and capture the characteristics of the students, the effect of immigration is one that deserves much of our attention. The influx of newcomers has strengthened existing programs such as bilingual education, and the immigrants have been the major beneficiaries of this cultural attention. Their presence has also added tremendous weight and impetus to the goals and objectives initially outlined by Chicano activists in the 1960s. What began as nativist acculturation (for example, learning the English language while retaining the Spanish one) has evolved into a trend of Mexicanization. This broader and deeper process has affected Mexican people of all generations, even if the signs for some are only symbolic. A sound, solid ethnic (and personal) identity in this context enables the students to feel good about themselves, as they strive to succeed and achieve.

Of the many factors that shape a successful school record for students, it is clear that family support stands out over the others, but never by itself, as we will see in the next chapter. A stable ethnic identity results from a well-developed acculturation strategy, but the family and family members must play a role here, too. Where family support is absent, the student usually shows lackluster effort to excel academically. However, conditions of acculturation, ethnic identity, strong family support, and all the rest, will carry a person only so far. As we have seen, institutional and personnel changes from the different levels (macro to meso to micro) must also be a part of the equation. To return to the analogy at the beginning of this chapter, snapshots serve fine for the details of the moment, but a movie strings these portraits together to help us understand why change happens and in what directions change is taking us.

8 / *Personas Mexicanas:*
Multiple and Shifting Identities

Evidence is still being gathered to more accurately gauge the dynamics behind Mexican-American academic achievement. Many writers have looked at Mexican-American cultural styles and academic achievement since the 1960s. These investigations have broadened and deepened our understanding, despite the fact that some of these studies have been confined to more rural and small-town populations and constricted cultural styles. Many of these works also were developed with evidence and insights from one point in time. As we have seen, culture change and ethnic identity must be examined over a period of time in different places (Delgado-Gaitan 1993a).

The brief review in Chapter 7 of social and cultural transformations in recent decades shows that new habits have been introduced and old conditions revamped. These changes include graffiti "tagging," persistent dropout rates, and deepening of poverty and worsening of problems such as crime, drugs, and gangs. Increased immigration into the Los Angeles area has also altered, and undoubtedly frustrated, Americanization processes and efforts. Recent research nevertheless shows that Mexicans are rapidly becoming acculturated despite the obstacles (Myers 1995). Concurrently, cultural reforms, such as bilingual education, have gained a partial foothold in some educational circles, even as resistance against these changes mount.

This investigation was conducted in a heavily populated urban area, rich in history and intracultural variances, with continuous immigration constantly remaking the human landscape. It is an area that in general reflects and represents the Mexican people's experiences as city dwellers. The suburban locale initially served as a place of contrast and comparison to the East Los Angeles environs. But even here, what once was a suburban bedroom community has become a working-class enclave. Bedroom communities are moving farther from the central cities, and the diffusion of urban gangs and gang behavior has found its way there, too.

Charting changes in these two neighborhoods and schools also served to monitor the developments that have occurred during the past two decades. We can say with certainty that changes in the schools' populations and policies can make a difference. It is also clear that educational performance and achievement spring from a mesh of social and cultural forces and influences and not from one single cultural or socioeconomic factor. Thus, to advance our understanding of Mexican Americans, we need to again heed the instructive advice of Manuel Ramirez noted in Chapter 2: we must ". . . do studies in rural and urban . . . different states of the Southwest and Midwest . . . Texas and California . . . East Los Angeles and Chicago" (1971, 407).

For example, the midwestern Mexican and Latino population has grown and evolved significantly. When I first visited Chicago as a young teenager in 1954, the southeast Chicano community was small and adjacent to the lake. At the time, the community was growing, but the increase was slow. However, by the time I revisited the city in 1988, the explosion was astounding! A ride down Eighteenth Street reminded me of East Los Angeles, circa the 1940s, as one after another *panaderia, tortilleria, cantina, marqueta* or *mercado* passed before me. The expansion and deepening of Mexican culture and peoples continues, as I also noted in a visit in late 1995 (see Horowitz 1983 for a glimpse of this relatively new barrio). Interestingly, there are so many Mexicans and other Latinos in the United States today that they finally have qualified for a generic ethnic label: Hispanic, a name largely promoted by the federal government (Vigil 1990b).

Mexicans, however, are not a generic population, and a single label cannot address the variability within the group (Suarez-Orozco and Suarez-Orozco 1995a). Thus, we need a broader framework that encompasses the differences in time, place, and people. Once we have defined and established this framework, we can then reassess the complex network of factors that affect the academic performance of Chicano students (Ready 1991).

TIME, PLACE, AND PEOPLE

The facets of time, place, and people are important features that can aid future researchers and investigations on the question of acculturation and education. The *time* period reflects the economic, social, and political habits that shape people and events, whereas *place,* such as the neighborhood or school, reflects changing realities. People change over time and in places, and new and different forces, such as immigration or economic restructuring can significantly alter an individual's feelings, thoughts, and actions. As the Spindlers have noted (Spindler and Spindler 1990), such shifts can tax and strain enduring (past), situated (present), and endangered (stress between first two) notions of self.

The two time periods of this study, 1974 and 1988, provide an in-depth elaboration of acculturation and schooling. Earlier fieldwork in the 1970s and follow-up investigations in the 1990s, along with these two points in time, enable us to chart the different levels and degrees of changes through two decades. In effect, there are two types of acculturation continuum. One is intragenerational, as was documented for each of the studies; the other is intergenerational, as the two studies show how the changing nature of acculturation and ethnic identity evolved over time. As we have noted, an accelerated increase in immigration coupled with the residential movement of earlier immigrants to suburbia combined to generate a current of Mexicanization. Associated with this change was a higher expectation to succeed among immigrants as compared to third- or fourth-generation Mexican Americans who had suspended or lowered their level of expectations (Phelan and Davidson 1993; Suarez-Orozco and Suarez-Orozco 1995a). This underscores and further documents an observation I made back in the late 1960s when I accompanied a group of teachers in visits to farm laborer camps and noted the same difference in attitude and spirit between immigrant and native residents. The immigrants were decidedly more optimistic and filled with the expectation that they would eventually find success in America. In sharp contrast, the natives had already experienced setbacks and disappointments in America and appeared to be riding out their lives.

The Mexicanization current has also fortified the groundwork initiated in the aftermath of the Chicano Movement and set the direction and tone of ethnic self-identification among Mexican students of all generations. For example, Spanish language usage and pride in Mexican and Latino cultural habits and customs have become the norm.

But while this Mexicanization process was unfolding and gaining ground, a political backlash was also forming. This process was complicated by the simultaneous arrival of large numbers of Asians and Central Americans in the same time span. Political pressures to counter the effects of massive immigration have taken especially destructive, and in many ways, ugly turns (Macias 1995b). Elected political leaders at both the federal and state levels have used these demographic and multiculturalist changes to appeal to the worse fears of the public. The passage of Proposition 187 in 1994 in California mirrors this sentiment, and aims to bar undocumented immigrants from certain health and education services; as of this moment, it remains tied up in the courts.

Demography, however, follows its own rules, and a high birthrate in the Latino population has augmented the process of Mexicanization. As an example of these changes, what once was a working-class suburban neighborhood and school peopled mostly by Anglo-Americans, has now become primarily a second- and third-generation community of Mexicans. This change suggests that we must now start talking about a "greater (South) East Los Angeles," particularly in light of the Mexicanization of the southeast sections closer to the center of Los Angeles, such as Huntington Park and South Gate (Kotkin 1995; Inside Metro 1995; Ramos 1995).

Thus, the concept of *place* has changed. Urban and suburban locales have become radically altered during this time. For instance, East Los Angeles gradually stopped being the primary port of entry for immigrants as housing units and neighborhoods filled up with newcomers, even in some instances displacing Chicano residents in older, traditional barrios. In turn, third- and fourth-generation families, some of them gang-oriented, moved to suburban residences farther out from the city to replace (or create) the voids left by whites. Suburbia became the new community for these offspring of much earlier waves of immigration. For the recent immigrants, the new port of entry became South Central Los Angeles and Pico Union (west of downtown), where older, cheaper housing and neighborhoods were closer to the many jobs that downtown garment and sweatshop industries offered.

The presence of a larger Mexican population that relies more on the Spanish language and follows Mexican customs in both communities makes for quite a different environment. It has not been just a matter of cultural regeneration and retention but also a more assertive cultural pride that commands our attention (as witnessed by the number of Mexican flags brandished during the anti-Proposition 187 rallies in the fall of 1994).

According to some older informants who attended the urban school, as far back as the late 1950s and early 1960s, the shift from an Anglicized to a Mexicanized perspective was beginning to show clues. At one time, speaking Spanish, even among themselves, was avoided, and anyone who did so was branded a T.J. (literally from Tijuana, a border town, considered a lower class of Mexican), but the gradual change of embracing one's cultural heritage and ethnic identity peaked by the time of the 1968 Walkouts (Vigil 1996). Interestingly, this intraethnic habit of 1.5-generation or second-generation youths putting down newcomers has recently reappeared in sections of Los Angeles. Newcomers there are called "wetpacks" (a new spin on wetbacks, implying they had swum across the border, because of the school backpacks the newcomers often use with Mickey Mouse or other designs on them); as in the 1970s, students strongly resent this type of internal racism (Quintanilla 1995).

Meanwhile, both the urban and suburban locales witnessed an increase in street gangs and gang members. Some of this growth was the result of families persistently mired in poverty who produced generations of gang members (Moore and Vigil 1987; Jencks and Peterson 1991). However, the bulk of the expansion stemmed from marginalization or "choloization" of an even larger number of disaffected youth, making more of them at risk to become gang members (Vigil 1988; 1990a; Suarez-Orozco and Suarez-Orozco 1995b).

This choloization also was intensified among the children of the new immigrants, something nearly unheard of in previous decades as attachments to traditional Mexican culture enabled many to steer clear of street gangs. Two new developments probably account for this radical shift. One is that many of these new arrivals come to the United States with a background of urban poverty. For them, the process of marginalization actually began in Mexico. This is especially the case for those who are border dwellers and have gained some exposure to cholo culture and styles (Valenzuela 1988). The other reason is simply understood as being the "new kids on the block," having to contend with and react to the established street-youth population. Thus, learning the culture of America in some cases has come to mean learning the culture of the street.

Schools, as mentioned, have written off this element of the adolescent population. This change worsened matters, as gang members of high school age were now free of the classroom and allowed to roam the streets. Relegated strictly to the street life, the conflict with other gangs and gang members, as well as with law enforcement officers, takes center stage.

It seems amazing that difficult, troubled adolescents are dealt with in this way, as if by turning our backs on them we will make them disappear. When they appear in ever larger numbers some place else, we then wonder at the increase in gangs. As usual, we cite some such problem as a breakdown in family values or lack of responsibility and accountability, admittedly a part of the equation, but neglect to consider that troubled youth are a hot potato that no one wants—or knows how—to handle.

Equally important as a *place* factor is the changing nature and dynamics of sources of immigration, as immigrants bring with them many of the cultural attributes of their place of origin. The difference between rural, town, and city and between central, southern, northern, and bordertown Mexico, add significantly to an appreciation of the cultural variance that is Mexico. Immigration studies show that the 1910 Revolution immigrants (Gamio 1930), *braceros* (from *brazo,* arm, equivalent to fieldhand)

An all-girls alternative high school.

in government-contract labor programs of the 1940s and 1950s (Samora 1971), and more recent arrivals (Chavez 1992; Portes and Rambaut 1990; Portes and Bach 1985) have been drawn from contrasting regions, places, and socioeconomic classes in Mexico. How we examine and ponder the backgrounds of the students from the two time periods should, of course, be guided by such contrasts. Recently, it appears that more immigrants have arrived from large town or city backgrounds, and are less peasant-based in their orientation (Chavez 1992). (Nevertheless, a sizable number of them are peasants, especially among the tens of thousands who claim an Indian heritage). These immigrants are thus more familiar with modernized mass media and relatively more prepared for a life in a modern urbanized area such as southern California. Directly linked to the preacculturation dynamic addressed earlier, some immigrant families and their children get a "kickstart" in their acculturation to Anglo-American lifeways and customs. It also shows up when a student, such as Lidia from the impoverished *vecindades* (neighborhoods) of Mexico City, is thwarted and held back because of the limited opportunities unique to certain places (Lewis 1959).

The *people* dimension is the last of our three-fold framework, and intersects with both time and place. Cultural evolution and the movements and migratory experiences of people create contrasting effects for different families. Robert Alvarez' book *Familia* (1987) details just how this might unfold for one family, tracing the almost one-hundred-year path from the mines of Baja California to the fields of rural California and on to residence and life in modern San Diego. All the while, the family through several generations underwent ethnic and cultural adjustments and alterations. If any members of this family had decided to skip one of these phases, their acculturation and adaptation experiences would have been quite different, and whatever cultural refashionings and ethnic identity strivings that resulted would have taken different routes (Rueschenberg and Buriel 1995).

Consider the 1970s individuals from both locales in the first study. Those in the urban group who desired an Anglo way of life could not find it in the barrio (no exposure and no access, and thus, no identity). Suburban parents moved away from East Los Angeles, and their children believed that they had "made it" (being relatively affluent), but cultural marginality erupted in that time period when the school population was only 30 percent Mexican. Further, the 1980s informants showed that suburbanites of that era felt more comfortable with being Mexican because political and demographic changes had facilitated the Mexicanization process (by this time, 70 percent of the students were Mexican). Urban students, similarly, found their cultural environment was revitalized and challenged by the work ethic, optimism, and idealism of new immigrants.

More important to the transformations of people over time and in various places, however, are their racial, cultural, and socioeconomic attributes and characteristics. Such personal and group qualities prefigure their departure from Mexico and entrance into the United States in ways that have not been adequately addressed, much less understood. Using the category "immigrant" and assuming that it is fixed in time and place is a mistake, as the above discussion on the changing nature of immigration shows. Focusing on personal traits and qualities, the people who immigrated to the United States, including Los Angeles, in the 1920s were considerably more Indian and mestizo in physical appearance and rooted more in the rural indigenous cultural ethos of Mexico. They were also the products of sharp class distinctions that persisted in the aftermath of the 1910 Mexican Revolution. This cataclysmic event released millions of debt peons and peasants from *haciendas* (landed estates), and a large portion of them found their way to the United States. As noted earlier, the more modern immigration patterns are much more complex. Although rural, indigenous populations still figure prominently in the influx, especially in many of the Maya, Zapotec, and other almost pure Indian settlements in Los Angeles, there has been a marked rise in working, middle-income, and more educated professional settlers, constituting a "brain drain" of sorts. All these human variations must be integrated into the analysis; otherwise, researchers will be missing important aspects of a large, heterogeneous population. This is grasped, for instance, in the range of income, family structure, and cultural repertoire in the 1980s 1.5-generation urban students. The variations in their goals, study habits, and academic performance are striking.

REASSESSING EDUCATIONAL PERFORMANCE AND ACHIEVEMENT

Under this framework of time, place, and people, we can now turn back to the students and see how the complex set of social and personal factors we have discussed relates to their educational performance. In general, by comparing the life events and forces of students with higher GPA versus those with lower GPAs, we can see that factors such as immigrant aspirations, lower economic status, family structure, ethnic identity, and gender issues also figure into grading and schooling issues (Grant and Sleeter 1986). For example, students appear to do well when they have a stable ethnic identity, secure family environment, an adequate socioeconomic status, access to successful role models, and active parental involvement and support. Students who had all of these factors in their favor seemed to do especially well; although the sequence or the weight of each factor is still unclear.

For example, immigrant aspirations can be a strong motivating factor in educational performance. For several of the students, their concept of the American Dream fueled their success in school; this was particularly true for the 1974 urban Mexican-oriented students. As relatively recent immigrants (they had come to America within a year of the 1974 study), these students expressed hope in the idea that they could succeed later in life if they worked hard in school. As Matilda pointed out, "In the United States, I know there is work; and if I want an education, this is a good place to get it."

In contrast, several students from suburbia believed they had already achieved all that the American Dream could offer and generated minimal motivation to work harder in school. Relatively affluent, especially when compared to their parents' early days in the barrio or their grandparents' status in Mexico, these students had become satisfied with their current socioeconomic status and felt little pressure to advance. For example, Veronica, the 1974 suburban Chicano-oriented female, commented, "I live better here (in the suburbs) than my cousins in East Los Angeles. . . . I want a nice house and a nice yard. Something to show for yourself; the level would be like my parents'." The 1988 suburban Chicano-oriented students voiced similar arguments, and they too appeared satisfied. Rather than striving for higher dreams, they seemed to have settled into a blue-collar respectability. This attitude of relative affluence echoes another student's words: "From East L.A. to Pico Rivera, seven miles to the American Dream," which shows that advancement to perceived affluence can be highly subjective.

If relative affluence can sate the desire for the American Dream, then low-income status can also sour the American Dream (Chapa 1988). This is illustrated in the case of Eduardo, a 1974 urban Chicano-oriented student, who clearly was beset by economic stresses and problems. One of eight children, he lived with his mother and siblings in a small apartment within a government-operated housing project. The family was supported by welfare assistance; his absentee father earned too little to make meaningful support payments, and none of the older siblings had found long-term employment. Eduardo's hopes for the American Dream had been trampled, and members of his family, having lost their coping skills, were more cynical about the benefits of education.

Working-poor status was also the major deterrent to reaching higher pinnacles for Lidia, a 1988 urban Mexican-oriented student. Although a recent immigrant, she lacked the same immigrant aspirations we noted in the 1974 group of urban youth, and even the 1.5 generation in 1988. Coming from one of the countless *vecindades* in Mexico City, a struggling, disoriented life has clearly affected her attitude and that of her parents. They evince few aspirations and express limited strategies for an achievement orientation. This is reflective of their shaky economic roots in Mexico, a poverty stricken lifestyle, which they, in part, carried with them when they immigrated to the United States. They emerged from a caste-like system in Mexico, in which they understood that a ceiling over their heads was part of the reality. This mindset continued to undermine their adaptation and social mobility aspirations in the United States. Lidia's mother was notably negative toward school, and Lidia also experienced some gender conflict as her stepfather encouraged only his son. Not to be overlooked is the simple fact that Lidia was too tired to do well in school; working late into the night at her uncle's restaurant overtaxed her and diminished the importance of school. Here the gender scheme explodes with meaning, especially in terms of how poverty and lack of education have solidified traditional demeaning roles for females—that is, in this instance, no school, just work late at the restaurant (National Council of La Raza 1991).

Working-poor status and economic dislocation, however, did not have the same effect on Norma and Hector, the 1988 urban Mexican-oriented students; a happenstance paralleled by Hortensia and Matilda in 1974, who were struggling but upbeat. Although they coped with low-income backgrounds, Norma and Hector did not see themselves as poor. For them, conditions in America were a step up from what they remembered about life in Mexico, and so they considered themselves as upper middle class. Thus, poverty in and of itself may not be the critical factor; as noted previously, it may instead be more important to examine the individual's own assessment of socioeconomic status, and whether parents were able to look above ceilings for the silver lining.

FOCUSING ON THE FAMILY

Social mobility aspirations are also strongly linked to the family's hard work ethic and support for high educational achievement (Gandara 1982). Combined with the structure of the family is the need for a sound, consistent family strategy that emphasizes the importance of an education (Delgado-Gaitan 1992). Such family features include establishing and maintaining stability within the household with clear lines of authority to provide a consistent and balanced childrearing ambience. Most important to learning is scheduling regular involvement and participation of parents, adults, and older siblings in the learning and schooling affairs of the child (Delgado-Gaitan 1991b). These are just a few examples of what would constitute beneficial family patterns (Delgado-Gaitan 1993b), a tradition that seems to persist among some families even after years of acculturation (Valenzuela and Dornbusch 1996).

The parents of Matilda and Hortensia, the 1974 urban Mexican-oriented students, are a good illustration of such practices. Matilda's parents clearly had placed a high priority on education, as her brother was put into a good school in Mexico. She and her sister were sent to the United States for the sole purpose of receiving a better education under the watchful care of a guardian. Hortensia's parents took the time and effort to mindfully expose her to the realities of life as a low-wage worker. There was regular family involvement in their lives, for the parents (a guardian in Matilda's case) constantly questioned how the girls spent their time. Matilda, in particular, said that she had to account for every minute of her day. She resented this attention, but she accepted it, and it helped reinforce the value that her parents placed on education. These Mexican immigrants were quite concerned about occupational mobility and realized that through hard work, education is a means to job and career goals.

Another example of this successful type of parent-child interaction is Norma, the 1988 urban Mexican-oriented student. Norma was doing well in school and even enrolled in Advanced Placement trigonometry classes. Her family was intact and functional, and her parents had high expectations. Moreover, they had given Norma a great deal of encouragement to do well in school by showing her that education is the way to escape poverty. Norma's father even went so far as to say he would work extra jobs to help his kids go to college, even though Norma somewhat resented favoritism shown toward her brothers. This ethic was transmitted to Norma and her siblings, who studied in their crowded home on whatever makeshift tables they could find.

Similarly, this kind of family consistency and parental support is depicted in Pascual's portrait (Pascual was a 1988 urban Anglo-oriented student). Both of Pascual's parents oversaw his studies at home, and they made sure that Pascual was prepared for his exams. The parents' successful strategy was guided by their own educational background and the fact that they were happily retired and so had the resources and the time to give Pascual direction. The same can be said for Valerie (the 1974 suburban, Anglo-oriented student), but with different family dynamics.

Family stability, however, is not always necessarily associated with a two-parent household, as seen in the case of Georgina, the 1988 Chicano-oriented student. Despite poverty and being unattached, Georgina's mother had done an admirable job in giving her daughter stability. Georgina's mother was strict and was willing to sacrifice for her child's education. Thus, Georgina did well in school.

In contrast, in families where there was instability and conflict, the family unit exerted a negative influence on the youth's academic performance. This is seen in the case of Jose, the 1988 suburban Anglo-oriented student, who was reared in a broken home in the absence of a strong father figure. Cecilia, a 1974 urban Chicano-oriented student, also experienced a great deal of family stress, but this was the result of negative influences of her father. Her father often awkwardly executed the role of the traditional dominant male, and Cecilia reacted as a rebel. As a result, her family was unable to exert a strong influence on her academic behavior.

Other students may have had relatively stable families, but their parents had little forethought or interest in helping their children perform well in academics. This seems to be the case for Randy, the 1988 suburban Anglo-oriented student whose parents seemed more concerned about his athletics. In the case of Christine, the other 1988 suburban Anglo-oriented student, parental support was apathetic, exemplified by her father, who viewed education as an ordeal: "I had to go through it, and if she wants to spend the rest of her life in it, go ahead."

Thus, in combination with cultural styles or influences, the point that emerges from this discussion is that the primary social unit of the family helps a child start and maintain a positive school performance.

GENDER INTERVENES

In the debate over the educational performance of Chicano youth, the specific issues and concerns of female students have often been ignored, as part of a "gender scheme" gap (McKenna and Ortiz 1988; Vasquez 1982; de la Torre and Pesquera 1993; Long and Vigil 1980). In general, the prevailing opinion has been that Chicanas, especially those from traditional households, have been easier to integrate into school (as compared to

Chicano males) because they perform to expectations. This is illustrated by examples such as Matilda and Hortensia, the 1974 Mexican-oriented urban students.

Recent research suggests that this situation may have changed and that Chicanas are having significant problems in school (Segura 1993; Achor and Morales 1990). Sally Andrade (1982), for example, studied the sharp disparities that exist between Chicanas and the wider society. She found that 70 percent of the Mexican-American women twenty-five years and older have not completed high school. For the same age group, another researcher found that the median years of schooling are 8.6 years for Chicanas as compared to 12.4 for all adult women in the United States (Gandara 1982). Even in comparison to Chicano males, women fare worse: In 1979, only 2.8 percent of Mexican-origin women twenty-five years and older had completed college, and men had completed college at twice that rate (Segura 1993).

In addition, although females may respond positively to the expectations of a traditional ethnic environment—Hortensia and Matilda, in 1974, were obedient and dutiful in following their parents' directives—the subservient female role expectation in traditional Mexican culture can also create a great deal of tension (Ruiz 1993; Vigil 1987). This was especially illustrated in the case of Cecilia, the 1974 urban Chicano-oriented student, who rebelled against her authoritarian father. She performed poorly in school and engaged in a chola behavioral lifestyle that included joining a girl gang. Indeed, my own studies have confirmed that a growing presence of Chicana female gang members has emerged in both urban and suburban areas (Moore, Vigil, and Levy 1995). A similar visceral reaction was found with Diana in the 1988 urban sample, who resented the special treatment accorded males in her family, but unlike Cecilia suffered in silence.

Thus, we cannot ignore the needs of female students, and we must refocus on new strategies for their success. They need role models, in particular, to encourage them, and males who are politicized on gender issues and can help break the traditions that prevent educational and social attainment for females. A promising development in this regard is that by 1988, the principals of both the urban and suburban high schools were female. The power of female role models is evident in the case of Cynthia, the 1988 suburban Anglo-oriented student, whose female high school teacher turned her on to school; as a result, Cynthia went from being a mediocre student to a B-average student. Counselors are now consciously encouraging and guiding female students to higher education institutions, and as researchers have demonstrated (Achor and Morales 1990), a traditional or caste-like background can be overcome and does not automatically reproduce itself (Ruiz 1993). Nevertheless, some Chicanas still view traditional culture as a hindrance and obstacle rather than something positive and worthy of replication, and the strain between past upbringings (*enduring self*) and present demands (*situated self*) continues today (*endangered self*).

ETHNIC IDENTITY: NATIVISM AND *PERSONAS MEXICANAS*

A stable ethnic identity is another key theme in evaluating the students' academic performance. A secure, comfortable, relatively stress-free ethnic and cultural identity is associated with strong educational pursuits. For example, the 1974 urban Mexican-oriented students exhibited more confidence in their ethnic identification and performed well in school. Indeed, even though the ESL program was just starting in the urban high school, it became a key to success for the Mexican-oriented students. This learning environment of cultural accommodation eased their acquisition of English and prevented the students from experiencing a serious educational slowdown or blockage. During the past twenty years, such programs have become more established and have made their mark on the urban setting, even though controversy still swirls around them (Colvin 1995). Recent trends indicate that school districts are leaning toward English immersion programs and tending to disfavor bilingual ones (Pyle 1995a). Trujillo (1996) provides a historical and ethnographic example of the see-saw effect on such programs and orientations in another southwest state, Texas.

In the suburban high school, the Expanded Horizons program helped students mediate the acculturation process. For example, Sara, the 1974 suburban Mexican-oriented female, could not speak Spanish fluently, but her family strongly encouraged her Mexican identity. Her involvement in the Expanded Horizons program reinforced this leaning so that she identified as being Mexican even though she lived in a predominantly Anglo neighborhood. Her identity strivings were also shaped by her dark skin, in reaction to ethnic slurs she encountered that in effect forced her to claim a Mexican identity in a positive way (see also Menchaca 1993, 1995). Thus, the program provided a cultural context and impetus for the suburbanite students. In the decades since then, this program has continued, and additional learning approaches have been introduced. For instance, the AVID program is a daring, innovative strategy for low-income or mediocre students who have been identified as "bright" on the basis of nontest, subjective criteria. These students are then placed in more academically oriented classes that address their potential and special learning needs. I recently gave a presentation to these students and was struck by their attentiveness and response. Within several weeks, I received letters from at least thirty of them, thanking me and commenting about how the talk made them rethink who they were and what they could do with their lives. I was touched by the warm, appreciative words, and researchers have demonstrated that this program is indeed making a difference among its targeted students (Mehan et al. 1994).

Thus, programs such as New Horizons and ESL (and AVID, to a degree) serve in different ways to preserve the Mexican culture and personal self-confidence of its students: the urban students retain their identity, and the suburban students regain theirs. I refer to this dual process of learning a new culture while affirming an old one as nativist acculturation (Vigil and Long, 1981). McFee (1968) referred to it as 150 percent acculturation. Nativist acculturation, in combination with familial support, has produced a relatively improved educational record for Mexican-oriented students. Both school programs have evolved and have been refined through the decades, of course, but each adjustment has strengthened bilingual education and multicultural learning environments, despite the resistance demonstrated by the principal of the suburban high school (in 1988) time and time again.

UNIDIRECTIONAL ACCULTURATION OR ASSIMILATION?

In the 1950s, traditional wisdom held that unidirectional (that is, Anglo-oriented) acculturation was a good predictor of school grades and academic achievement.

Unidirectional acculturation may have been a good predictor, but only under some conditions and sometimes at great cost. This was particularly true when attitudes became fixed and so rigid that there became only one way to succeed, the "Anglo way." Let us examine this path.

Many minority students are unable to go the Anglo way, because racial appearance is also a mediating factor in acculturation and is found to affect direction and rate in changing one's ethnic identity. For example, the two 1974 urban Anglo-oriented males who were physically dark in appearance still had a tenuous sense of ethnicity (see Menchaca 1995, 1993; Rodriguez 1991; Del Valle 1989). In contrast, the suburban students felt differently. Another Anglo-oriented student in 1974, Jeffrey, considered himself white but was confused about this position. For Valerie, the other 1974 Anglo-oriented student who performed well in school and was relatively confident with her identity as white, several other factors must be taken into account: her parents were of mixed backgrounds, she had a fair-skinned appearance, and her father had a *rico* orientation from the state of New Mexico, itself a distinct and unique region of the Southwest. Interestingly, and significantly, probably because it became more fashionable to be "ethnic," the mixed-race students in the 1988 suburban sample refrained from claiming white as a label. Indeed, several hint at problems with this aspect of identity. How times have changed!

Most of the lower-achieving students were those who failed to successfully "strategize" the acculturation process and were found primarily in the Chicano and, to some degree, in the Anglo niches of the acculturation spectrum (Vigil 1979; Suarez-Orozco and Suarez-Orozco 1993, 1995a). Even the 1974 suburban intermediates, Veronica and Juan, underwent identity conflict and confusion in the middle of a different context and situation (intermediate cultural orientation must be determined for each place and time and thus is not absolute). They occupied a marginal location in the acculturation spectrum, as they had failed to stabilize an ethnic identity (again, *enduring, situated,* and *endangered* selves in conflict).

In addition, several of the students were poorly rooted in both the Mexican and Anglo cultural traditions, especially in 1974 when there was a wider array of cultural lifestyles. In the 1988 spectrum, the cultural lifestyles were more closely grouped together. The 1974 intermediate individuals tended to gravitate toward more contracultural behavior, a lifestyle that included gang involvement, moderate drug usage, and school absenteeism. Cultural marginality along with street socialization has taken its toll in this regard. Southern California has experienced a sharp increase in gang membership and gang-related violence in the past two decades (Vigil 1988; 1993a). The two schools involved in this investigation have hardened their policy by getting rid of students before they might drop out. As a result, the problems apparent with the marginalized cultural intermediate students in the 1974 study are less visible in the 1988 sample; most such students were not attending these schools. An administrator at the urban school in the latter period said, "We send our gang kids over to_____ high school" (another East Los Angeles campus).

In sum, some major educational problems emerged when adolescents attempted to acculturate. Difficulties were especially acute for those in the intermediate range who were not well rooted in either the Anglo or Mexican culture. This, of course, changed somewhat with the shorter acculturation spectrum stemming from Mexicanization in the 1980s. Acculturation strategies among Anglo-oriented students were undermined by time, place, and people. Often, this meant they did not know who to identify with and how to gain access and exposure to Anglo-American culture—witness the three males in 1974 from both areas who were unsure of themselves. The Mexican-oriented cultural types were less conflict-ridden and performed commendably in school when a learning program was geared to them, and when difficulties emerged, their problems stemmed principally from socioeconomic forces. Indeed, early cultural and linguistic training helped mold a positive self-image, which later enhanced educational advancements. This was clear in 1974 and for Mexicans who grew up learning Spanish; their later acquisition of English was facilitated through ESL programs. As a result, strong bilingual students were more assured and confident and fared well in school.

REASSESSING THE CULTURE VERSUS STRUCTURE DEBATE

In this context of variability, the experts still agree that cultural and structural difficulties and barriers have negatively affected Mexican-American educational pursuits (Foley 1991). Language and cultural patterns have proven a hindrance in certain circumstances, but they are not the insurmountable barriers some 1960s and earlier writers suggested with their extreme "cultural deficit" explanations. An additional consideration is the "breakthrough" motivation some students bring with them (an unfocused striving to surmount obstacles to break through rather than to reach a particular goal), for culture shock can be only a temporary phase if the effort and work ethic is strong enough and the person is consistent and follows through. This appears to be the case for the new immigrant students, whose attitude, discipline, family orientation, and work ethic helped them achieve academic success despite cultural obstacles; their success should not surprise us, for modern urban Mexican culture, lest we forget, also stresses education and the acquisition of knowledge and skills to advance oneself. Additionally, the screening practices of schools that led to testing and tracking have continued in some districts, but elsewhere new approaches to gauge student abilities and kindle strivings have been introduced.

Some of these strategies and policy decisions have returned modest improvements in attitudes toward school and advances in learning. These alterations must be cautiously interpreted, for schools in other places might be entirely different. The fact that the urban school in this study had been designated an "informal" magnet school certainly skews its generalizability for East Los Angeles area units, as it most assuredly does for other schools in California and the Southwest.

In contrast, the structural argument that low socioeconomic status in various ways undermines school performance also appears to hold true. In tandem with institutional racism barriers, this has worked to historically root an oppositional attitude and lackadaisical approach to the dominant culture's school and learning routines; I suggest caution, however, about overinterpreting the political consciousness of this attitude and behavior, for some researchers have raised it to the level of a sort of "resistance movement" (Giroux 1983).

But structural barriers are not impermeable, as many of the individuals and families in this investigation have shown. Some of the racist comments and experiences that students confronted bothered them. Many used this event to steel their resolve to do well, while others complained and lamented how this treatment poisoned their attitude toward learning. Even more subtle teacher comments can be construed as biased, as, for example, when a teacher said: "His bilingualness shows up in his work." Also important are the time and place factor. Suburban parents in 1974 expressed stronger and more detailed accounts of racism in their lives and imparted the attitude of "watch the *gabacho*" (meaning "white person" or foreigner, from the label that Mexicans applied to the French troops during the 1860s intervention). This attitude was not quite as strongly imparted by the 1988 suburban parents. Racism, as contemporary reviews show, has gone underground (although it appears to have recently resurfaced in its old form) and is expressed in more subtle ways; the white female principal of the suburban school in 1988 showed it in a remarkably disingenuous way by refusing to address the latent cultural and youth problems festering there, even though most of the other teachers agreed the problems existed.

For these two schools, the structural record is mixed, and perhaps for the following reasons. First, East Los Angeles has become largely an immigrant enclave, with first- and 1.5-generation Mexicans dominating the area. Although low incomes and poverty are prevalent, the students in this area did not think they were poor. For these mostly immigrants and children of immigrants, the idealism of the American Dream and their aspirations for the future prevailed. In essence, feelings of being downtrodden or oppressed were not present in the students we studied.

In contrast, the suburban locale, although it includes some enclaves that can be classified as lower working class, hardly qualifies as a low-income area, and so its overall problems are different. In this instance, the children and families are later generations of Mexicans who have benefited somewhat from the American Dream and have stopped somewhere along the way to enjoy it. Relative affluence, in the metaphor "From East L.A. to Pico Rivera, Seven Miles to the American Dream," suggests another type of structural explanation: Success can abate further aspirations to strongly strive for a higher level of attainment. Educators in Mexican-American communities thus, while acknowledging parents' very real achievements and justified pride, nevertheless must impress upon youth and parents the need to build upon those achievements. The question to now ask is this: In this century of change, how do the Mexican-American people transform themselves to modern citizens by obtaining the formal education that is now a requisite for survival?

Although these questions seem to be outside the scope of this investigation, a second look is required, because no one has yet explained Mexican educational patterns in a way that accounts for historical considerations, particularly in the preimmigration and preacculturation Mexican context prior to arrival in the United States.

Strong, convincing arguments have been presented for both the cultural and structural points of view. Instead of counterposing these perspectives in a this-or-that-way rivalry, we must begin to reconceptualize them in a this-and-that-and-that way to synthesize and build rather than segment and isolate (Jacob and Jordan 1987).

In this broader cultural change canvas and landscape, the experiences of students before they enter the United States should also be included. Poverty in Mexico can also take its toll and persist in the United States even when the person immigrates. Cross-regional, binational, historical, and longitudinal studies are steps in the direction of capturing the answer to Mexican education pursuits and problems (Macias 1990; Suarez-Orozco 1991).

FINDINGS AND RECOMMENDATIONS

A combination of cultural and structural situations and conditions leads to successful school performance. As we have noted, stable and anchored ethnic identity, a solid family environment, a secure socioeconomic status, and a positive and influential role model all collectively contribute to enhance school achievement and behavior. A multilingual and multicultural strategy is the best acculturation route and one on which to build other elements (Ramirez 1985). It is a path of adding and combining, giving recognition and respect to various cultural influences that enrich one's *persona mexicana*. Academics have referred to it as additive (nativist) rather than subtractive (unidirectional or assimilational) acculturation, as a pathway to adaptation and integration into America (Vigil and Long 1981; Gibson and Ogbu 1991; Gibson 1995).

Another way to look at it is that a person can have "multiple" identities and not just "one self per customer" (Shweder and Markus 1995); a notion that has been recognized by some researchers who advocate a multidimensional measure for an individual's "selves" (Felix-Ortiz, Newcomb, and Myers 1994). Ramirez (1985), an early guide to this line of research (he was also a co-designer of the Experienced Teacher Fellowship Program, which I attended in 1968), has developed a model exploring how a broadening of one's linguistic and cultural persona aids cultural adaptation and participation. According to this analysis, *mestizo* (comprised of racial and cultural mixtures, amalgamations, and syncretisms) psychology better enables a person to function and operate in an increasingly cosmopolitan world. I have referred to this strategy of cultural expansion and incorporation as *personas mexicanas* (connoting many masks of Mexicans) because it reflects the history and cultural evolution of Mexicans and Mexican Americans (Vigil 1984, 1992a), a people of many cultural and linguistic influences; it closely approximates the "American cultural dialogue" notions proposed by the Spindlers (Spindler and Spindler 1990). Cultural and linguistic accommodation and integration is the one area where public institutions and political leaders can readily make a difference, because control is in their hands to make schools effective and productive experiences for the culturally different, politically underrepresented, and economically powerless (Samaniego 1994).

As shaped by socioeconomic backgrounds and forces, family life and parenting strategies and skills are extremely important in this context (Degado-Gaitan 1991b; Suarez-Orozco and Suarez-Orozco 1995a). Involvement of family members in school affairs and the learning process, with their holding higher standards and expectations, appears to make a difference. Suburban parents in 1988 demonstrated less of an influence here than what transpired for the urban children; the relative af-fluence aura seemed to undermine their efforts.

In the context of a more accommodating cultural climate of multiculturalism, parents have also contributed their own folk theories on doing well in school, be-cause they believe that their cultural background should be valued even if they have not attained an adequate education themselves. These parents can teach work habits, discipline, and responsibility by their example, and transfer this purpose to their children who will, in turn, be willing to entertain educational and occupational pur-suits once they understand the importance of aspiring to higher status than their par-ents. This premise is reflected in the statement of one parent who said, "Don't work like a burro, like me."

Parents who take the time and trouble to ensure that the hopes for their children are successfully realized can provide consistent guidance. Parents or other family members are the first, and perhaps most important role models in the initial phase of a succession of influences necessary to succeed. Similarly, research shows that teachers, the second most important role models for children (or, sadly, first if par-ents don't fill that function), can also make a significant difference (Abi-Nader 1990); as can school counseling and learning programs that follow a "culturally therapeutic path" (Spindler and Spindler 1994; Trueba et al. 1993).

Because educational changes have brought some improvements over the decades, it is advisable to underscore what innovations need to be continued and ex-panded. ESL and bilingual education programs in one form or another, controlling for poor and good versions, have made a difference (Pyle 1996; Garcia 1991); even, according to one writer, providing more "social capital" and in effect, more re-sources (Stanton-Salazer 1995; Stanton-Salazer and Dornbusch 1995). These pro-grams have helped students absorb the culture shock of the mainstream educational system, and equipped them with the linguistic tools to navigate in and between cul-tures (Montero-Sieburth and La Celle-Peterson 1991). Interestingly, the program in the urban school has undergone periodic changes, and recent evidence shows that a primarily native language (Spanish) program is less successful than one that leans toward English (Pyle 1995b; Colvin 1996); one author speaks to this rather contro-versial issue, heatedly debated among language experts, and suggests that Mexican-American people should emphasize the "right side of the hyphen" (Navarette 1995).

Other programs, such as the Expanded Horizons program, also have been ben-eficial. These programs, in combination with committed teachers and innovative schools, can make the difference in helping struggling students overcome socioe-conomic, cultural, and personal barriers. We have repeatedly seen this in our stu-dents' lives as well as in other studies (Abi-Nader 1990). These programs should be thoroughly surveyed and examined to determine which approach is best. Espe-cially important in this regard is how unidirectional acculturation can be reexam-ined and rethought to include an almost definitive multicultural strategy that teaches respect and interest in cultures other than one's own (King 1995). Indeed, many mainstream teachers have an inherent bias that leads them to unconsciously (and often even consciously) identify with students who they think are like them. That is, Anglo teachers identify more often with Anglo students (Suarez-Orozco and Suarez-Orozco 1993). This in and of itself is not a malignant bias, but it does

negatively affect students of other ethnic backgrounds who then receive less attention in the classroom, and so on. A multicultural strategy would mitigate the influence of teacher bias for *all* students. It also would contribute to a lessening of the
common human tendency of ethnocentrism (belief that one's culture and ethnic
group are superior to the exclusion of others) and at least turn us away from a *malignant* to *benign* ethnocentrism. (The former is a sense of superiority that shapes
prejudicial attitudes and nurtures discriminating practices, whereas the latter rec-
ognizes that it is common to feel that way, but that overstepping one's boundaries
to infringe on other people's rights and privileges is wrong and unacceptable).

In light of the vehement backlash to multiculturalism and in particular to the
Mexican culture, however (again, witness the English-Only movement and the
pro–Proposition 187 movement, and the glaring fact that less than 30 percent of students with limited English proficiency participate in such programs [Macias 1995a),
I must emphasize that multiculturalism does not mean anti-Americanism! Indeed, a
multicultural strategy can benefit Americans of all backgrounds. Milton Gordon
(1964) long ago pointed out that we can learn and maintain *primary* (American)
ethnic customs, practices, attitudes, and relationships and simultaneously cultivate
the dexterity to hold *secondary* (other culture) ones; this is known as ethnic pluralism or cultural democracy. Switching back and forth as the occasion warrants,
showing a cosmopolitanism that places us in the world culture, is much more beneficial because it encourages resiliency and openness and not rigidity and myopia.

Yet, detractors and critics of multilingual and multicultural programs continue
to argue that personal strains and tensions associated with binational loyalty and allegiance would undermine the stability and fabric of America (Porter 1989; Shogren
1995; Gingrich 1995). Assimilation, however, is an inexorable and inevitable
process and is an aspect of the much broader acculturation experience, and it is happening even now. Even the first-generation immigrants in the barrio realize that
their children and grandchildren will eventually take part in the American mainstream. Evidence shows that this is already a welcome pattern (Myers 1995); late-
night Spanish-language television features advertisements for language cassettes to
improve one's English speaking abilities. As the Spindlers, the pioneers of educational anthropology, noted, "This assimilative process will go on, for it is the American ethos, the central process of American culture and society. Ethnicity is not lost
but participation is gained. However, ethnicity is reshaped" (Spindler and Spindler
1990: xi–xii). Thus, a multicultural strategy would not work against assimilation,
but would in fact promote the participation of minorities into a more heterogeneous
American mainstream.

This America of the twenty-first century will play a leading role in the global
economy by showing an example of how acculturation can be a win-win situation.
By embracing multilingualism and multiculturalism to promote appreciation and respect for other peoples and cultures, America will not just make the global economy
an exchange of goods and services. In addition to, and as an essential corollary, it
will encourage cultural and linguistic exchange, communication, and understanding.

Appendix / The Quantitative and Qualitative Research Methodology

To study these complex issues requires a great amount of background research and systematic methodology. Many personal and professional impressions and preliminary observations (Vigil 1971, 1972, 1973) at both of this study's targeted high schools and communities served as my background research and preceded initiation of the "supra-formal" work in 1974. This initial fieldwork also helped to shape and develop a field-derived survey questionnaire that addressed acculturation factors (for example, birthplace and generation, language use and knowledge, ethnic identity, cultural beliefs and practices) and other personal, family, and social qualities, along with overall school achievement, performance, and behavior (for example, GPA, attendance, attitude toward school and teachers, and extracurricular activities). This survey instrument was developed and field-tested in high schools of contrasting environments and demographics. A representative semistructured sample of Mexican-American students was then selected at each of two high schools for its administration.

One of the schools was in East Los Angeles, a large urban area of Mexican-American barrios adjacent to downtown Los Angeles; and the other was in suburbia, a working- and lower middle-class enclave with a sizable majority of Anglos (60 percent). Because it was important to solicit a broad cross-section of the students of Mexican descent at the high schools, a sample was selected that was representative of female and male students of different ages. Thus, thirty-nine urban and forty-one suburban students were randomly selected in roughly equal numbers from each sex-age level category. The two subsamples also compared closely with the overall school populations on average GPA and percent of Mexican born.

Statistical analyses were conducted with the data collected with this survey instrument. With this early sample, an acculturation scale was developed to reflect the cultural and generational variance among the Mexican-American students in both schools. Included in this acculturation scale were birthplace (first, second, third, or fourth generation in the United States), language uses and abilities, preference for ethnic identity labels, and other cultural practices, to thus make a "cluster of factors" to broadly characterize each student rather than rely on one, such as the voluntary (immigrant) or involuntary (native) dichotomy utilized as a primary indicator in many recent studies (see, for example, Gibson and Ogbu 1991). The analyses indicated that the scale was significantly correlated with the students' own self-identification of ethnicity. The acculturation scale, then, was used as an index of a conceptual acculturation spectrum, ranging from "Mexican ness" on one end to "Anglo-ness" on the other, with "intermediate" or "Chicano" in the middle of the spectrum. (I use the term "intermediate" to refer to Chicano because this term captures the middle area where the Mexican and Anglo cultures merge, and bilingual and bicultural styles are forged if and when there is a set strategy of development.)

With this acculturation spectrum index for all the informants, six key informants were selected from each school who represented the polar opposites and intermediate placement on the spectrum: two Mexican-oriented, two Anglo-oriented, and two in the middle (see chapter 1 for the acculturation spectrums for both schools and time periods). Thus, although statistical testing and comparisons were derived from this quantitative analysis, the key to unraveling the issue of acculturation and school performance among students was to follow up with an *in-depth*, detailed ethnographic investigation of selected respondents that were representative of the spread of cultural styles found on the acculturation spectrum. Over a period of several months, I was able to gather ethnographic information on the habits and daily routines of these individuals. I was also able to observe and interview various members of their families and communities, as well as take note of situations in the classroom settings when I interviewed their teachers. The findings from this 1974 study are available elsewhere (Vigil 1976, 1979, 1982, 1987; Vigil and Long 1981).

In addition to the publications cited above, I also used data from the 1974 study to explore the role Mexican culture had on impeding or enhancing female students' lives and schooling experiences, as in a 1987 conference at the Claremont Colleges, sponsored by the Tomas Rivera Center, on Education Among Hispanic American Women. *Broken Web,* edited by Teresa McKenna and Flor Ida Ortiz (1988), stemmed from that seminar. This event and interaction rekindled my interest in the subject, as I had periodically continued to visit each of the two sites to keep abreast of matters and had also spoken to students about culture and history as a guest lecturer. I thus decided to pursue a restudy of the two sites along the same dimensions, to gauge the many changes that had occurred in the fifteen-year hiatus. This approach provides a longitudinal dimension to a complex and persistent problem.

The qualitative focus, embedded in a representative sample and guided by a composite acculturation scale, depicts a broader, deeper cultural orientation that enables us to appreciate and understand *in situ* what the dynamics of life are in minority communities (Mexican Americans in this case) and how that life affects the schooling habits and accomplishments of individuals and groups.

The same general procedure for selecting informants for 1974 was followed for the restudy in 1988: a semistructured, representative sample for each school, followed by informants selected for in-depth examination. From the thirty-nine students from the urban high school and thirty-one students from the suburban high school, we selected twenty-four students for in-depth follow-up (twelve from each high school). This time, however, we purposely selected according to educational performance as well: high performance students and low performance students in each niche of the acculturation spectrum.* This was intended to permit a focus on other factors besides cultural lifestyle that might affect educational performance.

---

*The acculturation measure for the 1988 sample was constructed from a reduced number of variables, those which had proven most salient in the analysis of the 1974 data. These variables were: generation, Spanish fluency, and self-selected ethnic group label.

A mix of quantitative and qualitative approaches, then, constitutes the means by which evidence was gathered and analyzed to shed light on the issues of culture change and adaptation, acculturation, and school achievement and performance.

A NOTE ON THE QUANTITATIVE FINDINGS

Although *Personas Mexicanas* is based primarily on longterm ethnographic observations and comparisons of the two research sites, both the 1974 and the 1988 sample data were subjected to quantitative analysis as well. In the first study, it had been expected, on the basis of most earlier and contemporary research on these issues, that acculturation-level scores (computed by summing indicators of generational distance from Mexico, ethnic identity preference, English language ability, and nonparticipation in various typical Mexican activities) would correlate with grade point average and other indicators of educational success. Instead, the correlations obtained were in the opposite direction; for example, acculturation was inversely and significantly correlated with grade point average. (Detailed explanation of the 1974 findings is available in Vigil 1982.)

The scores from the initial sample were subsequently reanalyzed within a framework of nativist acculturation (Vigil and Long 1981). A bilingual ability score (based on English and Spanish skills) was computed as an indirect index of bicultural adeptness. Although this measure's correlations with indices of school success were marginal, all were direct (not inverse) correlations. Moreover, the measure performed similarly within the urban and suburban subsamples.

A similar strategy for quantitative analysis was employed with the 1988 questionnaire data, and Table A-1 presents examples of the findings from the two periods for comparison. In 1988, the acculturation scores (based on generation, English language, and ethnic identity preference) were not inversely related to GPAs; rather, there is a (nonsignificant) direct correlation. Bilingual abilities in the second study correlated virtually the same as before with GPAs—marginal, but direct. Acculturation scores were significantly related to the students' self-assessment of their socioeconomic status in both studies, whereas bilingual abilities were only marginally correlated with social class status, but in opposite directions in the two samples.

The self-perceived social class measure is important for adding perspective to the differences between students at the urban high school and those at the suburban school. Suburban sample students estimated their social class status higher than did the urban students, and that difference persisted in 1988 (urban mean 2.95, S.D. 1.04 versus suburban mean 3.78, S.D. 1.06, T=-3.13, p<.01). Urban and suburban students also differed significantly in average acculturation scores (mean 5.46, S.D. 1.23 versus mean 7.94, S.D. 1.51, t=7.06, p<.001). Bilingual scores in 1988 differed only marginally between the two subsamples (urban mean 3.13 versus suburban mean 2.83, N.S.) and average GPAs for the two groups were nearly identical (2.46 versus 2.48).

These differences contribute to the different results of statistical analyses within the subsamples (see Table A-2). A strong direct correlation between acculturation and GPA exists for the urban sample, but not for the suburban students who

TABLE A-1 RELATIONSHIP OF ACCULTURATION AND BILINGUAL ABILITY WITH
GRADES AND SOCIAL CLASS, 1974 AND 1988

Correlation (r)	1974	1988
Acculturation scale with grade point average	−.30**	.20
Acculturation scale with social class status	.61**	.26*
Bilingual ability with grade point average	.16	.16
Bilingual ability with social class status	.18	−.08

*p<.05
**1<.01

are more acculturated. Conversely, the marginal correlation between bilingual abilities and GPA is clearly stronger for the urban students. Neither of these indices is
strongly related to social class status within either subsample; rather, the strong
overall correlation of acculturation with class is simply a reflection of the urban-
suburban differences on these measures.

These examples, thus, tend to reinforce the overall ethnographic impression of
what changes have been occurring, what urban-suburban differences persist, and what
the relationships among these factors relating to acculturation and education are.

TABLE A-2 RELATIONSHIP OF ACCULTURATION AND BILINGUAL ABILITY WITH
GRADES AND SOCIAL CLASS, URBAN VERSUS SUBURBAN

	Urban School	Suburban School
Acculturation with GPA	.33*	−.09
Acculturation with social class status	.08	−.04
Bilingual Ability with GPA	.29	.17
Bilingual ability with social class status	−.02	.03

* < .05

References

Abi-Nader, J. (1990). A house for my mother: Motivating Hispanic high school students. *Anthropology and Education Quarterly 21*(1): 41–58.

Achor, S. & Morales, A. (1990). Chicanas holding doctoral degrees: Social reproduction and cultural ecological approaches. *Anthropology and Education Quarterly, 21*(3): 269–287.

Acuna, R. (1988). *Occupied America.* New York: Harper and Row.

Alvarez, R. (1987). *Familia: Migration and Adaptation in Baja and Alta California, 1800–1975.* Berkeley: University of California Press.

Alvarez, R. (1988). National politics and local responses: The nation's first successful desegregation court case. In H.T. Trueba & C. Delgado-Gaitan (Eds.), *School and Society: Learning Content Through Culture,* (pp. 37– 52). New York: Praeger.

Andrade, S. J. (1982). Family roles of Hispanic women: Stereotypes, empirical findings, and implications for research. In R. E. Zambrana (Ed.), *Work, Family, and Health: Latina Women in Transition.* New York: Hispanic Research Center, Fordham University.

Arvizu, S. F. (1974). Education for constructive marginality. In W. Dillon (Ed.), *The Cultural Drama,* (pp. 122–135). Washington, D.C.: Smithsonian Institute Press.

Arvizu, S. F. & Snyder, W. (1977). *Demystifying the Concept of Culture: Theoretical and Conceptual Tools, #1.* Sacramento, CA: Cross Cultural Resource Center, Sacramento State.

Bernal, M. E. & Knight, G. P. (Eds.). (1993). *Ethnic Identity: Formation and Transmission Among Hispanic and Other Minorities.* New York: State University of New York Press.

Blum, J. (1978). *Pseudoscience and Mental Ability: The Origins and Fallacies of the IQ Controversy.* New York: Monthly Review Press.

Bogardus, E. S. (1926). *The City Boy and His Problems.* Los Angeles: House of Ralston, Rotary Club of Los Angeles.

Bowles, S. & Gintis, H. (1976). *Schooling in Capitalist America: Educational Reform and the Contradictions of Economic Life.* New York: Basic Books.

Boyer, E. J. (1995, October 24). Changing of the political guard. *Los Angeles Times.*

Buenker, D. & Lorman, A. R. (Eds). (1992). *Multiculturalism in the United States: A Comparative Guide to Acculturation and Ethnicity.* New York: Greenwood Press.

Buriel, R. (1984). Integration with traditional Mexican American culture and sociocultural adjustment. In J. L. Martinez & R. Mendoza (Eds.), *Chicano Psychology,* 2nd ed. New York: Academic Press.

Buriel, R. & Cardoza, D. (1993). Mexican American ethnic labeling: An intrafamilial and intergenerational analysis. In M. E. Bernal & G. P. Knight (Eds.), *Ethnic Identity: Formation and Transmission Among Hispanics and Other Minorities.* New York: State University of New York Press.

Carter, T. P. & Segura, R. D. (1978). *Mexican Americans in School: A Decade of Change.* New York: College Board.

Chapa, J. (1988). The question of Mexican American assimilation: Socioeconomic parity or underclass formation? *Public Affairs Comment 35:* 1–14.

Chavez, L. (1992). *Shadowed Lives.* New York: Harcourt Brace Jovanovich College Publishers.

Colvin, R. E. (1995, June 5). Bilingual education rift divides state teachers union. *Los Angeles Times.*

Colvin, R. E. (1996, April 12). Panel OKs overhaul of bilingual ed. *Los Angeles Times.*

Del Olmo, Frank. (1995, November 13). Latino youth rekindle the spark of activism. *Los Angeles Times.*

Delgado-Gaitan, C. (1991a). *Crossing Cultural Borders: Education for Immigrant Families in America.* New York: The Falmer Press.

Delgado-Gaitan, C. (1991b). Involving parents in the schools: A process of empowerment. *American Journal of Education 100*(1): 20–46.

Delgado-Gaitan, C. (1992). School matters in the Mexican-American home: Socializing children to education. *American Educational Research Journal 29*(3): 495–513.

Delgado-Gaitan, C. (1993a). Researching change and changing the researcher. *Harvard Educational Review 63*(4): 389–411.

Delgado-Gaitan, C. (1993b). Research and policy in reconceptualizing family-school relationships. In P. Phelan & A. L. Davidson (Eds.), *Renegotiating Cultural Diversity in American Schools.* New York: Teachers College, Columbia University.

Delgado-Gaitan, C. (1994). Literacy acquisition in an elementary school. *UC Linguistics Minority Research Institute, 4*(1).

De la Torre, A. & Pesquera, B. M. (Eds.). (1993). *Building with Our Hands: New Directions in Chicana Studies.* Berkeley: University of California Press.

De Leon, M., (1970). The hamburger and the taco: A new cultural reality. In H. S. Johnson & W. J. Hernandez-M. (Eds.), *Educating the Mexican American* (pp. 33–45). Valley Forge, PA: Judson Press.

Del Valle, M. (1989). *Acculturation, Sex Roles and Racial Definition of Puerto Rican College Students in Puerto Rico and the United States.* San Francisco: R and R Associates.

De Vos, G. (1982). Adaptive strategies in U.S. minorities. In E. E. Jones & S. J. Korchin (Eds.), *Minority Mental Health* (pp. 74–117). New York: Praeger.

Diaz, D. R. (1993). La vida libra: Cultura de la calle en Los Angeles Este. *Places 8*(3): 30–37.

Donato, R., Menchaca, M., & Valencia, R. (1991). Segregation, desegregation, and integration of Chicano students: Problems and prospects. In R. R. Valencia (Ed.), *Chicano School Failure and Success: Research and Policy Agendas for the 1990s.* London: The Falmer Press.

Eaton, J. (1952). Controlled acculturation: Survival technique of the Hutterites. *American Sociological Review, 17.*

Elsass, P. (1992). *Strategies for Survival: The Psychology of Cultural Resilience in Ethnic Minorities.* New York: New York University Press.

Ernst, G., Statzner, E., & Trueba, H. T. (1994). Alternative visions of schooling: Success stories in minority settings: Theme issue. *Anthropology and Education Quarterly 25*(3): 199–393.

Estrada, R. (1995, September 10). Dole is half-right on 'English only.' *Los Angeles Times.*

Felix-Ortiz, M., Newcomb, M. D., & Myers, H. (1994). A multidimensional measure of cultural identity for Latino and Latina adolescents. *Hispanic Journal of Behavioral Sciences 16*(2): 99–115.

Fishman, J. (1986). Bilingualism and separation. *Annals of the American Academy 487:* 169–180.

Foley, D. (1991). Reconsidering anthropological explanations of ethnic school failure. *Anthropology and Education Quarterly 22*(1): 60–86.

Foley, D. (1990). *Learning Capitalist Culture: Deep in the Heart of Tejas.* Philadelphia: University of Pennsylvania Press.

Gamio, M. (1969). *Mexican Immigration to the United States.* New York: Arno Press (originally published 1930).

Gandara, P. (1982). Passing through the eye of the needle: High-achieving Chicanas. *Hispanic Journal of Behavioral Sciences 4*(2).

Garcia, E. E. (1991). Bilingualism, second language acquisition, and the education of Chicano language minority students. In R. R. Valencia (Ed.), *Chicano School Failure and Success: Research and Policy Agendas for the 1990s*. London: The Falmer Press.

Gibson, M. A. (1988). *Accommodation without Assimilation: Sikh Immigrants in an American High School*. New York: Cornell University Press.

Gibson, M. A. (1995). Patterns of acculturation and high school performance. *UC Linguistic Minority Research Institute, 4*(9): 1–3.

Gibson, M. & Arvizu, S. F. (1977). *Demystifying the Concept of Culture: Methodological Tools and Techniques*, no. 2. Sacramento, CA: Cross Cultural Resource Center, Sacramento State.

Gibson, M. A. & Ogbu, J. (1991). *Minority Status and Schooling: A Comparative Study of Immigrant and Involuntary Minorities*. New York: Garland Publishing.

Gingrich, N. (1995, August 4). English literacy is the coin of the realm. *Los Angeles Times*.

Giroux, H. (1983). *Theory and Resistance in Education*. London: Heinemann Educational Books.

Gonzales, G. (1990). *Chicano Education in the Era of Segregation*. Philadelphia: The Balch Institute Press.

Gordon, M. (1964). *Assimilation in American Life*. New York: Oxford University Press.

Grant, C. A. & Sleeter, C. E. (1986). Race, class, and gender in education research: An argument for integrative analysis. *Review of Educational Research 56*(2): 195–211.

Graves, T. (1967). Acculturation, access, and alcohol in a tri-ethnic community. *American Anthropologist 69:* 306–321.

Griswold del Castillo, R. (1990). *The Treaty of Guadalupe Hidalgo: A Legacy of Conflict*. Norman: University of Oklahoma Press.

Hallowell, A. I. (1955). *Culture and Experience*. Philadelphia: University of Pennsylvania Press.

Hayes, K. G. (1992). Attitudes toward education: Voluntary and involuntary immigrants from the same families. *Anthropology and Education Quarterly 23*(3): 250–267.

Hayes-Bautista, D. E. & Rodriquez, G. (1994, May 5). L.A.'s culture comes full circle. *Los Angeles Times*.

Helfand, D. (1995, June 10). Garfield high grads return and deliver. *Los Angeles Times*.

Hill, M. (1928). An Americanization program for the Ontario schools. Reprinted in Leonard Pitt (Ed.), (1968) *California Controversies*. Glenview, IL: Scott, Foresman, and Co.

Horowitz, R. (1983). *Honor and the American Dream*. New Brunswick, NJ: Rutgers University Press.

Hurh, W. & Kim, K. (1984). Adhesive sociocultural adaptation of Korean immigrants in the U.S.: An alternative strategy of minority adaptation. *International Migration Review 18*.

Hurtado, A. & Gurin, P. (1995). Ethnic identity and bilingualism. In A. Padilla (Ed.), *Hispanic Psychology*. Thousand Oaks, CA: Sage Publishing.

Inside Metro. (1995, August 29). Community profile: South Gate. *Los Angeles Times*.

Jacob, E. & Jordan, C. (1987). Explaining the school performance of minority students: Theme issue. *Anthropology and Education Quarterly 18*(4): 259–391.

Jencks, C. & Peterson, P. E. (1991). *The Urban Underclass*. Washington, D.C.: The Brookings Institute.

Kamin, L. J. (1974). *The Science and Politics of IQ*. Potomac, MD: Erlbaum.

Katz, M. (1986). *In the Shadow of the Poorhouse: A Social History of Welfare in America*. New York: Basic Books.

Keefe, S. & Padilla, A. (1987). *Chicano Ethnicity*. Albuquerque: University of New Mexico Press.

Kim, E. Y. (1993). Career choice among second-generation Korean Americans: Reflections of a cultural model of success. *Anthropology and Education Quarterly 24*(3): 224–248.

King, C. (1995, September 21). Too narrow a view of who's American. *Los Angeles Times.*

Kotkin, J. (1995, May 28). Latinization of South Los Angeles. *Los Angeles Times.*

Lambert, W. E. (1990). *Coping with Cultural and Racial Diversity in Urban America.* New York: Praeger.

Laskin, D. (1994, September 5). How do you say 'Catch 22' in Spanish? *Los Angeles Times.*

Lavin, E. (1995, March 23). Escalante math and science program turns F's into A's. *Los Angeles Times* (Southeast Edition).

Leacock, E. (Ed.). (1971). *The Culture of Poverty: A Critique.* New York: Simon and Schulster.

Lewis, O. (1959). *Five Families: Mexican Case Studies in the Culture of Poverty.* New York: Basic Books.

Long, J. M. & Vigil, D. (1980). Cultural styles and adolescent sex role perceptions: An exploration of responses to a value picture projective test. In M. Melville (Ed.), *Twice a minority: Mexican American women.* St. Louis, MO: C. V. Mosby Co.

Long, L. K. & Padilla, A. M. (1971). Evidence for bilingual antecedents of academic success in the groups of Spanish American college students. *Journal of Cross-Cultural Psychology 2:* 53–58.

Macias, J. (1990). Scholastic antecedents of immigrant students: Schooling in a Mexican immigrant sending community. *Anthropology and Education Quarterly 21*(4): 291–318.

Macias, R. (1995a). CA LEP enrollment continues slow growth in 1995. *UC Linguistic Minority Research Institute 5*(1): 1–2.

Macias, R. (1995b). California's bilingual education under siege. *UC Linguistic Minority Research Institute 4*(10): 1–2.

Macias, R. & Garcia Ramos, R. G. (1995). *Changing Schools for Changing Students.* Santa Barbara: University of California Linguistic Minority Research Institute Publication.

Martinez, R. (1994, January 30). The shock of the new. *Los Angeles Times Magazine.*

Matute-Bianchi, M. (1991). Situational ethnicity and patterns of school performance among immigrant and nonimmigrant Mexican-descent students. In M. Gibson & J. Ogbu (Eds.), *Minority Status and Schooling.* New York: Garland Publishing.

McFee, M. (1968). The 150% man: A product of Blackfeet acculturation. *American Anthropologist 70:* 1096–1107.

McKenna, T. & Ortiz, F. I. (Eds.). (1988). *Broken Web: The Educational Experience of Hispanic American Women.* Berkeley: Floricanto Press.

McLaughlin, B. (1994). Linguistic, psychological and contextual factors in language shift. *UC Linguistics Minority Research Institute, 3*(4).

McWilliams, C. (1968). *North from Mexico—the Spanish-speaking People of the United States.* Westport, CT: Greenwood Press (originally published 1949).

Mehan, H., Hubbard, L., & Villanueva, I. (1994). Forming ethnic identities: accommodation without assimilation among involuntary minorities. *Anthropology and Education Quarterly 25*(2): 91–117.

Menchaca, M. (1989). Chicano-Mexican cultural assimilation and Anglo-Saxon cultural dominance. *Hispanic Journal of Behavioral Sciences 11*(3) 203–231.

Menchaca, M. (1993). Chicano Indianism: A historical account of racial repression in the United States. *American Ethnologist 20*(3): 583–603.

Menchaca, M. (1995). *The Mexican Outsiders: A Community History of Marginalization and Discrimination in California.* Austin: University of Texas Press.

Menchaca, M. & Valencia, R. R. (1990). Anglo-Saxon ideologies and their impact on the segregation of Mexican students in California, the 1920s–1930s. *Anthropology and Education Quarterly 21:* 222–249.

Merl, J. (1994, May 25). State dropout rate falls 38.8% in eight years. *Los Angeles Times.*

Moll, L. C. & Diaz, S. (1987). Change as the goal of educational research. *Anthropology and Education Quarterly 18*(4): 300–311.

Monroy, D. (1990). *Thrown among Strangers: The Making of Mexican Culture in Frontier California.* Berkeley: University of California Press.

Montejano, D. (1987). *Anglos and Mexicans in the Making of Texas, 1836 1986.* Austin: University of Texas Press.

Montero-Sieburth, M. & La Celle-Peterson, M. (1991). Immigration and schooling: An ethnohistorical account of policy and family perspectives in an urban community. *Anthropology and Education Quarterly 22*(4): 300–325.

Moore, J. W. & Pachon, H. (1985). *Hispanics in the United States.* Englewood Cliffs, NJ: Prentice-Hall.

Moore, J. W. & Pinderhughes-Rivera, R. (Eds.). (1993). *In the barrios: Latinos and the Underclass Debate.* New York: Russell Sage Foundation.

Moore, J. W. & Vigil, D. (1987). Chicano gangs: Group norms and individual factors related to adult criminality. *Aztlan 18*(2): 27–44.

Moore, J. W., Vigil, J. D., & Levy, J. (1995). Huisas of the street: Chicana gang members. *Latino Studies Journal 6*(1): 27–48.

Myers, D. (1995). *The Changing Immigrants of Southern California.* Report from the Department of Urban and Regional Planning, Los Angeles: University of Southern California.

National Council of La Raza. (1991). Upcoming report highlights gender and education: The relationship between Latino poverty and gender. *Newsletter of the National Council of La Raza 3*(2).

Navarette, R., Jr. (1995, August 20). Emphasizing the right side of the hyphen. *Los Angeles Times.*

Neisser, U. (1986). *The School Achievement of Minority Children: New Perspectives.* Hillsdale, NJ: Erlbaum Associates.

Ogbu, J. U. (1982). Cultural discontinuities and schooling. *Anthropology and Education Quarterly 13*(4): 290–307.

Ogbu, J. U. (1987). Variability in minority school performance: A problem in search of an explanation. *Anthropology and Education Quarterly 18*(4): 312–334.

Ogbu, J. U. (1989). The individual in collective adaptation: A framework for focusing on academic underperformance and dropping out among involuntary minorities. In L. Weis, E. Farrar & H. Petrie (Eds.), *Dropouts from School: Issues, Dilemmas, and Solutions,* 181–204. Albany, NY: State University of New York Press.

Ogbu, J. U. (1991). Immigrant and involuntary minorities in comparative perspective. In M. Gibson & J. Ogbu (Eds.), *Minority Status and Schooling: A Comparative Study of Immigrant and Involuntary Minorities,* 3–33. New York: Garland Publishing.

Olmedo, E. L. & Padilla, A. M. (1978). Empirical and construct validation of a measure of acculturation for Mexican Americans. *Journal of Social Psychology 105:* 179–187.

Padilla, F. M. (1992). *The Gang as an American Enterprise.* New Brunswick, NJ: Rutgers University Press.

Parsons, T. (1965). *Ethnic Cleavage in a California School.* Doctoral dissertation, Palo Alto: Stanford University.

Patthey-Chavez, G. G. (1993). High school as an arena for cultural conflict and acculturation for Latino Angelinos. *Anthropology and Education Quarterly 24*(1): 33–60.

Phelan, P. & Davidson, A. L. (Eds.). (1993). *Renegotiating Cultural Diversity in American Schools.* New York: Teachers College, Columbia University.

Phelan, P., Davidson, A. L., & Yu, H. C. (1993). Students' multiple worlds: Navigating the borders of family, peer, and school cultures. In P. Phelan & A. L. Davidson (Eds.), *Renegotiating Cultural Diversity in American Schools,* New York: Teachers College, Columbia University.

Pitman, M. A., & Eisenhart, M. A. (1988). Women, culture, and education: Theme issue. *Anthropology and Education Quarterly 19*(2): 67–196.

Plaschke, B. (1995, November 9). A proud struggle on the field—and off. *Los Angeles Times.*

Polgar, S. (1960). Biculturation of Mesquakie teenage boys. *American Anthropologist 62,* 217–235.

Porter, R. P. (1989). *Forked Tongue: The Politics of Bilingual Education.* New York: Basic Books.

Portes, A. & Bach, R. L. (1985). *Latin Journey: Cuban and Mexican Immigrants in the United States.* Berkeley: University of California Press.

Portes, A. & Rumbaut, R. (1990). *Immigrant America: A Portrait.* Los Angeles: University of California Press.

Pozzetta, G. E. (Ed.). (1991). *Assimilation, Acculturation, and Social Mobility.* New York: Garland Publishers.

Pyle, A. (1995a, July 14). State panel OKs flexible bilingual education policy. *Los Angeles Times.*

Pyle, A. (1995b, July 31). English fluency moves up the priority ladder. *Los Angeles Times.*

Pyle, A. (1996, January 12). Bilingual classes boost performance, study finds. *Los Angeles Times.*

Quadagno, J. (1994). *The Color of Welfare: How Racism Undermined the War on Poverty.* New York: Oxford University Press.

Quintanilla, M. (1995, November 17). The great divide. *Los Angeles Times.*

Ramirez, M. (1971). The relationship of acculturation to educational achievement and psychological adjustment in Chicano children and adolescents: A review of the literature. *El Grito 4*(4): 21–28.

Ramirez, M. (1985). *Psychology of the Americas: Mestizo Perspective on Personality and Mental Health.* New York: Pergamon Press.

Ramirez, M. & Castaneda, A. (1974). *Cultural Democracy, Bicognitive Development and Education.* New York: Academic Press.

Ramirez, M., Taylor, C., & Peterson, C. (1971). Mexican-American cultural membership and adjustment to school. *Developmental Psychology 4*(2): 141–148.

Ramos, G. (1995, November 20). Unassuming MTA leader takes the expertise route. *Los Angeles Times.*

Ready, T. (1991). *Latino Immigrant Youth: Passages from Adolescence to Adulthood.* New York: Garland.

Redfield, R., Linton, R., & Herskovits, M. (1936). Memorandum for the study of acculturation. *American Anthropologist 38:*149–152.

Rodgers, W. & Long, J. (1968). Male models and sexual identification: A case from the Out-Island Bahamas. *Human Organization 30:* 1–13.

Rodriguez, C. (1991). *Puerto Ricans: Born in the U.S.A.* Boulder, CO: Westview Press.

Rogler, L., Cortes, D., & Malgady, R.G. (1991). Acculturation and mental health status among Hispanics. *American Psychologist 46*(6): 585–597.

Romanucci-Ross, L. & De Vos, G. (Eds.). (1995). *Ethnic Identity.* London: Alta Mira Press.

Roseman, C. & Vigil, J. D. (1993). From Broadway to Latinoway: The reoccupation of a gringo retail landscape. *Places 8*(3): 20–29.

Rueschenberg, E. J. & Buriel, R. (1995). Mexican American family functioning and acculturation: A family system perspective. In A. Padilla (Ed.), *Hispanic Psychology.* Thousand Oaks, CA: Sage Publishing.

Ruiz, V. (1993). Star struck: Acculturation, adolescence, and the Mexican American woman, 1920–1950. In A. de la Torre & B. M. Pesquera (Eds.), *Building with Our Hands: New Directions in Chicana Studies,* 109–129. Berkeley: University of California Press.

Rumberger, R. W. (1991). Chicano dropouts: A review of research and policy issues. In R. R. Valencia (Ed.), *Chicano School Failure and Success: Research and Policy Agendas for the 1990s*. London: The Falmer Press.

Samaniego, F. (1994, December). New analysis of case study project data suggests stronger link between school characteristics and bilingual program success. *UC Linguistic Minority Research Institute 4*(4): 1–2.

Samora, J. (1971). *Los Mojados*. South Bend, IN: University of Notre Dame Press.

Sanchez, G. (1932). Scores of Spanish-speaking children on repeated tests. *Journal of Genetic Psychology 40*.

Sanchez, G. (1966). History, culture, and education. In Julian Samora (Ed.), *La Raza: Forgotten Americans,* 1–26. South Bend, IN: University of Notre Dame Press.

Santana, G. (1986). The Chachas. Unpublished student paper in University of Southern California anthropology course.

Sassen, S. (1991). *The Global City: New York, London, Tokyo*. Princeton: Princeton University Press.

Schlegel, A. & Barry, H., III. (1991). *Adolescence: An Anthropological Inquiry*. New York: The Free Press.

Segura, D. (1993). Slipping through the cracks: Dilemmas in Chicana education. In A. de la Torre & B. M. Pesquera (Eds.), *Building with Our Hands: New Directions in Chicana Studies,* Berkeley: University of California Press.

Shogren, E. (1995, October 31). Gingrich assails American bilingualism as 'dangerous.' *Los Angeles Times*.

Shweder, R. & Markus, H. (1995). Culture, identity, and conflict. *ITEMS: Social Science Research Council 49*(1): 11–13.

Siegel, B., Vogt, E., Watson, J., & Broom, L. (1953). Acculturation: An exploratory formulation. *American Anthropologist 55:* 973–1002.

Spindler, G. (Ed.). (1970). *Education and Anthropology*. Stanford, CA: Stanford University Press.

Spindler, L. (1984). *Culture Change and Modernization*. Prospect Heights, IL: Waveland Press.

Spindler, G., & Spindler, L. (1961). The instrumental activities inventory: A technique for the study of the psychology of acculturation. *Southwestern Journal of Anthropology 28*(1): 1–23.

Spindler, G., & Spindler, L. (1987). Teaching and learning how to do the ethnography of education. In G. Spindler & L. Spindler (Eds.), *Interpretive Ethnography of Education at Home and Abroad,* 17–33. Hillsdale, NJ: Lawrence Erlbaum Associates, Inc.

Spindler, G., & Spindler, L. (1990). *The American Cultural Dialogue and Its Transmission*. London: The Falmer Press.

Spindler, G., & Spindler, L. (1991). Reactions and worries. *Anthropology & Education Quarterly 22*(3): 274–278.

Spindler, G., & Spindler, L. (1993). The processes of culture and person: Cultural therapy and culturally diverse schools. In P. Phelan & A. L. Davidson (Eds.). *Renegotiating Cultural Diversity in American Schools*. New York: Teachers College, Columbia University.

Spindler, G., & Spindler, L. (Eds.). (1994). *Pathways to Cultural Awareness: Cultural Therapy with Teachers and Students*. Thousand Oaks, CA: Corwin Press, Inc.

Stanton-Salazar, R. D. (1995). Information networks and the social reproduction of inequality. *UC Linguistic Minority Research Institute 4*(5), 1–2.

Stanton-Salazar, R. D. & Dornbusch, W. (1995, April). Social capital and the reproduction of inequality: Information networks among Mexican-origin high school students. *Sociology of Education 68:* 116–135.

Stromquist, N. & Vigil, D. (1996). School violence in the United States. In J.C. Tedesco (Ed.), *Prospects: International Bureau of Education,* Paris: UNESCO.

Suarez-Orozco, M. M. (1989). *Central American Refugees and U.S. High Schools: A Psychosocial Study of Motivation and Achievement.* Stanford, CA: Stanford University Press.

Suarez-Orozco, M. M. (1991). Migration, minority status, and education: European dilemmas and responses in the 1990s. *Anthropology and Education Quarterly 22*(2): 99–120.

Suarez-Orozco, M., & Suarez-Orozco, C. E. (1993). Hispanic cultural psychology: Implications for education theory and research. In P. Phelan & A. L. Davidson (Eds.), *Renegotiating Cultural Diversity in American Schools,* New York: Teachers College, Columbia University.

Suarez-Orozco, M., & Suarez-Orozco, C. E. (1995a). *Transformations: Migration, Family Life, and Achievement Motivation among Latino Adolescents.* Stanford, CA: Stanford University Press.

Suarez-Orozco, M., & Suarez-Orozco, C. E. (1995b). Migration: Generational discontinuities and the making of Latino identies. In L. Romanucci-Ross & G. De Vos (Eds.), *Ethnic Identity.* London: Alta Mira Press.

Teske, R. H. C. & Nelson, B. H. (1974). Acculturation and assimilation: A clarification. *American Ethnologist 1*(3): 351–367.

The Tomas Rivera Center. (1993). *Resolving a Crisis in Education: Latino Teachers for Tomorrow's Classrooms.* Claremont, CA: The Tomas Rivera Center for Policy Studies.

Trueba, H. T. (1988). Culturally-based explanations of minority students' academic achievement. *Anthropology and Education Quarterly 19*(3): 270–287.

Trueba, H. T. (1991). From failure to success: The roles of culture and cultural conflict in the academic achievement of Chicano students. In R. R. Valencia (Ed.), *Chicano School Failure and Success: Research and Policy Agendas for the 1990s.* London: The Falmer Press.

Trueba, H. T. & Valencia, R. R. (1993a). Cultural ecology: A new type of anthropological determinism? Unpublished paper.

Trueba, H. T. & Valencia, R. R. (1993b). Cultural diversity and conflict: The role of educational anthropology in healing multicultural America. In P. Phelan & A. L. Davidson (Eds.), *Renegotiating Cultural Diversity in American Schools,* New York: Teachers College, Columbia University.

Trueba, H. T., Rodriguez, C., Zou, Y., & Clinton, J. (1993). *Healing Multicultural America: Mexican Immigrants Rise to Power in Rural California.* London: The Falmer Press.

Trueba, H. T., Spindler, G. & Spindler, L. (1989). *What Do Anthropologists Have to Say about Dropouts? The First Centennial Conference on Children at Risk, School of Education, Stanford University.* New York: The Falmer Press.

Trujillo, A. L. (1996). Bilingual/bicultural education and politics in Crystal City, Texas: 1969–1989. In R. M. De Anda (Ed.), *Chicanas and Chicanos in Contemporary Society,* 157–178. Boston: Allyn and Bacon.

U.S. Commission on Civil Rights. (1972). *The Excluded Student: Report 3.* Washington, D.C.: U.S. Government Printing Office.

Valencia, R. R. (Ed.) (1991a). *Chicano School Failure and Success: Research and Policy Agendas for the 1990s.* London: The Falmer Press.

Valencia, R. R. (Ed.) (1991b). The plight of Chicano students: An overview of schooling conditions and outcomes. In Richard R. Valencia (Ed.), *Chicano School Failure and Success: Research and Policy Agendas for the 1990s.* London: The Falmer Press.

Valencia, R. R. (Ed.) (1991c). Conclusions: Towards Chicano school success. In Richard R. Valencia (Ed.), *Chicano School Failure and Success: Research and Policy Agendas for the 1990s.* London: The Falmer Press.

Valencia, R. R., & Aburto, S. (1991). The uses and abuses of educational testing: Chicanos as a case in point. In Richard R. Valencia (Ed.), *Chicano School Failure and Success: Research and Policy Agendas for the 1990s,* London: The Falmer Press.

Valentine, C. (1968). *The Culture of Poverty.* Chicago: University of Chicago Press.

Valenzuela, A., & Dornbusch, S. M. (1996). Familism and assimilation among Mexican-origin and Anglo high school adolescents. In R. M. De Anda (Ed.), *Chicanas and Chicanos in Contemporary Society,* 53–62. Boston: Allyn and Bacon.

Valenzuela, J. M. (1988). *A La Brava Ese!: Cholos, Punks, Chavos Banda.* Tijuana, Mexico: El Colegio de la Frontera Norte.

Vasconcelos, J. & Gamio, M. (1926). *Aspects of Mexican Civilization.* Chicago: University of Chicago Press.

Vasquez, M. J. (1982). Confronting barriers to the participation of Mexican American women in higher education. *Hispanic Journal of Behavioral Sciences 4*(2): 147–165.

Vigil, J. D. (1971). Chicanos in suburbia: A preliminary excursion into the acculturative process by means of a questionnaire. Unpublished paper.

Vigil, J. D. (1972). Chicano acculturation: Individual and groups in an urban and suburban high school setting. Unpublished paper.

Vigil, J. D. (1973). Life-histories and autobiographies of urban and suburban Chicanos. Unpublished paper.

Vigil, J. D. (1976). Adolescent Chicano acculturation and school performance: The role of social economic conditions and urban-suburban environmental differences. Doctoral dissertation, University of California, Los Angeles.

Vigil, J. D. (1979). Adaptation strategies and cultural life styles of Mexican American adolescents. *Hispanic Journal of Behavioral Science 1*(4): 375–392.

Vigil, J. D. (1982). Chicano high schoolers: Educational performance and acculturation. *The Educational Forum, 47*(1): 59–73.

Vigil, J. D. (1983). Chicano gangs: One response to Mexican urban adaptation in the L.A. area. *Urban Anthropology 12*(1): 45–75.

Vigil, J. D. (1984). *From Indians to Chicanos: The Dynamics of Mexican American Culture.* Prospects Heights, IL: Waveland Press.

Vigil, J. D. (1987). The nexus of class, culture, and gender in the education of Mexican American females. In T. McKenna & F. I. Martinez (Eds.), *The Broken Web: The Education of Hispanic Women,* 79–103. Claremont, CA: Tomas Rivera Center for Policy Studies.

Vigil, J. D. (1988). *Barrio Gangs: Street Life and Identity in Southern California.* Austin: University of Texas Press.

Vigil, J. D. (1990a). Cholos and gangs: Culture change and street youth in Los Angeles. In R. Huff (Ed.), *Gangs in America: Diffusion, Diversity and Public Policy.* Beverly Hills, CA: Sage Publications.

Vigil, J. D. (1990b). U.S. Latinos. In D. Levinson (Ed.), *Encyclopedia of World Cultures,* New Haven, Connecticut. Human Relations Area Files.

Vigil, J. D. (1992a). History and place in the formation of Chicano ethnicity. Presentation to Conference on Hispanic History and Culture. Milwaukee: University of Wisconsin.

Vigil, J. D. (1992b). The Los Angeles riots. President's Panel Presentation, American Anthropological Association Annual Conference, December 2–6, San Francisco.

Vigil, J. D. (1993a). Gangs, social control, and ethnicity: Ways to redirect street youth. In S. B. Heath & M. W. McLaughlin (Eds.), *Identity and Inner-city Youth: Beyond Ethnicity and Gender,* 95–112. New York: Teachers College, Columbia University Press.

Vigil, J. D. (1993b). Points of contact between Mexico and the United States: Cultural styles and multiple ethnic identities. Presentation to International Congress of Anthropological and Ethnological Sciences, July 29–August 4, Mexico City.

Vigil, J. D. (1996). Que vive La Raza: The many faces of the Chicano movement. In S. Pe-draza & R. Rumbaut (Eds.), *Origins and Destinies: Immigration, Race, and Ethnicity in America*. Belmont, CA: Wadsworth Press.

Vigil, J. D. & Long, J. M. (1981). Unidirectional or nativist acculturation? Chicano paths to school achievement. *Human Organization 40*(3). 273–277.

White, L. (1949). *The Science of Culture*. New York: Farrar, Strauss, and Giroux, Inc.

Willis, P. E. (1977). *Learning to Labour: How Working Class Kids Get Working Class Jobs*. Farmborough, England: Saxon House.

Wilson, W. J. (1987). *The Truly Disadvantaged*. Chicago: University of Chicago Press.

INDEX

Aburto, S., xiv, 1, 4, 5
Acculturation
  problems of, xiii – xiv, 8, 18, 20, 33, 42, 124,
    134
  spectrum, 3, 14, 15, 26, 31, 35, 36, 40, 42, 47,
    55, 58, 60, 64, 70, 74, 83, 85, 98, 115, 124,
    135
  strategies, 8–9, 18, 35, 40, 75, 92, 133–135,
    138, 139
  styles, xv, 9, 18, 122, 133–135, 137
Achor, S., 132
Achievement orientation, 120, 129
Acuna, R., 20
AFDC (Aid for Families with Dependent
    Children), 25
Alvarez, R., 4
American Dream, 75, 87, 120, 129, 136
American Southwest, 20
Americanization
  see assimilation
Anglo residents, 89
Anti-immigrant legislation, 113
Arvizu, S.F., 8, 9
Assimilation
  Americanization, 3–5, 24, 31, 99, 138, 139
  Anglicization, xiii, xiv, 1, 24, 35, 79, 83, 92,
    101, 103, 107, 109
  Anglo-conformity models, 1, 3, 6, 35, 104,
    106, 108
AVID (Advancement Via Individual Determi-
    nation), 92, 121, 133
Bach, R.L., 18, 127
Banda, 9, 42
Baja California, 127
Barrios, xiii, 3, 13, 69, 75–76, 78, 109, 119,
    124
Barry, H., III, xiv
Behavioral environment, 11
Bilingual-bicultural
  education, 1, 2, 8, 9, 23, 41, 113, 114, 116,
    121, 123, 136, 138; see also ESL
  identity, 5, 8, 31, 64, 70, 96, 98, 115; see also
    ethnic identity
Bilingualism, 2, 53
Binational, 2, 91–92
Binationality, 2, 91, 137
Blum, J., 4
Bernal, M.E., 113
Blowouts of 1968, 24
Bogardus, E.S., 92
Bowles, S., 20
Braceros, 126
Boyer, E.J., 114
Buenker, D., 1

Buriel, R., 4, 9, 127
CABE(California Association of Bilingual Edu-
    cation), 116
California's jail population, 119
Canta Ranas, 69, 78
Cardoza, D., 9
Carter, T.P., 4
Castaneda, A., 5, 6
CETA(Comprehensive Employment and Train-
    ing Act), 6
Chachas, 8, 42, 54–55
Chapa, Jorge, 22, 129
Chavez, L., 2, 127
Chicano activism, recent reemergence, 115
Chicano Moratorium, 23
Chicano Movement, 5, 23, 119, 125
Choloization, 32, 41, 75, 126
Cholos, xiii, 9, 10, 15, 32, 34, 38, 42, 74, 121,
    132
Cinematic image as metaphor for longitudinal
    study, 11, 113
Clinton, J., 5, 138
Colonias, see barrios
Colvin, R.E., 7, 133, 138
Cortes, D., 8
CRASH(Community Resources Against Street
    Hoodlums), 119
Cross-cultural understanding, 9
Cultural deficiency, 4
Cultural deficit concept on education policy, 4,
    135
Cultural democracy, see ethnic pluralism
Cultural ecology, 18; see also Ogbu
Cultural imperialism, 20
Cultural nationalist, 6
Cultural resistance, 18
Cultural transition process, 70
Culture conflict, 31, 92
Culture shock, 8, 27, 28, 41
del Olmo, F., 115
Delgado-Gaitan, C., 1, 18, 121, 123, 130, 137
Del Valle, M., 134
de la Torre, A., 134
De Leon, M., 113
De Vos, G., 1, 113
Diaz, D.R., 3, 41
Diaz, S., 18
Diversification, 7
Donato, R., 2, 3, 4
Dornbusch, S.M., 130
Dornbusch, W., 25, 138
Drop-outs, 10, 25, 123
Drugs, 28, 32, 34, 55, 58, 74, 76, 78, 123, 134
Eaton, J., 5

Economic restructuring, 7, 124
Eisenhart, M.A., 15
Elsass, P., 2
English immersion programs, 133
English-only movement, 6, 113
Entrepreneurial enterprises, 41, 50
Environmental constraints, 11
Ernst, G., 2
ESL(English as a Second Language), 8, 27, 39,
　48–49, 53, 92, 94, 96, 116, 133, 138; see
　also bilingual-bicultural education
Estrada, R., 113
Ethnic identity, 5, 8, 20, 23–24, 27, 30, 31, 33,
　35, 39, 42, 74, 77, 84, 92, 103, 113, 114,
　122, 125, 131–132, 137
Ethnic pluralism, 6
Ethnic pride, 85, 115
Ethnocentrism, 12, 139
Expanded Horizons, 13, 70, 73, 85, 121, 133,
　138
Family as an achievement factor, 27, 46, 47, 49,
　51, 53, 54, 55, 56–57, 59–61, 62, 64, 71,
　76, 83, 91, 92, 94, 96, 101, 102, 103, 106,
　109–110, 115, 122, 127, 128, 130–131
Farm laborers, 11
Federal housing policy, 11
Felix-Ortiz, M., 137
Fishman, J., 2
Foley, D., 17
Gamino, M., 2, 126
Gandara, P., 130
Gang
　activity, 10, 13, 15, 28, 38, 55, 75–76, 77, 78,
　　91, 114, 117, 119, 123, 134
　diffusion to new areas, 75, 89–91, 109, 123,
　　126, 134
　members, 9, 10, 42, 75, 78, 119, 126
Garcia, E.E., 1, 25
Garcia Ramos, R.G., 17
Gender as an achievment factor, xiii, xiv, 2, 15,
　32, 53, 54, 56–57, 107, 130, 131–132
Getsmart, 117
Gibson, M.A., 5, 8, 18, 137
Gingrich, N., 113, 139
Gintis, H., 135
Gonzales, G., 3
Gordon, M., 6
Grant, C.A., 128
Graves, T., 10, 69
Great Society, 6, 116
Griswold del Castillo, R., 20
Gruin, P., 115
Hallowell, A.I., 11
Hayes, K.G., 20
Hayes-Bautista, D.E., 1
Head Start, 9, 57, 117, 118
Hefland, D., 120
Herskovits, M., xv
Heterogeneous population of Mexico, Mexican
　immigrants, 126–128
　see also preacculturation experience

Hill, M., 3
Hispanic label, 124
Horowitz, R., 129
Household income, 11
Hubbard, L., 121, 133
Hurh, W., 18
Hurtado, A., 115
Immigrant aspirations, 20, 27, 63–64, 128, 130
Immigrant versus nonimmigrant minorities,
　17–21
Immigration, 7, 8
Informal economy, 7–8
Inside Metro, 129
Institutional change, 116–120
Jacob, E., 19, 136
Jencks, C., 7, 126
John Wayne Thesis of Educational Change, 10,
　120
Jordan, C., 19, 136
Kamin, L.J., 4
Katz, M., 116
Keefe, S., 115
Kim, K., 18
King, C., 138
Knight, G.P., 113
Kotkin, J., 125
La Celle-Peterson, M., 138
Lambert, W.E., 113
La raza cosmica, 2
Laskin, Douglas, 8
Latinos in Los Angeles, 20
Lavin, E., 120
Leacock, E., 7
Lewis, O., 127
Levy, Josh, 132
Linton, R., xv
Lock, A., 2, 124
Long, J.M., 5, 9, 11, 15, 19, 131, 133, 137
Long, L.K., 18
Lorman, A.R., 1
Macias, Jose, 137
Macias, R., 17, 125, 139
Macro institutional levels,
　see Institutional change
Maintenance programs, 8
Malagady, R.G., 8
Manitos,
　see New Mexico
Marginality, xiii, 31, 40, 77, 126, 128, 134
Markus, H., 137
Martinez, R., 8, 42
Matute-Bianchi, M., 18
Mendez v. Westminister, 4
McFee, M., 5, 18, 133
McKenna, T., 131
McLaughlin, B., 1
McWASP(middle class, white, Anglo-saxon,
　Protestant), 119
McWilliams, C., 4
Mehan, H., 121, 133
Menchaca, M., 2, 3, 4, 11, 133, 134

Mexican political refugees, 21
Mexican Revolution, 20, 21, 128
Mexicanization, 1, 8, 14, 41, 53, 58, 71, 89,
    113–115, 120–126, 128, 135
Mexicans in the Midwest, 124
Micro institutional levels,
    see Institutional change
Moll, L.C., 18
Mongolingualism, 117
Monroy, D., 20
Montejano, D., 20
Montero-Sieburth, M., 138
Moore, J.W., 7, 20, 126, 132
Morales, A., 132
Multiculturalism, 2, 138, 139
Multiple marginality, 10
Multivariate anaylsis, 25
Myers, H., 37
NABE (National Association of Bilingual Edu-
    cation), 116
National Council of La Raza, 130
Navarette, R., Jr., 138
Neighborhood Watch, 91, 109
Neisser, U., 17
Nelson, B.H., xv
Newcomb, M.D., 137
New Horizons, 121
New Mexico, 79, 82, 109
Norteno, 9
Ogbu, J.U., 5, 18, 137
Olmedo, E.L., 1
1.5 generation 9, 42, 46, 47, 64, 92, 98, 114,
    120, 129, 136
Oppositional culture, 17
Ortiz, F.I., 131
OSS (Operation Safe Streets), 117, 119
Pachon, H., 20
Padilla, A.M., 1, 18
Parsons, T., 11
Patthey-Chavez, G.G., 1
Peasants, 127, 128
Personas mexicanas, 2, 9, 41, 92, 137
Pesquera, B.M., 131
Peterson, P.E., 7, 126
Phelan, P., 2, 124
Pico Union, 125
Pitman, M.A., 15
Pinderhughes-Rivera, R., 7
Plaschke, B., 119
Pocho, 40
Porter, R.P., 139
Portes, A., 127
Posadas, 51, 115
Poverty, 20–21, 46, 63–64, 123, 126, 130
Pozzetta, G.E., 1
Pyle, A., 133, 138
Preacculturation experience (before migration
    to U.S.), 5, 40, 63–64, 127, 136
    see also heterogeneous population of Mexico
Proposition 13 in 1978, 117
Proposition 87, 125, 138
Quinceanera, 57, 93, 97, 99, 115

Quintanilla, M., 126
Race as a factor in acculturation, 4, 21, 27, 38,
    73–74, 79, 80, 82, 84, 85, 89, 92, 96, 100,
    126, 134, 136, 137
Ramirez, M., 5, 6, 19, 123, 137
Ramos, G., 125
Reagan, R., 58, 117
Ready, T., 124
Redfield, R., xv
Relative affluence, 75, 83, 85, 91, 94, 109,
    128–129
Religion, 34, 50, 51, 54, 56–57, 61, 62, 78, 82,
    87, 94, 95, 97, 99, 103, 104–105, 106, 107,
    109, 116, 119
Rico,
    see New Mexico
Rodgers, W., 11
Rodriguez, C., 134
Rodriquez, G., 1
Rogler, L., 8
Romanucci-Ross, L., 113
Roseman, C., 41
Rueschenberg, E.J., 127
Ruiz, V., 132
Rumberger, R.W., 10
Rumbaut, R., 127
Samaniego, F., 137
Samora, J., 124
Sanchez, G.I., 4
San Diego, 127
Santana, G., 8
Sassen, S., 2
Schlegel, A., xiv
School funding decrease, 118
School performance, xv, 1, 2, 5, 9, 17, 23, 24,
    27, 33, 37, 38, 42, 46, 48, 50, 52, 53, 56, 57,
    58, 59, 61, 62, 63, 72, 74, 77, 79, 81, 83, 94,
    95, 96, 97, 100, 101, 102, 103, 105, 106, 108,
    109, 113, 123, 128, 130, 134
Segregation, 4
Segura, R.D., 4, 132
Self-identification
    endangered, enduring, and situated selves,
        xiv, 124, 134
    multidimensional, 137
    see also ethnic identity
Shogren, E., 139
Shweder, R., 137
Siegel, B., xv
Sleeter, C.E., 128
"Snapshot" as a metaphor for an ethnographic
    study, 5, 11, 113
Snyder, W., 8
South Central Los Angeles, 125
Spindler, G., xiv, xv, 2, 5, 12, 18, 19, 124, 137,
    138, 139
Spindler, L., xiv, 2, 5, 12, 18, 19, 124, 137, 138,
    139
Stanton-Salazar, R.D., 25, 138
Statzner, E., 2
Staysmart, 118

Stoners, 9
Street socialization, 10, 134
Stromquist, N., 118
Structural theorist, 17
Study design, 15–16
Suarez-Orozco, C.E., 124, 126, 134, 138
Suarez-Orozco, M.M., 21, 124, 126, 134, 137,
    138
Subcultural activity, 40, 98
Sweatshop industries, 125
Teske, R.H.C., xv
Texas, 133
Tijuana, 126
Tomas Rivera Center, 120
Tracking, 4
Traditional ethnic rituals and customs, 32, 34,
    47, 50, 51, 56–57, 59, 84, 95, 96, 97, 99,
    101, 104, 106, 114–115
Transition programs, 8
  see also ESL
Transitional, 91
Treaty of Guadalupe Hidalso (1848), 20
Trueba, H.T., 1, 2, 5, 10, 12, 18, 138
Underclass, 7, 21, 41
  see also poverty
Upheavals of 1992, 7
U.S. Commission On Civil Rights, 3
Valencia, R.R., xiv, 1, 2, 3, 4, 5, 7, 21
Valentine, C., 7
Valenzuela, A., 130
Valenzuela, J.M., 126
Vasconcelos, J., 2
Vasquez, M.J., 131
Vecindades, 46, 127, 129
Vigil, J.D., xiii–xv, 5, 7, 9, 10, 15, 19, 26, 27,
    41, 118, 119, 126, 131, 132, 133, 134, 137
Villanueva, I., 121, 133
Voluntary vs. involuntary minorities, 18
White, L., 121
Whittier Blvd., 41
Willis, P.E., 17
Wilson W.J., 7
Working class, 41, 92
Working poor, 7, 41, 129
Yu, H.C., 2, 124
Zou, Y., 5, 138